WHEN YOU'RE YOUNG

By

Trevor John Heath

Copyright © Trevor John Heath 2015
This book is sold subject to the condition that it shall not, by way of trade or otherwise, be lent, resold, hired out, or otherwise circulated without the publisher's prior consent in any form of binding or cover other than that in which it is published and without a similar condition including this condition being imposed on the subsequent publisher.
The moral right of Trevor John Heath has been asserted.
ISBN-13: 978-1517101213
ISBN-10: 1517101212

To Mum and Dad.

CONTENTS

1. Count up to 10 1
2. School Daze and Summer Haze 25
3. Thirteen Years and Nine Months 49
4. Hunting, Shooting, Flying 64
5. Rising Up 87
6. Flying Low 108
7. Sweet Sixteen 130
8. Going Solo 150
9. Summertime Blues 171
10. We Can Work it Out 197
11. Hip to be Square 225
12. Bombs Away 250

ACKNOWLEDGMENTS

Thanks to Martin Stevens and Colin Bell for their memories and photos, to Jenny Chapman and Pete Cole for their approbation, and to Holly and Freya for being typical teenagers.

1. Count up to 10

His face was of contorted evil. I had never seen a true evil face before, but somehow recognised it. What had made someone this way? Was it nature or nurture, or the lack of it? I had to get away. I was scared. Scared of what he would do to my bike. Scared of what he might do to me; reaction without thought. Fight or flight. I chose flight.

I came to know of Roger Berry during my childhood; this was my first encounter. I had ridden up the hill from my home, No. 60 Mansfield Road, in Basingstoke. My sister, Alison and I were on our nearly new bicycles, mine was a bright orange step through and it had a small carrier over the rear wheel. I was seven years old. Alison, two years older, was riding nearby, as we often played at the swings by King's Road shops. Berry had appeared from nowhere, a couple of years older, intimidating.

'That's a nice bike. Give's a go,' he demanded. I tried to ignore him, and ride away. He was quick. He grabbed the rear carrier, and was shaking it violently, slamming the rear wheel down. He was trying to dislodge me. His face was of instant fury, which is like instant mash, but without the boiling water. I could feel his hate. It was indeterminate of origin, but radiating towards me. I was panicking, tearful, desperate to find my pedals. A moment in time stretched to eternity. Eventually, my feet found their mark, and with a final slam of my wheel I managed to prise myself free. I rode away, triumphant, intact. And suddenly, at seven years old, wiser and wary of strangers, whatever age. Psychopaths evidently start early.

*

Me, at 60 Mansfield Road, Basingstoke 1963. I was banished to the back garden for being so messy. (Trevor Heath Archive)

Trevor John Heath was born on the 2nd of March, 1963. My mother, Winifred Margaret Heath, was 30 years old, and I was the last of four children. Mum suffered for years afterwards with bladder issues, and apparently I was the cause; ever the troublemaker.

As were many others, I was born in the Shrubbery. Not a small bush besides the family home, but a Victorian nursing home, which disguised itself in the 60s as a maternity ward. I had terribly sensitive skin; Mum told me that the starched sheets of the hospital caused me to bleed. As a child, plasters would cause more irritation than the injury. Eventually someone invented non-irritant plasters. It was probably someone with a similar issue.

The winters of 1962 and 1963 were amongst the longest and coldest of the 20th century. It also coincided with a baby boom. We should scrap IVF and just book into ice hotels.

Basingstoke, until the late 1950s, was a small market town. The population in 1958 was around 20-25,000. It expanded rapidly as part of the Greater London Plan of 1944, to accommodate overspill from London. Part of that spill arrived in the form of my mum and dad, who had had enough of living with my dad's parents in Mitcham. They left 18 Milton Road with just my one-year-old brother, David (maybe some clothes), and set up in a bungalow on the brand new Berg Estate. The Berg is on the south-western side of Basingstoke and I remember it still being a building site when I was small.

Dad, Frederick George Heath, was a true cockney. He was born on May 6th 1927, in Drury Lane, 'within the sound of the Bow Bells'. He had a good sense of geography even from birth. Dad had five sisters, all older, including his twin sister, Joan. They had lived for years in the Peabody Buildings in London, two rooms, eight in a bed, and no running water. Well, apart from their noses. Ostensibly a slum, they were bombed out in the war and moved to Mitcham, in Surrey. Grandfather Heath was also called Frederick George. Imaginations were obviously narrow when it came to naming offspring in the 20s. Grandfather was a painter and decorator, and his wife Mary was a cleaner. Mary was my grandmother, Nanny Heath. She lived to nearly 98, which must be a recommendation of sorts to inhale disinfectant.

Frederick Heath Senior was allegedly half Irish and was born in 1900. He fought in the Great War and was in Ireland during the civil unrest and early IRA activity. He described the Black and Tans, the regiment sent to control the insurrectionists, as a 'cutthroat band of criminals and mercenaries'. His actual words might have been 'evil thugs biggest bastards ever' but at this point of my story, I'm only seven and can't hear such language. Churchill had learnt to fight fire with even bigger fire. It worked for a while in Ireland, hence Grandad came home.

Dad's early life was not easy. As a small boy, he had cotton reels which he played with as toy cranes. One time, his eldest sister, Helen, arrived with some roller skates. Little Freddie had a great time with those, until the angry owner arrived to reclaim them. In Dad's words, they didn't have 'two farthings to rub together.' I don't know why you'd want to, except maybe to keep warm. Big families were normal back then, which was insane, as they had hardly any money. It certainly instilled a sense of family, as you couldn't escape the buggers.

The War was a huge distraction to a 12-year-old. Dad would often 'hop the wag', in other words, play truant. More often than not, he would frequent the London markets, Billingsgate fish market or elsewhere, cadging food from the sellers. Otherwise, he and his mates would break into one armed bandits to steal the coins. Formal education, therefore, was not at the top of the list for young Fred. Education was discovering the best places to find shrapnel from anti-aircraft guns, even shell cases and ammunition; observing Spitfires dogfighting above the City skyline, amongst the smoke of fires raging over the bombed buildings. Dad's early life could not have contrasted more to my own, in peaceful, semi-rural Hampshire. But in one sense, they were similar, as I was also part of this large extended family of the Heaths.

Mum and Dad had met whilst Mum was working at the Foreign Office, in Downing Street. Dad started his working life at 14, helping on a milk round. At age 18, he was called up for National Service, missing the Second World War by days. By May 1945 it was all over, bar the shouting anyway. Dad was posted to the Service Corps, in Logistics, and spent three years in Palestine. He said that period of his life put him off travelling, as he did so much in those three years; in troop ships, trains, multiple vehicles. The Army gave him a trade; he became a first class driver and was expert in handling multiple vehicles including amphibious craft such as the D.U.K.W., a two and a half ton beast heavily used in the war. His HGV licence was to follow, and Dad became a lorry driver.

Mum had been evacuated during the conflict. It must have been all that cod liver oil. She was put on a train from London to Devon, and arrived with her name on cardboard hung over her neck with string. She was the last to be collected; the family in Devon had forgotten to pick her up! She was seven years old. Her sister, Doreen, stayed in London with their mother, as she was deemed too young at five to leave. My grandmother, Nanny Smith, had lost her first born, Raymond, at 18 months to pneumonia. She hated the countryside and only visited once while my mum was there. Grandfather Smith, 'Poppy', came down about once a month to visit. Mum was staying on a farm and at that young age was expected to help with all the chores. For all her efforts, she only saw an egg the weekends her father visited. She was so hungry most of the time; she would extract vegetables from the soil on the way to school, wash them in the river and eat them. The farmer's daughter was of a similar age, and hated my mum being there. It was not a happy time, and she was moved after about a year to a family in Crediton. She enjoyed it there, apart from the one time a stray Dornier bomber dropped its load in the valley, which blew out the window of the bathroom; when Mum was in the bath. Thankfully, she was unhurt. It was a good excuse to avoid bath night for a while, though. Good job he didn't drop the bombs the other side of the valley, or Mum wouldn't have been here and this typing would be fading away a la Back to the Future.

After the worst of the Blitz, Mum moved back to Mitcham. She left school in quite strange circumstances, as she had taken it upon herself to attend business school in the evenings to learn typing and shorthand. When she became proficient, she started teaching typing and shorthand, although the school didn't actually know she was working. Apparently, this caused a bit of a kerfuffle. Kerfuffle is an old word for shitstorm, if you didn't know. She was teaching young ladies only slightly younger than herself, and obviously found her forte before she was twenty. I don't know if she found her twenty before she was forty, but that's another story.

Winifred Margaret worked as a secretary at the Foreign Office in Downing Street for a while. This was the time of Burgess and Maclean, spy scandals and Cold War paranoia. Mum was posted to New Zealand (it was a big envelope), and although she was engaged to my Dad, she stayed for two years. Dad waited for her. It was a long wait; she said she was only popping to the shops.

After Mum returned in 1956, speaking like a kiwi and free from the clutches of Civil Servantdom, my parents lived for a while at the Heaths' in Milton Road. After a pastoral childhood and being exposed to the ways of the world via the Antipodes, Mum was not going to be content in a two up, two down semi in post-war Surrey. So soon after my brother was born, virtually dragging him along with the umbilical, they upsticked to Basingstoke, mentioned in the Domesday Book, site of the siege of Basing House with Oliver Cromwell, and where I had just been born. Keep up, I know there are 1,000 words since it happened but stick with it.

My sister, Jacqueline Margaret, was born in April 1959, followed by Alison Joan in March 1961. My brother, David, had been born in Carshalton in January 1957. Mum had it all worked out that we would have birthdays in January, February, March and April. I managed to mess that up by being a week late. Sorry, Mum.

By the time I came along, the family had moved to 60, Mansfield Road in South Ham, about one mile east of their bungalow. The house was a three bed semi and was unusual in that our side of the road was privately owned; the other side was council housing. That sort of delineation doesn't happen today. Our house was opposite a long layby, which in the 60s was not home to many cars. Not many of my friends' parents owned cars, or a telephone for that matter. We had both. The phone was a big red number that sat in the hall, and we were Basingstoke 24162. Dad owned a red Morris Oxford as well, wonder if he bought a job lot of red stuff. Anyway, the car was great; it housed all six of us comfortably. So long as you read 'comfortably' as Trev on Mum's lap in the front and three kids in the back. Seatbelts were rarely fitted in those days, let alone used. Often, the car would only start with the application of the starting handle. We had a radio, but it wasn't fixed in the car; Mum would bring the kitchen transistor with a large antenna, which used to stick out of the passenger window and be jammed in by the top of the glass. Not that the reception was very good, either LW or MW, it was just a buzz most of the time.

Opposite and to the right, were the Waters family. David was my age and was a right budding little entrepreneur. He could sell a fridge to the Eskimos and throw in an electric fire with it. His dad, Cecil, sometimes took us to school in his Zephyr. His car had a *fitted* car radio – now that was posh. Directly opposite were the Browns. Their eldest son died of asthma at 12 years old. I always found that shocking as a child. To always feel so safe, smothered with family, but death had come knocking just across the street to one so young.

Opposite to the left were the Youngs, three boisterous boys and a younger girl. Stewart was the youngest boy and in my class at school. Their dad was away quite a bit so they were a bit wild. I recall Stewart breaking school pens under the desk in the classroom when we were six years old. His face was covered in ink as he was biting them too. Strange kid.

Behind the row of houses opposite, was Camrose football ground. My brother and I avidly collected the free football cards that you received on buying petrol. Totally irresponsible for garages to sell petrol to seven-year-olds but there you go. Actually, it was probably from our parents' purchases. It was also unusual that my mum could drive, as most mothers didn't work or drive.

David and I shared the smallest bedroom, which is the size of a lot of people's walk-in wardrobe today. To say it was small is to call Warwick Davis a little bit on the short side. Somehow, we had bunk beds, a wardrobe, a chair and an electric heater in there. It was often a juggle to determine what went on top. From our window, we could see right into the football ground. We watched the matches, and could determine the score through the loudness of the cheering. It was like trying to watch a tennis match with blinkers on and your head fixed to the floor; the view was partial and you couldn't see the goals.

My sisters had the other bedroom at the rear of the house, also with bunk beds, and my parents were in the main bedroom, at the front. Later on, they extended the house with a conservatory and brought the kitchen out further into the rear garden. The neighbours on the left, with whom we shared a wall, wouldn't allow the two-storey extension we wanted, claiming 'right to light'. All well and good, but soon after the extension was finished, they moved, the bastards.

The other side of our house were the Wilkinsons. Silkie was the young, blonde mum and she was married to Peter, who was a copper. They had two kids, a boy and a girl. Sue was a year below me so she never really registered. Peter did though. It's hard enough to be naughty without the fuzz on your doorstep. Not that I was badly behaved though. It was growing up. Back then, the main entertainment was ball games. The kids from the street would congregate, mostly in the layby or the garage block behind our house, to kick a ball around or play marbles. There were hardly any cars so play was only interrupted occasionally. When we reached the grand old age of five, David Waters, Stephen Waters, David's older brother, Kenneth Looe and I ventured afar and outside the confines of our determined environment; we walked into the football ground. It was only 100 yards from our homes but might as well have been 100 miles. A small squad car turned up, probably a Morris Minor, pale blue and white with a noddy light on top.

'How old are you?' the first copper asked David. He burst into tears.

'Five!' he wailed.

'How old are you?' he asked Kenneth, who was of Korean parentage and was also wailing.

'Six!'

Same question to Stephen: Eight.

And to me, who answered 'Five,' but for some reason, had no compulsion to cry or be fearful. We had done nothing wrong, and couldn't tell why we would be in trouble.

'You shouldn't be in here,' intoned the copper, 'where do you live?'

We indicated the hole in the fence. 'Over there,' sobbed David.

'Well, you better get back there then, now.' With that, they drove off. We went home, but the football ground remained a source of great attraction.

On Saturdays, we would go into the stands with the other punters, and buy fizzy drink and crisps; bubble gum, Bazooka Joes, all things sweet and sickly. We would often find coins that people had dropped in the stands, or had left their winnings in the slot machines. The joy of finding a thruppennybit, or even a sixpence; the PA was deafening to our young ears, the smell of beer, sweets and tobacco all merged into this exciting admixture of the forbidden, drunkenness and adulthood.

It seemed the whole world descended on our doorstep via the portal of the Camrose ground. Travelling fairs and circuses would set up there, two minutes' walk from my door. The fairs were wonderful, the stall holders were all these rufty-tufty, foul-mouthed itinerants with poor hygiene and a wonderful way of luring you in, to just 'aveanuvver go'. We all used to go so often that our house was always full of goldfish. It didn't matter if they died, we could go and win another half a dozen next week. I became a dab hand with a pellet gun; I won reams of Hong Kong produced plastic shit. I remember winning eight or nine times in a row and came home with a large eagle with a snake in its beak, that you could bounce on the attached elastic. That took pride of place hanging from my bedroom ceiling.

The circus was always a separate fascination. They used to turn up with elephants. Elephants! Did anything go in 1970? David Waters would be first to attend the scene. 'Could we help water the animals, or odd jobs for you?' I don't remember us ever receiving payment in kind for the work, but at least we got close to the animals. We helped water the elephants and run small errands. Over the years, David inveigled himself with the circus people, as he that gift of the gab. I was shyer than Lady Di at her first photo call, and wouldn't have said 'boo' to a goose. Not that the circus had geese.

Once, my friend Martin and I were sneaking around the outside of the circus tent, trying to find a way in without paying. Martin was sure he had found an aperture, and turned to me to say, 'Over here!' Before he got the chance, BAM! He was floored by a fist that emanated from the tent. It was another young lad, probably all of 10, preventing unlawful entry. Suffice to say, we gave up that day.

Dad took us one year, and it was truly wonderful; there were horses, lions, elephants, clowns, tumblers, acrobats; all this on our doorstep. It was a big doorstep, mind you.

Unfortunately, in the 21st century, animal shows are seen as either cruel or too expensive, and travelling circuses are few and far between. The idea of health and safety is a little bit different as well, charging horses around a small tent and lions behind mobile cages would give modern organisers the collywobbles.

Our housing estate, South Ham, was on the south west edge of the town. Our limits, before we fell off the edge of the world or bumped into the invisible glass dome enveloping us, were the King's Road shops, school, or the swings near the shops. Everything was constrained by distance, as we could only walk so far. But we were free to roam, so long as we were back for tea or before dark. In the days before mobile phones, so long as we avoided strangers and Roger Berrys, we were deemed pretty safe. Therefore, we were also free to engage in terrible mischief which although not intentionally malicious, could have escalated beyond the capacity of us all to restore to pre-juvenile activity.

One of these activities was shoplifting. A group of us, five or six, would get together and buy sweets from Groves, the Newsagent. Penny chews (or two for an old penny), blackjacks, fruit salads, lollipops, sherbet dib dabs, flying saucers; it's amazing we had any teeth left before we were 8. Lee Butler, who lived across the road from me, had a little sister who pretty much lost all her baby teeth almost as soon as they arrived, thanks to the propensity for the rush of sugar.

Lee had an older brother and sister, and the Butler family had unfortunately inherited the sticky out ears gene. This gave them the look of various size scale models of the FA cup when seen en masse and from behind.

Dean Smith lived on Baird Avenue, just around the corner of Mansfield road. He was the youngest of three boys and was part of the gang. Also the youngest of four boys was Neil Tickner. He was a lanky, awkward-looking child and had a semblance to the character of Rodney Trotter. Along with David Waters one day, someone had the bright idea of stuffing chocolate and drink under our coats and walking out without paying.

'Won't we get into trouble?'

'Oh, no, I've done it tons of times,' one of us lied.

Without even thinking too hard about it, and under strict peer pressure from the group, I entered the shop. Casually, I walked around, and spotting some literal eye candy, noticing no one was observing me, the hollow chocolate Santa suddenly was in my clothing, where it rapidly began to melt. To disguise my crime, I bought some cheap sweeties and dutifully paid for them, from my meagre pocket money. We regrouped, right outside the shop. We immediately compared notes, i.e. stuffed our faces with hooky cocoa products. Neil Tickner produced a large bottle of Tizer from under his coat and started swigging it.

'How did you get that?' I exclaimed.

'Ah, it was easy,' he said. 'Look at this!' He then emptied his pockets of enough appropriated confectionery we could have started our own shop.

We were so brazen. I can't believe no one came out of the newsagent's and copped us. It was as if the Great Train Robbers had stopped at the garage down the road and asked for change from a million pound note. The visceral thrill of winning a few sweets at the expense of the poor shop owner was shortly lived. Neil Tickner tried it a few too many times, was caught, and the worst possible – a visit from the police to his parents. The shame! That stopped us in our tracks. That was unthinkable, our parents discovering we were not the angels they knew us not to be, but what we thought they might think us to be.

Another great wheeze was long burn, coloured matches. They tended to be on sale close to Guy Fawkes Night, and burned longer, brighter, flaring up with a green or red flame. I have no idea why they sold them to us kids, but they did; shame on them. We would start small fires with them in allotments or woodland, and when the conflagration would start to get as tall as us, stamp them out. Only, often, the fires would have other ideas. One allotment behind the Kings

Road shops was especially tinder dry – rife for a good old arson experiment. We put it out – just – and were chased out by an allotment holder, some old git who didn't appreciate pre-cooked potatoes and carrots. It was a scary exit over the wire fence and then we ran as fast as our little wayward legs would carry us. As so often, we would regroup, panting and exhausted, ready to do it all again somewhere else.

It was little different from my dad during the war, hunting ammunition, killing boredom. What else to do in a small market town, except create your own entertainment? We were all fascinated by the war; all we saw on our little black and white tellies were war films, Pinky and Perky, and the black and white minstrel show. Most of us couldn't relate to puppet porkers or racist productions patronising America's Deep South, so we latched onto recent history instead.

A few hundred yards from the Camrose ground was the Pied Piper Garage. It was there the circus people often used to pitch up, as behind it were open fields and plenty of space to congregate. We loved it too, as there was an old wartime bunker just behind it. It was abandoned, effectively a rubbish area behind the garage, and to enter it you had to open the wooden door which was effectively on the floor. Then, you could walk down a few stone steps into this wondrous damp, smelly den, maybe 15 by 10 feet in size, six feet down. It had probably been home to many a tramp or part-time visitor over the years. To us, it was a bolthole, an exciting room, somewhere to hide away for a while. Across the road, which was the main A30 from London to the west, was an old transport café and the Stag and Hounds pub. Surrounding them were acres of open land, turned a golden straw colour in the summer sun. There were pressurised beer containers dotted around outside the pub, and we would sometimes press down on the pressure valves to release a few lickfuls of beer. We hated the taste, but it was fun, more importantly, *it wasn't allowed*. In the middle of the field, close to the café, we lit a few of our satanic matches. Soon enough, we had started a fire in the middle of an area dryer than Bill Murray's wit. Stamping on it wouldn't put it out. David Waters tried to roll a rusty old barrel on it. We all helped. All we achieved was potential tetanus. The flames laughed at us and spewed black smoke into the sky, contrasting with the azure backdrop. Panic was setting in. Do we run? Do we continue? Someone was bound to see it, capture us and throw us in prison for the rest of our lives. All attempts were seemingly futile. Neil Tickner got his dick out. *Not now Neil*, we thought. Next thing, he's pissing on the fire. Great idea! We all do the same. Amazingly, it works. With the inferno now just a big, black smouldering patch of straw, we legged it back to the bunker, and lived to fight another day. No more fires, though.

Fireworks. A bit more bang for your buck than coloured matches. They were a little harder to obtain, maybe, but with definitely more entertainment potential. Bangers were the weapon of choice. Light one, throw it at your mate/little sister/passing cat, and bingo! Tinnitus forever. A top trick was making a genie. Collect all the used fireworks you can find, empty out as much unignited gunpowder mixture on the pavement, and drop a coloured match on it. Not recommended if you value your eyebrows; or your face.

Dad used to buy a clutch of fireworks and every year, we'd light them in the garden. Our rear garden was narrow and probably 35 feet long. Catherine wheels would be attached to a fence post and we would stand well back, to avoid any potential hazards. Roman candles would be lit in mud, at arm's length, nice and safely. We would have gloves on whilst swirling red hot pokers at each other, I mean, sparklers. All this was pointless as soon as you lit a jumping jack. Whichever way my sister Jackie ran, the neon caterpillar would still be at her ankles, tracking her egress, narrowly missing inflicting third degree burns. One year, Dad went all out and bought a 'finale' rocket. 'Explodes in a beautiful cascade of multi-coloured stars,' said the label. This one took extra preparation; the milk bottle holding it was more forcefully semi-buried in earth, and the firelighter was especially started for the occasion. Eventually, the blue touch paper was alight; it took ages to lift off, shot up 40 feet above the garden, arced over into the garages and went 'bang!' completely out of sight. The only stars Dad saw were when Mum whacked him over the head.

For all our life preparatory excursions around our manor, we never particularly injured ourselves. There was the occasional cut or bump, especially after falling off bicycles. I am allergic to normal plasters, so after just a few hours of applying a plaster to my skin, I had to remove it or it itched like hell. So it was quite a shock to hurt myself quite badly in the least likely environs, Kings Furlong Junior School.

I was the youngest of four, so it seemed like an age before I could start at school. I remember being at home with Mum, aged around four, where the day would disappear in a whirl of washing, visiting her friends or Watch with Mother. The house would seem empty in the day without my brother and sisters, so I relished starting school to be with others, to experience, to learn. When I finally started at King's Furlong, aged five in 1968, I was an ophthalmologist's training tool, i.e. a model pupil. Well, apart from playing with my Dinky Thunderbird 2 in assembly once, this was subsequently confiscated. Mrs Duke, my teacher, didn't relinquish it until the end of term, when I had completely forgotten about its iniquitous hijacking. I was overjoyed at our reconciliation, it was my favourite toy, and I had hardly missed it all.

The playground should be exactly that: a ground within which to play. Oh no, in 1970 some nutter thought it would be great to put three large industrial concrete pipes on their side, for us kids to play in. The smaller pipe was about six feet long inside, with a bore just big enough for one person to slide through. The two larger pipes were in a row behind it, and were large enough to stand up in. Often, children would sit inside the small pipe, curled up in a ball. This microcosmic industriana became a cornucopia for the imagination, one day it would be a spaceship, another day, a time machine. Sometimes, it became a handy vessel within which to shelter from a shower. One particular day, about eight of us boys and girls were playing the delightful game of kiss chase. Golden-haired Donna was chasing me, and I certainly wanted to be caught. Giggling, I ducked through the first pipe, with her in hot-lipped pursuit. I slowed down through the second pipe, hoping she was right on my tail. On approaching the small, third pipe, I ducked down with the aim of diving through it. Wham! I was on my bum, what had happened? I couldn't think straight, there were lights in my vision, had my head exploded? My thoughts were somehow coalescing in my brain, I realised I had hit the top of the pipe mouth. In a contest with concrete, flesh and bone, concrete wins. I put my hands on my severely raging scalp, and brought my hands down toward my eyes. Red. All I could see was red, all over my hands. Blood; blood, fear, panic and more blood.

I staggered to my feet. All around me, the cacophony of youth was shrieking, yelling, oblivious to my horror. Donna was impervious too, not having realised I was hurt and pursued another lucky victim. I reached the edge of the playground, to where a teacher was on duty. I can't remember her name, only the ridiculously controlled, unemotional manner in the way she spoke. She turned to my friend, Phillip Maltby, to assist.

'Phillip, take Trevor in to see Mrs Ticel.'

That was it. No airlift helicopters, no sirens. Get another little boy to take me in to see the school secretary. Dammit woman, can't you see my brains are hanging out and I'm bleeding to death? As Phillip led me up the path into the building, large droplets of deep red blood delineated our path, macabre, sanguine echoes of Hansel and Gretel's gingerbread trail. *Plop... plop...* the blood was now falling in the corridors, up the stairs to the assembly level, across the assembly hall. Eventually, we reached the secretary's office. Mrs Ticel was a nice lady, matronly, and obviously had the medical training of a herring. Mr Read was the headmaster, old, stuffy, upright, with a greying 'tache under his nose and the demeanour of a dusty book. The pair of them totally ineptly wrapped my head with what seemed like vinegar and brown paper. I thought about changing my name to Jack just for the hell of it. They called my parents, who put me in the Morris Oxford and drove with alacrity (I don't know who Alacrity was, a neighbour possibly) to the General Hospital A&E. Every roundabout, the wheels screeched and as I tipped with the car, more blood would spill from my head. Oh, the poor (fake) leatherette seats.

Eventually, at the hospital I was stitched up. It was agony upon agony as the needle was passed through the top of my head. After receiving seven stitches to my cranium, I was x-rayed. It was really exciting to see the results. After what seemed like hours, and it probably was, I was wheelchaired to the car. I felt fine now, and was about to walk to the car. Dad stopped me, and carried me into the crimson chariot of choice. That was it, a week off school. It was nearly Christmas, and I distinctly remember being upset that I missed playing in the end of year production. It was something Greek, mythical, as we had made crepe hats like flames to signify our entrance to Hades. I couldn't fit my hat over my bandaged bonce, let alone float around a stage. One of my schoolmates turned up on our step with a box of Maltesers, as an end of term/get well soon gift from the school. That made it all alright. Sod the play, I got the chocs!

Today, children's playgrounds are cosseted enclaves of designer caution, with springy, soft surfaces and low height obstacles. At least we weren't wusses. Today, we would have sued the arse out of that school.

Christmas 1970 was one of only four years it snowed on Christmas Day in the 20th century. Well, it might have done more often at the North Pole, but not in Basingstoke. There is nothing more magical to a child than snow at Christmas. I would be wrapped up in my hand-me-down woollens, jumpers that David would have worn out only for me to wear out all over again. With a coloured hat, more often than not red, I would venture into the garden with Alison and Jackie and build snowmen. In reality, they were genderless blobs of compacted snow, but let's not get picky with detail after all this time. Utterly, utterly futile, as the first rays of winter sun would see the overlarge, anthropomorphised freezer pops dissolve into an amorphous flurry of slush. Then it would all freeze again, creating rigid ridges of ice that were treacherous to walk on. It was dangerous, so we'd try to ride our bikes on them, only to slip and fall over. Everything was a test, a challenge. If at first you don't succeed, try, try and try again. Unless you were told to stop, you wouldn't. The implication being, although something was risky, unless you hurt yourself, the life training helped the next time to overcome the barriers placed in your way. With the impeccable logic of a child, life learning is implicit. Taking risks in order to learn by doing is as natural as breathing; the trick is to only fall out of trees with cushions underneath.

*

Cushions were obviously in short supply when I was growing up. My adult body is like a map through the travails of life, scarred with the vestiges of long recovered traumas.

Dad was a lorry driver. He worked for Thorneycroft Limited, an old Basingstoke firm, for 15 years before Eaton took over and made him redundant. He loved the freedom of the open road. Early years in the job took him often to Scotland in the foulest weather; he would drive an open chassis with only cardboard across him to protect him from the wind. One trek north of the border, in heavy snow, with vehicle abandoned, left him with no choice but to try and sleep in the back of some Good Samaritan's car. He would be away most of the week, and his arrival home would be heralded by the sharp release of pressure from the lorry's airbrakes as he pulled up outside. The cab and trailer would block the light coming into the living room.

'Daddy's home!' would be the cry. I'd run out into the street and attempt the Everest-like assault to enter the cab. He would climb down from the driver's seat, and greet me, beaming, unshaven, and dressed in his green overalls, stinking of grease and diesel. I would sit behind the huge steering wheel and play with the horn, stamping on and off the airbrakes, giving the neighbours indigestion.

By the time I was eight or nine, and big enough to see out of the cab, he would take me on the road with him. This would be a short trip, normally to Watford, which took hours before the M25 was built, so it would be a full day out on the road. I loved it. Sitting high above the road, it seemed like we were genuinely Kings of the Highway, in charge of all we surveyed. We would stop at depots to collect the loads, and it gave me an early insight into the working life of not only my dad, but anyone who was destined to work in smelly, dirty factories. Everybody seemed happy to see him, and it was weird to hear everyone call him George; although he was Dad to us and Fred to friends and family, he insisted to be known as George at work. This was because at his first job on the milk round he was labelled by his middle name, as there was already a Fred working there. Obviously milkmen have difficulty with two people called the same thing.

'You mean he's Fred – and he's Fred – no, I don't get it. My brain hurts. What's your middle name? We'll call you George then.'

At the factories was my first experience of sampling drinks from an automatic machine. Tea was disgusting, and I was too young for coffee, so it was often hot chocolate or the weakest orange squash known to man. After a few hours on the road, we would stop at the Green Parrot transport café, and have egg and chips. It didn't matter how many times we went on that trip, it was always egg and chips. Finally, on the journey's last legs, we would pull up at the Wagon and Horses in Hartley Wintney. I'd be left in the cab with enough Coke and crisps to incite a seizure, and half a dozen comics to while the time away, while Dad had a few pints in the pub. I have no idea how many pints, probably two or three, but his driving was always impeccable before and after the visit.

Ron Kane was Dad's best mate at Thorneycroft's. He and his wife, Val, left Tadley, just outside Basingstoke, to a new life and job in Ilford, Essex. Ron now worked for British Rail. They had three girls and one boy, Denise and Jackie were Jackie and David's age, Avril was my age and Chris was five years younger. We used to visit them at weekends; the interminable journey to Ilford would be punctuated by the rapid lowering of the passenger window and me chucking up out of it. I was not a good traveller in those days. It would often be at Kingston or Staines that I would be getting hot, nauseous, and desperate to get out. David counted the number of parked cars I painted with one particular technicolour yawn into double figures.

Part of the problem was the poor circulation and suspension of old cars. Kids often get travel sick, but being stopped and started at multiple traffic lights and being bounced around certainly did not help. The street lights burned a headachy sodium glow of red or yellow, and I always found the journey hellish. David used to show his true future accountancy colours, and count the number of red or green lights we encountered on the journey. Geek.

In Ilford, we all had our particular arrangements for the night. I would always be on a camp bed (dunno what was camp about it, perhaps it did Frankie Howerd impressions), downstairs next to the tropical fish tank. The hum and bubbling from the tank used to soothe me to sleep. I was a very fussy eater; my subsidence was established on ingesting cheese, bread, marmite, crisps and Yorkshire pudding. I hated the texture of meat and vegetables and fruit were the Devil's spawn. Thankfully, Val was extremely understanding, having four of her own, and we were all looked after pretty well when we were there. There were other items on my menu, but I was an extremely challenging child when it came to cuisine.

The back garden was a long, thin strip in between other fenced off back gardens. It was large enough for multiple children to play in, with an area set aside for burning rubbish. Bonfires are less practical and moreover, less socially acceptable now but in the 70s it was quite normal to inhale everyone else's carbonised crap every day. Avril and I were little sods; we lit the bonfire one night while Val still had all her washing out.

Ron and Dad were quite similar in their behaviour. Both liked to shout, swear, fart, have a drink and a bet on the horses. Most of the time, the kids would pair off with our respective age peers. Denise and Jackie were like extended family sisters, but Avril was my playmate; at this stage Chris was too young to join in. They also had a dog, an Alsatian, which also loved to join in with the children's games, especially when kicking a ball around. One evening, just as dusk descended and the vestigial smoke from the bonfire wafted into the darkening sky, Avril and I were grabbing the last few minutes of light to punt the ball up and down the garden. I kicked the ball in the direction of the house, and my shoe came flying off with a similar trajectory. Avril grabbed it, laughing her head off, and disappeared through the kitchen back door. I was not amused, and running toward the back door, I thrust my left arm forward to turn the handle. Just at that moment, the Alsatian ran through my legs, not exactly tripping me, but distracting my gaze for a fleeting moment; enough distraction for me to miss the handle and thrust my hand and wrist through the glass instead.

CRASH! The ear wincingly sharp report of smashing glass and tinkling shards followed. Mockingly, the door opened from the impact, sans its insides. I stood there, not believing what had just happened, and let out a deep, primeval bellow. It might actually have been a girly scream, but my macho memory won't admit to that.

'ARRRRRRRRRRRRRRRRRRRRRRRRRRRRRGHHH HHHHHHHHHH!'

In the few seconds after, I thought, *Why did I scream? I feel no pain.* Surrounded by a wrecked glazed door, I stood in the doorway, oblivious to the subsequent realisation; I had cut my arm. Badly.

I looked at my left wrist. A circular section of skin around the size of a watch face had departed from me and was hanging on a small fleshy hinge. Blood was starting to pour and encircle my arm as I twisted it for a better view. Fingers on my right hand were protruding small sections of glass and even more alarmingly, there were lacerations to my right wrist. Somehow, I had missed a vein or artery, or I would not be here to type this. Now I let out a bigger cry – one of genuine panic and fear.

A few more seconds, and pandemonium broke out. I know we should have tied him up better.

Mum and Dad burst into view, bumping into each other as they crashed out of the living room, through the hall and into the kitchen where I stood. Mum had the wide-eyed expression of someone who had seen a ghost, maybe it was behind me.

'Oh my god, his arm is hanging off!' Mum exclaimed. I looked down. Nope. The arm was resolutely intact. Half my wrist though, was not exactly tickedy boo. Within a minute, both families were crammed into the kitchen. Dad took my wrists, and pushed the flap of skin into place. As he did so, it squeezed more blood out of the wound. Ron and Dad started binding me with bandages. The glass was rapidly swept up.

Another lovely journey to A&E. It was ages before we were seen. I was sure I would bleed to death before someone came. Eventually, I was wheeled into the procedure room, and surrounded by doctors and nurses. The doctor, who had a foreign accent, seemed aggressive and tried to calm me down as needles were pushed into my arms. They were administering local anaesthetic; all I knew was it hurt like hell and was having none of it. Eventually, the pain slipped away, and with 13 stitches in my left wrist, the final mopping up was left to a single nurse. I was bound tighter than a turkey at Christmas, with large dressings over both wrists, and plasters on my poor, cut fingers. The nurse found small splinters in my right little finger, it hurt as she carefully swabbed the blood off. Eventually, I was ferried back to Ron and Val's home, very sore and feeling completely sorry for myself. More than anything, it was embarrassing; I had damaged their home, and caused a lot of worry for everyone, especially Mum and Dad.

The wound on my left wrist took an age to heal. Christine was a nurse, who lived a few houses away behind us, in Baird Avenue. She often came in and changed my dressings, which were sticky due to the various creams applied to my damaged skin. Years later, I was told it was very lucky it had healed as well as it did, as the doctors thought they might need to perform a skin graft. Today, the nerves are still not fully recovered and never will, there is numbness to the touch.

I had one other nasty incident before I was 10. I was happily riding my bike in the garage block behind our house. I rode with my feet on the handlebars. I rode no handed. Unfortunately, trying to ride no handed with my feet on the handlebars didn't sustain balance; or momentum. I hit the concrete and part of the bike with a fast and painful impact. Ow. That bloody hurt. Extreme pain. In the juvenile pre-teen era, I was still wearing short trousers. I pulled up the left trouser leg to look at my thigh. Those of a queasy disposition should look away now and skip the next line. A large chunk of my thigh had been scooped out, exposing raw flesh and various constituent gristly bits. That was it; I was definitely going to die from this one. Amazingly, it didn't seem to be bleeding much. I semi-hopped and ran back into the house, plopped myself down on the chair in the kitchen, grizzling, and pulled up my trouser leg to shock the waiting world. That waiting world was Dad, 14-year-old Jackie and a visiting insurance man.

'Oh my god!' exclaimed the witless chap, on viewing my X-certificated limb. He almost choked on his sweet, before proffering a green packet: 'Would you like a polo?'

No I wouldn't, you numpty. Bring me the best plastic surgeon in the world or get outta my face.

'I'll have one,' Jackie said, accepting a hoop of sugar. What's the matter with this lot, can't they see I'm on the verge of death?

Dad drove me to A&E in Basingstoke. The car knew the way. So did I, up on the operating trolley, waiting for the murderous jabs of anaesthetic. Maybe it was because I was getting used to it, but I was inured to the process now. Please get on with it so I can go home. Three measly stitches later, I was on my way.

2. School Daze and Summer Haze

The seventies was a dull decade. Film and TV of the era show interiors to homes were decorated in shades of brown and beige. Clothing was similar; grey, grey, grey. Industrial disputes, strikes, power cuts and oil shortages. To me, this was just a backdrop. My world was full of Dinky Toys, school, conkers and Airfix kits. I didn't need to become a glue sniffer as a teenager; I had inhaled so much polystyrene cement that I was burnt out by the age of 12.

My first kit was a 1:72 scale model of the Apollo 11 Eagle. Like my peers, I was obsessed with astronauts and the moon landings. Dad mainly built this first kit, to show me how it was done. We would sit at the dining room table as the plastic jigsaw came together in a whirl of sprue, decals and stuck-together fingers. That was the secondary joy of poly cement, peeling it off the fingertips when dried to produce exact copies of one's fingerprints. It was like a spy film come to life.

As time went on, I became extremely adept at painting my kits and had beautiful recreations of aircraft, WW2 vehicles, sci-fi characters and spaceships. My favourite was the Saturn 5 rocket which separated into sections and stood three feet tall. When I was 14, David bought me an air pistol. I shot all my models to bits in the garden, some after setting fire to them, to make their demise 'cinematic'. I dunno how Dad managed to grow his tomatoes, there must have been bits of Airfix kits, fireworks, BB pellets and all sorts in that soil.

'Mary, Mary, quite contrary, how does your garden grow?'

It doesn't, it's full of Trevor's exploded crap.

We used to collect Brooke Bond tea cards. There were complete sets to collect; my favourite was The Space Race. Every box held two cards, which we would swap at school if there were duplicates. It took ages to collect all 30 or so cards, and then we would mount them in the respective booklet. The cards were full of facts about space travel, and a lot of speculation. The writers postulated there would be a moon base by the early 80s and we would send men to Mars by the year 2000. It didn't happen, we drank all that tea and they lied to us. Swizz.

My fave TV programme was Gerry Anderson's 'UFO'. *They* had a moon base. And women in purple wigs, which I didn't know until 1975 as we only had a black and white telly until then. A magnificent, top of the range TV in the 60s would cost a fortune, so most people rented them, and you only had two channels. Oh, and an off switch. It wasn't exactly a techie's paradise. If it went wrong, a repairman would come to your house, take the back off this leviathan and risk electrocution whilst the screen showed variations of Noel Edmonds' jumpers, i.e. a mass of geometric and jagged lines, albeit none in focus. In 1964, the huge event of the year – a third channel! BBC 2 was launched, part-time. It only ever seemed to show a picture of a 12-year-old girl, a clown puppet and a blackboard, or the Open University. Sometimes it was hard to tell which was which. In 1967 they started broadcasting in colour, so there was the strange spectacle of people staring at test cards at TVs in the shops, because they were now no longer monochrome.

Our colour telly arrived when we were watching 'The Generation Game'. Bruce Forsyth was suddenly brought to life, wearing a red shirt and a black and white checked jacket. We should have got a refund on our colour licence for that jacket.

Prior to the internet, our window to the world was through the TV. Whether it was bad news in Africa, Northern Ireland, London or the Middle East, Black Beauty still gambolled across the screen on a Sunday afternoon, followed by a bath and the regimented clipping of nails; except when there was a power cut, of course.

Our namesake, Ted Heath, the alleged Prime Minister, initiated the three-day week in late 1973 to conserve energy, which meant power supplies were severely rationed between January and March 1974. Sometimes we would remember the power was about to go out, other times we wouldn't know. It was good fun playing cards with David for hours by candlelight, not so when it was freezing. The only heat we had was from the gas cooker in the kitchen, around which we would huddle for warmth. We were lucky; most of my friends' houses were electric only.

I became quite adept at various card games, as David was 16 by then and had started gambling for money with his pals, so he was never short of a deck. The lights went out once when I was in the bath, which is most disconcerting. With all the street lights out, it was dead quiet, pitch black and very eerie; the perfect conditions in which to scare your sisters. Wooharr!

One night, the lights went out when I was practising with my violin. At first, I thought it was David playing a joke, except he was nowhere in sight, and wouldn't have been able to switch all the house lights off at once. At least the neighbours were spared one evening of the sound of a strangled cat.

I had been playing the violin from the age of eight. David was given it by Dad's sister Helen, tried and gave up after a short time. Jackie had a go and she gave it up, too. I started and persevered, failure was not an option. The major downside to learning an instrument is that it bonds you to practice time, time which is better spent outdoors if you are a young boy. My teacher, a peripatetic spinster named Miss Morton, was my first introduction to the upper middle class.

She would ask for your violin to tune it. On handing it to her, she'd respond, 'Thenk yew.' For a long time I thought she had a speech impairment. Surely she had a plum stuck in her mouth? She favoured tartan tweed skirts and smelt of old woman, like Grandma. She was probably about late thirties then, definitely ancient. She seemed a good teacher, but she could be fearsome. Any perceived lack of effort was met with a pursed lip irritation and a berating that felt like a whipping.

She made me and the other neophyte musicians perform solo in front of the school. I didn't know what nerves were until I stood there, a lump of sculpted wood under my chin, bow at the ready. I played along with Miss Morton at the piano, shaking like a leaf. At least it added vibrato. At the end, I received a warm clap from the assembled throng. My first gig, aged eight and a bit.

I lost my first friend aged nine. John Bailey lived on Hill View Road, close to the King's Road shops. We used to get the bus together early on a Saturday morning, into town. Then we would have a great splash in the Sports Centre swimming pool before a towel whipping session in the suffocating, dense, and humid changing rooms. Afterwards, we would wash down all the chlorine swallowed in the pool with a derisorily small portion of hot chocolate from the drinks machine. Then it would be a bus home, starving, ready for egg and chips.

John was a typically good mate. He would be calm, and never be inflammatory toward his friends. We were taught Country Dancing at King's Furlong. It was not popular with most boys. Clinton Bassett seemed to love it. Go figure, he was called Clinton, after all. Mrs Shepherd, our teacher, asked us to pair off one lesson with a respective girl. At the end, it was John left and Dawn Clarke.

Dawn was a very pleasant girl with a baby face, and the intellectual capacity of a cabbage. She probably became a politician. In our weekly times table tests, she always scored naught out of ten. Apart from the fact I always scored 100%, I couldn't understand anyone not getting 1 x anything wrong. Not Dawn. It was obviously too quickfire for her. Suffice to say, to be paired with Dawn for anything was like being paired with the fattest turkey on Christmas Eve.

'John, come and join with Dawn,' instructed Mrs Shepherd.

'Awww, noooo,' moaned John, genuinely distressed as being asked to leave behind any semblance of cool he had fostered from birth.

'JOHN! COME HERE NOW!' intoned Mrs Shepherd, intent on letting the poor girl have some dignity in her country dance thirty-minute session of need. John sulked across the school hall and sheepishly took Dawn's hand, and suffered the indignity of gaily skipping around the room with the plainest girl in school. He took it well. Of course, we teased him mercilessly about it for a week.

Sadly, John was hit by a car on the Winchester road, the busy main road down the hill from his home. He was on his bike and was killed. His death hit me hard, albeit not as hard as the car hit him, poor sod. He was my first friend to die, and it was especially difficult to handle as he was such a nice young chap.

After such incidents, the school would have a major health and safety push, where all sorts of do-gooders would turn up and tell us how to do things we had been doing for years; such as crossing the road, avoiding strangers, not drinking bleach, etc. I had my own incidents to contend with already so I could add not throwing your arms through glass doors being a particular one to avoid. It's true that we learn from our own experiences and vicariously through the lives of others. Riding bicycles on the road was and is always dangerous. But we lived for our bikes. We all took our cycling proficiency test in the grounds of the school, spread over a few summer evenings. No one ever tried to make us wear helmets though; the technology wasn't available to make them cheap enough as they are now.

I had to tell my other best mate, Martin Stevens, about John. Martin lived on Kelvin Hill, an adjoining street to mine. It was a small terraced council house and I always noticed the smell of the house differed from ours. I suppose because the door I always entered was via the utility room, and it smelt of fresh laundry. Martin couldn't hold back the tears when I told him. I don't think I'd seen him cry before that.

Martin's dad had fought in Normandy in WW2 but didn't ever talk about it. I suppose if I had received an arseful of shrapnel on a French beach, it wouldn't be the prime topic of coffee table conversation. Father John was a turner working for Smiths Industries, and had worked there for years. It was five minutes' walk to work.

Mum Doris was a housewife and both she and John had quite broad Hampshire accents. That always seemed strange to me but we were the invaders; London overspill, extra-terrestrials in some people's eyes. My accent seemed to me untraceable, except unspecific Southern England. Many people in Basingstoke spoke with a discernible London influence. 'Oi, mate' was a bit of a giveaway.

Martin was the youngest of three, and had an elder brother and sister. Most of my friends were the youngest, how did that work? Sister Sue was lovely, she always reminded me of Suzy Quatro. It must have been the leathers and the bass guitar.

Stewart Young was always in the thick of everything. I think he was mildly hyperactive. Any queue at school, he would work his way up the line and ask seemingly obscure questions. Do you have a penis or vagina? If you got it wrong, he would collapse in a fit of laughter and proceed to the next victim. Clinton thought he had a vagina. Mind you, that was probably wishful thinking.

Stewart and Dean Smith had a falling out over the price of fishing tackle. David Waters sold on some hooks at a profit which upset one of the others, who thought it 'not what mates do'. Commercial enterprise, I call it. I witnessed Dean and Stewart furiously biffing each other in the school toilet. The fists were literally flying. It was all over in days and then they were mates again. In the meantime, you were expected to pick sides, and risk being biffed just for giving agreement to one side or the other. It was a bit like World War One in miniature. Dean and David Waters tried to get me to smoke a fag, behind the Camrose ground. 'Go on, it'll make you feel good.' I already feel good, thanks. Besides, cigarettes cause cancer. 'No, it's lovely, try it.' I had no desire or need for it. No temptation, threat or coercion would work. We were only nine, for goodness' sake.

Dad had smoked from a young age. He rolled his own in Rizla paper and smoked in the house. Everybody smoked in front of the kids then. No one batted an eyelid. They couldn't, they were stuck down with nicotine. Visitors and relatives would light up in the front room and soon it would be a blue haze of swirling smoke and choking fumes. How they thought it wasn't harmful to passive inhalers is beyond me, the killer smogs of the fifties were behind us. If it wasn't ignorance, it was blissful insouciance. Mum would occasionally have a 'social' cigarette, i.e. she would drag on it but not inhale, just to join in with the group.

The worst thing to happen at school was the decision to allow packed lunches. I got fat. Now I was eating, as opposed to starving all day in the past. School dinners were pretty horrible, even though I was biased with my limited diet. I would only eat the chips or roast potatoes, and half of the desserts. Any meat, veg or fruit product would be examined and disdained. The mash was served up from an ice cream scoop and was full of lumps. The only thing I really liked was lemon curd sponge in custard; they could have served me that all day. Mrs Duke noticed my almost full plate and forced me, under the microscope of my watching peers, to sample some unspeakable brown meaty shite on my plate. On the arrival of said offal on my tongue, I almost retched before spending minutes chewing a gristly piece she had pointed out. She left, my humiliation complete, satisfied she had cured me of my spurious eating deficiency. Except I spat it out, and was determined never to be force fed again in my life. It doesn't work; a child will only eat what they like. Mum tried for years to get me to eat normally. I would be sent to my room without food, and I would happily starve than eat unpalatable muck. She would always acquiesce, and bring me the food I would eat.

Hence, my parents, and others, lobbied the school to allow packed lunches. The shock to my system of actually receiving nutrition during the day made me put on weight, and I was definitely fat by age 9. I ate the wrong things, sure, too much cheese and crisps, but I don't remember it being that much. I liked dairy, milk, eggs, cheese; but not tempered with fruit and vegetables, and sustained with meat, I guess the body decided to do its own thing. I was always very active, running around, cycling, swimming weekly; all the things boys do. In the seventies, most youngsters were pretty skinny; hamburgers were not commonplace in the High Street. It was inevitable that I was going to get bullied, and boy, was I bullied.

If there was anything different about you, you would get picked on; verbal abuse, name calling, racial slurs. And that was just the teachers. I became friendly with one boy called Colin Bell. We called him Ding Dong, naturally. His dad was English but his mum was Malaysian. When other kids mocked his Asian parentage, I wouldn't stand for it. I was already tired of being called every single Anglo-Saxon variation of Fatso, it was time to stand and be counted against mental terrorism. He was called things like Chink and Chinky nosh; he got used to it, but it wasn't right.

Martin sometimes called me Oliver, after Oliver Hardy, much to my chagrin. It was ok for your mates to tease you, but not others. The worst was Doughnut, after the much fatter kid on the TV show, 'Double Deckers'. Some girl called me that on the bus once. I didn't wish her well. In fact, I wished the 'wheels on the bus go round and round.' On her head. Not that I would say anything, or bite back. I was far too polite for that. I was raised a good Christian, and was a choir boy at our local church, St Peters. Every Sunday, I had to don an ecclesiastical frock and warble in my best falsetto.

At Christmas, I had a solo spot and had to sing the first verse of 'Once in Royal David's City' whilst leading in the choir. I was getting used to being listened to and looked at, understandable attention whilst performing than for looking odd. We occasionally got paid for our choir services; it was pocket money, but it was welcome all the same. I didn't know it at the time, but it was superb training for my voice, and taught me how to use my diaphragm when I sung. It was all good until my voice broke. It coincided with me becoming fed up with attending church every Sunday morning, anyway, but it seemed that overnight my voice went from falsetto to tenor with no inbetween. I would speak to Nanny Heath, Dad's mum, on the phone often when Dad made his weekly call to Mitcham.

'Sounds like a man, dunnee?' Nan would say, ad infinitum.

Gary Webb was my main nemesis at King's Furlong. He was a tubby hard nut, literally; he had a large head and would like to contact it with yours to make his point when attempting to intimidate. No one was really scared of him, he was in my year, but he made life difficult. He would start an argument over nothing and try to start a fight. Sometimes people would give him one. He would tuck his tongue in between his teeth and dig in. Aged seven, he annoyed Mrs Gardner so much in class, she pulled down his trousers and pants in front of everyone and smacked his arse. The girls didn't know where to look. Well, they did. It wasn't really worth the attention, though. Today a teacher would be struck off for such an action. He deserved it so we understood her dilemma.

Coincidentally, the musician Gary Numan's real name is Gary Webb. He is an analogue synth pop pioneer. Our Gary Webb was an anal ogre who popped pies in his mouth.

To escape all our troubles, Martin, Colin and I took solace in a tree outside the Camrose ground. We imaginatively named this haven, 'The Tree'. It had a wonderful branch about eight or nine feet up, partly overhanging the pavement next to the busy Winchester road. We would sit in there for hours, hidden away from the world under the carapace of leaves, and discuss *everything*; the meaning of life, UFOs, girls, teachers, UFOs, alien life, girls, UFOs, etc. We were particularly obsessed with the possibility of life on other planets, and there had been a lot of media coverage of supposed UFO incidents. We would spook each other with ghostly tales and all sorts of nonsense. When we were ready, we would swing out from a handy 'escape' branch and drop to the ground. Oh it all happened at The Tree.

In the summer, we would pluck the arrow-like seeds from the grass, collect bundles of them and throw them at each other. The little darts would stick in your clothes and it would be really irritating. Once we got bored of that, we would throw bundles at passing cars. They would hit and make a sound, but couldn't damage the cars in any way. One Mini driver slammed on his brakes, and chased us through the football ground. In the winter, we would throw snowballs at each other, gradually escalating into coordinated ice ball attacks on passing vehicles. Buses were good targets, as contact with the upper deck wouldn't alert the driver. Snowballs into the windscreens of cars didn't go down too well, we would often have to slip slide away fast. We would duck down into the underpass below the Brighton Hill roundabout, and re-emerge when the coast was clear. Martin had a predilection for setting traps. We would often make little dens in the bushes and undergrowth, using the abandoned materials that always seemed to be available around the Smiths industrial site. Martin once spring loaded the entrance to one such den; we moved a few small and quite light containers and held them in place with a few angled sticks and cardboard. Martin thought he would try it out and stamped on the cardboard entrance to the den. It worked too well. The containers chased us a few metres and clattered into the road, where cars swerved wildly, horns blaring. We sheepishly removed the containers from the road and hid in the tree.

One of the final indignities to the end of my early childhood was the realisation I could no longer see too well. I was squinting at road signs when we travelled around the town, and the blackboard at school was getting hard to read. So before the jump at age 11 to Big School, I was prescribed glasses for short sight. In 1974, you couldn't choose top designer frames. Oh no, you were handed NHS specs with enormous rectangular ones. There was a choice of colour though, black or brown. I had black. What difference did it make? I was wearing glasses. I was fat. My life was over.

Just before my eleventh birthday, in January 1974, I had a day where I had terrible stomach and groin ache. It lasted all day and made me sick. Mum called Doctor Hamber, our family doctor, who instead of removing himself from his pack of cigs and gin and tonic, recommended I was sponged down in the bath 'and make an appointment if you need to.' The sponging down took away the ache but I ended up with a very uncomfortable feeling in the unmentionables. Well I will mention them; it felt like I had been kicked in the nuts. It hurt to walk even, so Mum let me off school for a few days. Nanny Heath was staying, and challenged me, thinking I might be faking it to get off school; the cheek of it. Here I was with achy bollocks and no one was doing anything but ignoring it or making out I was imagining it. Following a trip to the Doc, his diagnosis was a twisted testicle, and would involve a small op. I was terrified; I didn't want to go into hospital. People go in and don't come out, I thought. I went in on a Saturday and the operation was the next day. They put a sign on the bed that says, 'Nil by Mouth'. So it would be ok to feed you up the bum, then?

The day of the op, the nurse injected me with a pre-med; an injection because I was a 'big boy', unlike the slightly younger children on the ward, who appeared to be given blackcurrant to drink to make them drowsy. I remember looking at the strip light above me, and I just couldn't keep it in focus. It was lovely – I was drugged and relaxed. Trepidation? What's that? Wheeled down to the operating theatre on the trolley, I was then given an injection in my arm that felt like liquid fire. The next moment, I was awake. The clock didn't say that time just now. Two hours of my life had disappeared. Unconsciousness was like an edited film, the splice was indeterminable. Drowsy and unspecifically sore, I was plopped back on my ward bed. The nurse took off the dressings and there was blood on my groin, which alarmed me greatly. I had a four-inch stitched line on the right hand side of my groin. What had they done? It was found on inspection I had a cyst, and the surgeons removed it. They also left a long plastic drain tube that fed in from my undercarriage. That was horrendous. Not just that they had to use it, but it would have to come out whilst I was awake.

I absolutely detested being in hospital; the smell of disinfectant, the constant traffic of nurses, doctors, consultants, visitors, the horrible food. A younger girl on the left to my bed lay listless, facing me; she threw up without moving, the acrid brown concoction hitting the floor with a loud splat. She was too exhausted to move. I rang for the nurse, horrified by the image and the smell. I had to endure near constant injections in the thighs, antibiotics, and painkillers, whatever. I felt like a human pincushion.

'How long do I have to stay in here?' I asked, almost constantly. I was told if I moved around it would shorten my stay. That was it, I was never still. I paced the corridors like a trussed up turkey, as the stitching down below and the ever present drain tube curtailed my hightailing it out the door. The nurses commented I never stopped; Good, now let me outta here. I recall seeing Lena Zavaroni giving it her all on the black and white telly in the ward, on 'Opportunity Knocks'. She was my age or slightly younger. One of the nurses was really pretty and kind; she gave me a kiss one night. I must have had a constant upturned crescent moon face, I was so miserable. After five excruciating days, I was going to be allowed home, but only after the drain was removed.

If I had known what was coming, I think I would never have left the hospital just to avoid it. I had to lie on an op table, whilst the male and female nurse cut the stitches holding the drain in place, and then removed it. That's 26 words, sounds simple. In reality, it was half an hour of me hollering the place down in agony. They didn't use any kind of anaesthetic or painkiller, and I was 10 years old. The worst is when the drain was carefully extracted, I felt like the bottom of me had fallen out. My God, it felt good when it was out, though. I could walk. It didn't hurt anymore. Time to go.

Back home, I lay on the settee in the living room, still miserable as sin, feeling terribly sorry for myself. This was alleviated in two ways. Firstly, Dad handed me an Airfix kit of a Boeing Vertol helicopter, which brightened me up considerably; secondly, from nowhere, Mum produced a tabby kitten and dropped him gently next to me. A puddy tat! We had a puddy tat! We called him Tinker and he was great. From my juvenile viewpoint, it was great fun to have a kitten, for a therapeutic measure it was also the perfect move. My attention shifted off myself to an external focus. I didn't take too long to get well.

It was a short-lived wellness. I had experienced tonsillitis more times than I could recall in the last year or two. It always resulted in a few days off school, which was a pain, because then I would have to catch up with what I had missed. In May, another consultant looked down my throat and said it was time they came out. Oh, no, not hospital *again*. It was a little different this time; it was a scheduled op, I knew what it was like in hospital. 'You'll get lots of ice cream,' everybody said with glee.

Great. I bloody hate ice cream. Well, I did then. So that was going to be poor compensation for letting some demented butcher hack off my last defences against infection. Hang on, I kept getting tonsillitis – they weren't working very well, were they? Today, doctors are reluctant to remove them. I can't say I missed them.

Fast forward – year 2000. Drinks party, New Year. 'Let auld acquaintance be forgot...' Me in tears. 'I miss me tonsils!' No, it wasn't going to happen.

The worst part was going down for the operation. Pre-med made me drowsy, as before. It was a female Indian doctor, garbed in the omnipresent surgical green, who tried to instruct me to clench my fists to raise a vein. I clenched away, and not just my fist. Sure enough, the syringed volcano was pumped into my arm; except I didn't go under. They missed. She tried the other arm. Arrrrrrrrrrrgh! More searing pain, two out of two misses. They tried top of my foot. Are they taking the piss? It's all bone. Well done. Three tries, three failures. I was a sobbing wreck on the gurney, and they decided to grab the rubber mask to gas me. The sight of the mask coming toward my face freaked me out. It was a clichéd device used on every spy film or TV programme, the view of the mask coming at you from sinister medical staff. I fought them but they held me down. Bastards. A few sniffs of the gas and I was weakening.

A northern voice was saying, 'A little bit more, Trevor, a little bit more...' I was looking up at four or so masked individuals, and I was feeling really calm. The voice was echoing, and I had the sensation of descending; my view telescoped and it all went wibbly wobbly just like a druggy film. The wibbly wobbliness continued for a while, and I was waking up. It was all over. Apart from feeling incredibly fatigued, I was astounded at not feeling any pain at all; until I swallowed. Oh my god! My throat has been ripped out! Give me ice cream! The staff tried to awaken me enough to look down my ravished cakehole. It was too painful to even consider allowing a lolly stick on the tongue, but they persisted. What were they looking for, had wedding rings gone missing? I'll tell you where I think they are, if I could a) talk, and b) wake up. It felt like they had used a blowtorch on me. Perhaps they did.

Another five days in hospital, and then we had a week's holiday in Cornwall. The chalet complex we stayed in had a pool, but I couldn't use it. I had to stay away from swimming pools for quite a while, which was a blow. I was a member of the BDASC, the Basingstoke District and Amateurs Swimming Club. Every Saturday morning, I would catch the bus from Western Way into town and go swimming at the Sports Centre. That was probably why I kept getting an infected throat.

The jump to Big School loomed large. One more summer, and it would be goodbye to King's Furlong Junior. I had enjoyed my six years there, and I had progressed very well. Mum was told I should do very well at secondary school. We had to sit a series of tests to assess our IQ, our Intelligence Quotient. The braining I received from the playground pipe must have set me back a few points. I demand cash back.

The Eleven Plus exam had been discontinued before then. Elder sister Jackie passed hers, and won a place at the local Girl's High School, Harriet Costello. It was now an ordinary secondary school, a comprehensive, albeit with some clever girls in the final, fifth year. I was sent there in the late summer of 1974, a lowly first year. Jackie would be there for one more year, which was good for me. I only knew one other person when I started, Nicola Tigwell, who also attended King's Furlong. But she wasn't a mate, worse, she was ugly. The back end of a bus was infinitely more attractive. The remainder of my mates went to Cranbourne, predominantly, or Richard Aldworth. Both were geographically closer to home, but Mum sent me to a good school. Aldworth seemed to have a reputation for churning out young mothers of 14, so it was obviously the best for sex education.

Mum took me to Heelas, the department store in Reading, to kit me out with the requisite uniform. A burgundy blazer, white and grey shirts, navy tie, black trousers, grey socks, sports kit, football boots, satchel; the bill was over £100, an absolute fortune in 1974. Deviate from the designated uniform and you were likely to be hung, drawn and quartered. Some kids' heads were sitting on spikes on open day.

The first day anywhere is horrible, but that day at Secondary School was probably the most fearful. I sat at the front of Class 1T, next to a boy called Guy Berger. Our Form Tutor laid out our timetable on the blackboard, which we dutifully copied down into our spanking new notebooks. Guy utilised rulers and protractors to make his lines neat and tidy; I avidly copied him, having absolutely no clue how to perform. I told him years later I was lost and that he seemed confident and knowing what to do. He admitted he didn't have a bloody clue either.

The first school assembly was eventful. We entered the school hall by classroom, and filed in a straight line down the long parquet-floored hall. This meant either side of us were pupils from other classes, and my first encounter with Tony Mortimer, who was on my right. We know no reason why some people don't like us. In his case, it was because I was breathing. As we weren't allowed to talk in Assembly, he showed his hatred, apart from through his venomous eyes, by kicking me hard in the shin. Not having established any pecking order in this place, and shocked by the sheer audacity of his cowardly act, I kicked him back in his. Unfortunately, the poor behaviour and nastiness of the school bully knows no bounds, and he continued to assail the same shin with his boot three or four times. Each time, the pain grew in stupendous intensity, and I resolutely found the opportunities to kick him back. His eyes burned with incandescent rage, who was I to return his attack on him? Finally, he got the last blow in that made my eyes water, and I was left to limp out from the hall in agony after 20 minutes of war. The next five years were to be filled with similar incidents; all I wanted was an education, not to be a punch bag for the douchebags; inadequate, psycho, spoilt little bastards who relied on strength of numbers most of the time to dole out their ridiculous, belittling intimidations. The same individuals would exploit the weaknesses in certain teachers, and virtually get away with murder, until the eventual karma and retribution of fate would rain down on them; in time.

David Potter was a tall boy from Old Basing. At first we were quite talkative and matey, but he found his calling as one of the worst of the bad lot. Being tall and quite strong, he would learn to assert his new found ability to dominate those of a less aggressive tendency, i.e. speccy fat boys who didn't want any trouble. Alas, I always seemed to get it. Potter became best mates with Andy Clark, and between them besieged us all for the remainder of our schooling. I had felt sorry for Andy Clark, as he had lost his mum at a young age, but it was a misjudged empathy. Single parent families were rare back then, anything less than one mum, one dad and a stable home and you were considered a pariah. Potter's dad was a silversmith, something quite different, and he felt destined to go into the family business.

His business now was being an absolute arse. The rowdy ones would sit at the back of the class and terrorise in various ways, mostly before or between classes, sometimes during. Gobbing spoons, disgusting – the assailant would flick spittle across the room with a small spoon or a ruler. In Latin, I once turned to receive an eyeful from Guy Berger. Nice. Potter sat one day chewing gum for hours, came over to me and declared, 'I've had enough of this Trevor, you can have it.' With that he pressed it into my hair. My black thatch was unfashionable enough without masticated rubber sticking it together. My attempts to remove it were ineffective so I had to trudge to matron's office. She spent an hour with white spirit, and got most of it out, complete with multiple clumps of hair. My scalp felt red raw. Thank you, Potter.

Potter sat quietly next to me at his desk, avidly tracing the outside jagged edge of a broken plastic ruler with his pencil. He then stabbed the broken tool between my forefinger and middle fingers of my right hand, leaving a graphite tattoo dot still present today.

Various indignities followed. Invariably we played rugby and football in the winter, so it was always freezing and extremely muddy. Playing rugby was a joke when wearing glasses. The first scrum I got into, the earpieces were scrunched together between various heads and my new steel framed glasses fell into the central spider of kicking legs, almost lost in the churned up mud. I managed to retrieve them before they were smashed, but they were bent all over the place. I seemed to be always walking into the town centre after school to get them professionally re-seated at the optician's. The bane of our life was cross country running. It was only a mile and a half, incorporating our football field, the path along the road beside the school, and around the War Memorial Park. Running with studded boots on frozen concrete was lethal; it was easier in heavy snow. I had the dubious honour of being half of the shortened route team – Adrian May being the other half. I was overweight but Adey May was very fat. He also had asthma, which made it worse for him. Even with the shorter route, we were always last – thankfully I always beat May. Later on, we made excursions into Old Basing along the dried up Basingstoke canal route, and also into Basing river itself. This culminated in a game of Murder in a muddy field; the game basically being an exercise in bringing everybody down into freezing mud. I had somehow escaped the worse of the filthing up, so Potter kindly came over and cupped his mud filled hands over my face.

'You're a bit too clean, Heath!' The mud was cold and disgusting. There was no escape. It dried hard and became quite warm. Free mud pack, thanks Dave. Cue extra scrubbing in the welcome hot showers.

We would always arrive at the subsequent lesson rosy cheeked, clean and knackered.

It wasn't only me that received the treatment. Ian Goodyear was a pleasant, goofy lad with a pronounced lisp. Potter and team were merciless. His games bag always ended up in the girl's toilets and he had to somehow retrieve it. Once, Potter and a few others picked up the long cupboard in our form room and stuck the loop of his bag under a corner, pinning it under a huge weight. He had no hope of picking it up himself. We would all laugh, because this time, it wasn't one of us on the receiving end. There but for the grace of God.

Potter overcooked his behaviour a few times. In the third year, we had a form room in the new Music Block. He thought it fun to stick silver foil into the fire alarm junction box. It set off the alarm, so the whole school of 1,000 pupils and staff dutifully assembled on the school playing fields. It was still the days of corporal punishment (getting rid of it being a Major Mistake), and Dave received a slap for that. He got gobby – too gobby – with the teachers. He broke a strip light in our form room and argued with Mr Macgregor in front of the class. That was a marching off to the Headmistress's office. Miss Everest was the Head, and she was of the formidable old school – no messing.

I nearly had him once. He deliberately knocked a chair off a desk that hit my head, which hurt considerably. I saw red. I picked up the chair by the legs and tried to bring it down on his head, and with a lot of force. I didn't care – he had pushed me for years. He grabbed the chair on its descent, missing his head, and deflected the blow. He was too tall, too strong – but for the first time I saw fear in his eyes. It didn't stop him, perhaps made him worse for a while – but I wasn't prepared to take his shit anymore. My antipathy had turned to hatred. I seethed about Potter. His demise filled my waking moments. He was omnipresent, unrelenting, and irrepressible; but not invulnerable.

Looking back, he was a persistent pain in the arse, but he was by no means the worst. We had never actually come to blows, through all his meanness and overbearing character; if for once he had shown contrition, a little human kindness or respect, it could have been forgiven as larking about or misjudged encouragement to harden the spirit. It took 22 years for me to bury the hatchet, and thankfully not in his head.

Dave was a lad, a bit of a troublemaker, but he was not a hard nut. They were the real ones to avoid. Of course, they would always act in pairs, or three, or more; a miniature mafia of malcontent. Steve Abbott, Jeff Yearly, David Champion, Nick Townsend. I would come into contact with the lot of them at various times, in the case of David Champion, with his solid forehead, and Nick Townsend, his fist. I think I just had 'victim' tattooed across my face. I knew Townsend's girlfriend, Julie, as she sang with us in the choir. He obviously didn't like me acknowledging her at school – hence the punch in the chin. Thankfully, it was just before the end of morning break, outside the school door; I pushed him away with my hand over his scabrous, ugly fizzog to prevent further blows and escaped into the corridor melee. That punch really hurt. I wouldn't hit back, it was best to avoid fights – I didn't want to end up as ugly as him. Being short sighted, I could end up with smashed glasses; glass in my eye or face – and then half blind when the glasses were gone. I stood up to bullies but wouldn't fight – bad combination. It made me weak and seem meek; I suppose I was, but it was more a lack of aggression. I was happy in myself, who were these personality failures to spoil my day?

My eyesight continued to deteriorate. They eventually went down to minus seven dioptres – on the blindness scale, there's mole, bat and Mr Magoo. I was now Mr Magoo and the glasses were like looking through the bottom of milk bottles. It seemed natural to team up with other myopic creatures blighted by nature; I became friends with Dave Langley and Simon Coates, and also Cheryl Barton. We joined chess club, which was a good way to avoid going outside in the winter. It was useless for me, though, Mr Coates was a demon behind the chequered board. I never beat him. Dave and I shared a love for science fiction, especially Dr Who. We were always drawing daleks and cybermen, or writing rude comments about teachers in our rough books. Simon loved making up limericks, so that became an obsession for a while. It was all innocent stuff. We were all academically oriented and not sporty, a real issue in the seventies, where most schools concentrated on excellence through athleticism. We were speccy, running was difficult. It made your glasses bounce.

Not that I hated sport; it was more my peers treating me as less worthy due to my weight. I was never going to be Pele, but I could pass well at football. I always found a space but the prima donna players would take a shot and miss instead of passing to me. Our Games teacher, Mr Critchell, was quite adept at maintaining a good atmosphere. He was, *cough cough*, a good teacher; definitely a role model for boys. Tall, athletic, good-looking, and most importantly, he ruled with an iron hand that was always deemed fair. Boys respect that, strength and discipline. He had a penchant for purple tracksuits – very 70s. I once spoke to Dave Langley during a PE lesson in the gym; I was beckoned to the front, and Critchell slapped me in the arc of the neck and back with his flat hand. It stung like a bastard, and made my eyes water. At no time did I think it undeserved, as we were warned of the consequences, and discipline was always swift and immediate. It made us respect him. On the other hand, we had a younger teacher who taught us for a while, who was a bit too handy with his punishment, and was rightfully removed.

Brother David was a huge cricket fan. We played Subbuteo cricket, we played in the garden, and there was always a cricket ball around. Therefore, it was unsurprising I was pretty good at it at school, to many people's surprise. Pity it was only a summer sport. I chased a high ball and tripped one afternoon; the ball plopped into my open left hand. A wonderful fluke but it won a huge clap.

The worst teacher was a hopeless, Glaswegian drunk. Mr Penman 'taught' chemistry. The science rooms, 34 and 35, were atop the building, and every ascent of the stairwell risked a soaking from yobs gobbing down from the top. Dave Langley obtained a detention for once indulging in this delightful habit. Physics was one of my best and favourite subjects, but chemistry was hard. It would have been difficult enough, but Penman would appear late, mumble in his thick, Gorbals brogue and then disappear again. We found out later it was to imbibe certain chemicals of the alcoholic variety. I had no clue what he had said or what the task was. He would mention something about moles and percentages and I would think he was moaning about an infestation from the Basingstoke Common. The man was a nuisance. Not only would he not teach he would reappear a little later, raise his voice in an unintelligible rant and complain we had not followed his brief. Unsurprisingly, I didn't do very well in that lesson.

The summer of 1976 has gone down in history of one of the longest and hottest ever. The grass everywhere started to turn yellow, then brown, until it had virtually given up. The sunshine was gorgeous, the heat relentless. At night, you could only sleep on top of the sheets; it was often over 20 degrees. The temperature gauge in our back garden hit the high nineties a few times. Martin and I bought cheap water pistols and spent the summer shooting each other to keep cool, or splashed around in our paddling pool. We have cine film of us all throwing buckets of water around, it was unbelievably hot. Coupled with the extended days were the violent summer storms; clouds would bubble up and late afternoon we would have thunder and lightning akin to tropical areas. There is that specific smell just before it rains, reminiscent of chlorine. Colin Bell and I sheltered under the

Camrose ground pavilion building just as the heavens opened. A bolt of lightning struck a cable overhead with a loud clack, followed by an enormous thunderclap. We abandoned that place as fast as our legs could carry us and dived into the nearby bus shelter a hundred yards away, hearts pounding and absolutely soaked. When the sun came out, our clothes would steam away and we would be dry in no time, and continue to enjoy our long, school summer break. Six weeks off is a long time and the sky was blue for most of it. Nostalgia can't brighten the memory; it was a blazing season and is indelibly scorched in the mind as well as the earth.

July 6th, 1976. It was a Tuesday. Two days earlier, the Yanks had been celebrating 200 years of independence. I don't know why, we don't celebrate 1,600 years since the Romans left. It was a lovely balmy evening, and Martin and I were pushing each other on Martin's Tuscan; a Raleigh Chopper lookalike as neither of us was bought the Choppers we desired. The path along the Winchester road was stony and loose, and Martin pushed on the rear bar of the bike a little too hard. The front wheel skidded and I was tipped off.

Martin was aghast. 'Look at your leg!'

I looked down. A hole had appeared just below my right knee. I don't know if the pedal or the ground caused it, but nearly three inches of flesh had been crushed inward. I pulled out as much gravel as I could, then on Martin's insistence, pedalled furiously home on his bike. It was around 6pm. I walked in, Dad was there. I was calm, aware that although I was injured, it could be fixed and I wasn't in danger. Maybe from Dad, though. He was angry, with restrained intent.

'You stupid sod,' he went on. Blood trickled down my shin.

'I've hurt myself,' was my opening understatement, later adding 'badly' as he came to view it. I've no idea why he was so grumpy; probably because he hadn't had his tea yet.

At A&E, they spent ages picking out the gravel with tweezers. It was uncomfortable as well as tender. Four stitches later, I was hobbling home in time honoured fashion. It led to a week off school, and I adopted a backward walk as the knee was so painful. The gravel wasn't completely removed, the wound got infected and seeped pus for a few days. Eventually, it healed but it took ages to catch up with my school work. It didn't stop me cycling for long; we lived for our bikes. It was our only form of transport except our feet.

When we were younger, David and I used to play 'Chicken' in the garden. We would throw gaming darts at each other, aiming as close as possible to our feet. Whoever moved was the chicken. On this occasion, David's dart entered the bone of my knee.

I struggled to extract it as it was in pretty well.

'Don't move,' David said calmly. 'I still have my second throw.'

Martin and me as cub scouts in Martin's living room, 1971. (Trevor Heath Archive)

3. Thirteen Years and Nine Months

The room was spinning. I was certain I was going to collapse. I felt as if I was swaying from side to side and my feet were fixed to the floor, like a circus trick about to go badly wrong. The music stopped. Miss Morton halted her piano playing and subjected me to a petulant rant, an ego-driven and spittle-flecked invective.

I had not practised enough her precious showpiece, so I was not going to be allowed to enter it in the forthcoming music festival. Good. I stayed silent, collected my violin case and slipped away.

Peripatetic lessons had become a bind. Violin lessons would interrupt the flow of general schoolwork, and my timetable had suddenly become very tight. This was the year of subject options, dropping less important or relevant subjects and concentrating on the ones that would determine our careers. Miss Morton was a miserable old cow, anyway.

Over the last couple of years, violin had been fun. I had performed with other pupils in local music festivals; one very memorable year, our music stands were sited so close every bow stroke I took meant the end of the bow went into my mate's ear. He thought he had intermittent deafness. I also often played in a quartet, which I had found wonderful. The mix of tones, violin, cello, bass and viola were magical. Now, I had the school orchestra, a larger, louder platform within which to perform. Miss Mason, the music teacher, was the standard, impetuous dragon, coordinating this seething mass of tone deaf, inharmonious, hormonal teenagers. It was a big group, with big sounds; first, second and third violins, cellos, bass, woodwind, brass, percussion; the French horns used to blow and the school walls would come tumbling down. Or so I hoped. It was an exciting group and we would play at lunchtime and after school.

I told Mum I didn't want lessons at school anymore. Conveniently, the new church choir mistress taught violin. Her name was Barbara, she was young, she was hip, more importantly, I thought she was hot. Yes please, teach me violin, Barbara, drool. She was dark-haired and very slim. Married? Bah. Ditch the bearded buffoon; I'll see you again in five years when I'm old enough.

Barbara taught me violin for the next few years. Under Miss Morton's tutelage, I had barely scraped past Grade 1. Now I was soaring through the grades, and enjoying my playing more and more. The local dogs and cats were no longer joining in. I could pick out and play along with parts on records – David was impressed that I could emulate the fiddle on ELO's 'Roll Over Beethoven'. I was just happy to be shot of the old bag – she had made life a misery. I had begun to fear the approach time to her lessons, culminating in the near fainting event as I failed to master my unprepared piece. It was probably a subconscious desire realised, I wanted to fail, to escape. One prima donna was enough, Miss Mason fulfilled that role perfectly.

Although I was still shy, the orchestra was my avenue to meet and talk with girls. Susan Davies was in my form and also played violin. She seemed quite plain-looking then but was actually fundamentally pretty. I used to get the raging horn being surrounded by the cello players – their legs would be splayed to accommodate their instruments. How I wished they would accommodate mine. I was getting older, puberty was kicking in strongly. I would think about the cello girls in other lessons, and sometimes it would be a while before I could stand up when the bell rang.

Harriet Costello School Orchestra, 1975. I'm fifth from left with the black shiny hair. (Hampshire County Council)

Some girls are bigger than others. That was certainly true. All the girls with big breasts seemed to be called Karen. Mind you, there were probably two Karens in every class. Jackies, Julies, Sharons. All years have predominance toward the popular names of the times. There weren't many Trevors. Guy Berger started to call me Fatty Bum Bum after the Carl Malcolm hit record. It was an endearing epithet from his point of view, I hated it. No one chooses their nicknames. I'll bash that no one. At King's Furlong, it had been Beefy Heathy. Ironically, they called Dad that at school too. I dunno why he didn't beat them up, he was 49 now.

Development wasn't limited to the girls, obviously. Shaun Roe had a man sized one already, what would it be like when he was twenty? Adolescence progressed at its own individual rate, but we compared notes as if we were lagging behind our Latin homework. Which in essence, we were also. It was deemed more important to watch 'The Sweeney' on a

Monday night than translate the Aeneid. Cue furiously cribbing together the Latin class members on a Tuesday before first lesson and in break, to collectively crack the code and reiterate the text before Miss Bagley's lesson. It didn't work. All we received was a collective detention.

Colin Bell's dad had been in the RAF. He had been stationed in Malaya, where he met Colin's mum. Col had started talking about the ATC. What's the ATC? Apparently, it was the Air Training Corp, the youth organisation set up as precursor to joining the RAF. You could learn to shoot, fly, visit RAF camps and all sorts. I couldn't resist all sorts. Let's join. You also had to be 13 years and 9 months minimum age. Ah, bugger, to join together, we would have to wait until Col, as the youngest of us and Martin was this age, and that would be April 1977.

Col lived on the Brighton Hill estate. We had witnessed the construction of the ever expanding town by playing on all the major building sites. Brighton Hill itself was still being built, and just by walking around we would always encounter a new play area. This play area involved walking along planks across half-built stairwells, dropping nails into central heating pipes and trying to start diggers. Col fiddled in one JCB cab and inadvertently set off the horn. It was deafening, so we legged it.

If there was a wall, we'd surmount it. The toilet block by the shopping centre had such a wall, atop the wall was access to the public toilet skylight. Martin and Colin had a ball viewing the ladies until they got bored or risked being seen. We bought Frisbees and would have hours of fun perfecting the wrist action. It was all glorious, healthy, outdoor activity, loads of walking and running around. Entertainment was cheap because there really was nothing else to do. We lived to be outside – indoors was boring. On a wet weekend, I would stay in and watch telly, there were endless black and white films to view from the preceding decades. It was a cosy time, surrounded by the whole family. That was all about to change.

David had totally messed up his 'O' Levels. He went to Tech College and retook them successfully, but was still unsure of his ultimate direction. He worked in a bank for a while, as he was always good with numbers. Aah, Numbers liked him too. After discussion with Dad, he decided to join the Army. At 19, he was off and disappeared from my life all of a sudden. It made things easier, as we had fought for sibling supremacy all our lives. He, being the eldest, assumed the mantle of Commander. I was having none of it. He would wrestle me to the floor and try to get me to submit under the worst torture imaginable; Chinese burns, knees into my arm muscles (the petrol pumps), farts, everything. I became more resilient and refused to submit, eventually becoming big enough to turn the tables on him. We always fought, verbally and physically. But it was brothers growing up, and it never became really nasty. Now he was out of the picture for a while and it was strangely quiet.

Soon, Jackie was to follow. She had always been very academic and conscientious, spending hours into the evening working toward achieving her 'A' Levels. Her linguistic skills won her a place at Cambridge. She was off to university and I lost someone to do my Latin translation.

Now it was Mum and Dad, and Alison at home. There was a big void to fill. The ATC couldn't have beckoned any louder. Hang on, we found out you could attend at 13 but couldn't join properly until 13 and 9 months. Wahay, we're off!

September 1976. Martin, Colin and I cycle to the headquarters of 443 Squadron, Air Training Corps. HQ was a large hut close to the Technical College, where Mum worked as a senior lecturer. Parade started at 6pm. All we could do those first few attendances was to soak up the atmosphere, which seemed to consist of young lads dressed in military uniform being shouted at. That and BO. *Oh, this looks great*, I thought. Posters lined the walls of the hut, showing images of gliders, light aircraft, and cadets enjoying the outdoor life. It was all tantalising and tempting, except it was also extremely scary. Would I be able to live up to these potential experiences? Will I make a complete fool of myself? Will I crap my pants firing a rifle? These questions were academic at this stage; firstly we had to enrol and get a uniform, learn the terminology, meet the people, and get home before it rained.

The storms of that year were almost as legendary as the hottest summer itself. We left the hut at 9pm into the scariest thunder and lightning storm I had ever seen. The sky was black, suddenly cracked open by a fluorescent vein of lightning. The deep, cavernous bowels of the earth must have opened, the whip like thunder followed by the reverberating kettle drums in the heavens. The rain was relentless; every rising of the knee in the pedalling cycle showed a shinier and shinier pair of jeans, water flowing off in a steady stream. The lightning was lighting up the sky like day. It was about two miles to home, and we all arrived absolutely drenched.

'Is it raining?' Mum inquired, as I stood flooding the hallway.

To our surprise, Adey May joined up at virtually the same time.

'They'll need a bigger uniform,' quipped Colin. They certainly did. Also joining was Ian Ross, a speccy, skinny, good-looking lad from the South Ham estate, and Phil Rolfe from Kempshott. Both of these guys became good mates. Ian was quite quiet, the silent type. Phil was more garrulous and had a Hampshire accent. I felt like a foreigner in my own town, sometimes. Everyone had to have a nickname. Phil had a bob-like haircut, so he became Purdey, after Joanna Lumley's character in 'The New Avengers'; Ian was his mate, so he naturally became Gambit, from the same show. May was just known as a fat bastard.

Adey May was also in one of my English classes. He was always giggly and disruptive, often erupting into helpless laughter and turning puce. One memorable afternoon, he began throwing paper planes around the room with abusive messages on them, when the teacher's back was turned. Eventually he was rumbled, shouted at and moved to the front. As I was now behind him, I repaid him for flecking my shirt with pen ink; Dave Langley and I virtually turned his white shirt blue with Quink.

Adey was quite a character. His dad was absent, divorced I think, so it was his mum, younger bro and himself. In art, we were able to discuss various topics whilst working, and the order of the day was often music. Adey bonded well with the art teacher over music, as somehow he had acquired a wonderful collection of eclectic records. He was generous with the lending, too. Kraftwerk, Tangerine Dream, Vangelis, Captain Beefheart. Not all to my taste, but it was great to play this stuff. We were all into Bowie, my bro was a big fan; Alice Cooper, Slade. Punk rock exploded in 1976 with the Sex Pistols, back then the headlines were more about the spitting than the music. I hated them as I was a clean cut youth intent on attaining some 'O' Levels, whilst they represented anarchy, violence and general yobbishness. Great guitar sound, though. Adey also turned me onto Ian Dury, Devo, The Stranglers, and various new wave acts that we loved because they were a little bit naughty. Their records contained swearing, no less. The girls were all into the Bay City Rollers and Smokie. Choh. I was also getting a taste for more commercial rock; Thin Lizzy, Boston, as well as the up and coming post punk bands. A lot of the art crowd liked poncey crap like Genesis when they were still prog, King Crimson, Led Zeppelin. I was having none of it. I know what I like, and I wasn't going to pretend just to fit in.

Back in the Air Cadet world, we were starting to find our feet. Literally. Square bashing, or drill, was a skill we all had to master. The ranks were the same as in the Air Force, so we would learn them, as well as the equivalent ranks in the Army and Navy. On December 1^{st,} 1976, as my service record states, I was inducted fully into the Air Training Corps.

Flight Sergeant Hatcher issued our uniforms. The tunic,

trousers and beret looked the same as those from about 1950. The last guy who wore it was probably dead. In fact, I think he was still in it. The material was the prickliest wool, and was a nightmare in the heat. There was also a pale blue granddad shirt with *separate* collar. We had never seen such a thing. I had to borrow collar clips from Dad. I also took to wearing braces too, as the trousers never seemed to connect with the tunic. The beret fit took a while to master; at least I discovered my hat size, 7 and 1/8. Hair had to be kept short, or it looked awful and felt like you were trying to squeeze your brain into an elastic band.

All told, I always looked like a sack of shit tied around the middle.

*

'How's it going, lads?' enquired Flight Lieutenant Bloxham. He was our CO, Commanding Officer. Not a real officer, but as defined by his lapel badge, VR, or Volunteer Reserve. My god, the ATC has so many volunteers they even have a reserve! Bloxham, or Blockhead as we not so affectionately dubbed him, was an inveterate smoker with a tendency to sound like a blocked drain when he inhaled. The exhale would normally be followed by the standard 40 a day cough. He was about 50, and had the worn grey face that always looked unshaven. Mind you, it could have been fag ash.

Bloxham always mistook me for May; so much so, my record book has the name 'May' crossed out and corrected by the old duffer. This was to prove much to my detriment.

We had to provide our own boots. Staffords in the town centre stocked outdoor gear. It was run by two guys called Ivor and Neville. Ivor was a screaming queen; I think the first I'd ever seen. About six feet, curly dark hair and a vague resemblance to Elliot Gould; the attitude was pure Frankie Howerd. It was a laugh hearing him speak. Mum asked him if he had anything suitable for me because I needed it for ATC.

'Oh, yes, we have lots of styles especially for ATCs,' he lied. He would mince off, engage with Neville midway between shelves, and mince back with the box.

'Try these on, love.' Shiver.

Once we had said boots, to make that satisfying 'crunch' on gravel noise, we would add Blakeys. These were steel heel caps that would make walking treacherous until they had worn down a bit. We would ride our bikes at speed and scrape our heels on the road, producing a trail of impressive sparks. Once we started to look the part, now we had to learn how to actually parade. Line up, square off, checkpace, right wheel, stand easy, attention; it was straight forward and we were keen to learn. It was always pretty funny when someone started 'tick tocking', i.e., right leg and right arm forward, or vice versa. It's pretty difficult to do it deliberately.

It was a disciplined environment. You did what you were told, when you were told. Stick it, and the world of aviation and responsibility would envelope you. Play up, like a petulant child, and you would be out. I don't remember anyone not sticking it.

All the adults were volunteers, from various walks of life. I can't remember Blockhead's profession, but it was probably white collar. Mr Bourne, a smooth, urbane, well-spoken gentleman, was a Truancy Officer, and ex-RAF. He had that Patrician air about him. He was always polite and well thought of, so he was always just Mr Bourne, no nickname. 'Silky Wilky', on the other hand, was Sergeant Wilkinson of the Hampshire Constabulary. He had a burly frame and a jovial air, always straight to the point but with plenty of natural authority. His daughter, Jeannette, was our age. She used to help out with the tuck shop; we could buy fizz, crisps and chocolate footballs after parade. She was a welcome bubble of oestrogen within a testosterone flood. She knew her power over these hormonal boys, and she wielded it.

Warrant Officer Ledger worked on the dust. He was a

laugh. Mid-forties, moustache, balding, he had a wonderful way with words, albeit strangled in a Hampshire twang. We had .303 and .22 calibre rifles on site, to learn range practice, handling of weapons and how to drill with a rifle. With muzzle aimed to the sky, he would throw these weighty weapons at you from a few yards away, God help you if you dropped it.

'This is how you check a weapon. With the naughty end facing up, open the breach with the bolt, so; check the breach is clear, close the bolt; bring the weapon to the firing position; pull the weapon in to the shoulder, and fire off the action. Don't ever jerk a trigger! Squeeze it gently, like your girlfriend's tits (cue smirking cadets). Treat your weapon like your woman. It deserves respect. Treat it right and it will serve you right,' and so on.

We would have to learn how to strip the weapons well before we would be let loose on a firing range. I removed the bolt from a .303 one night and strafed the edge right down my left thumb. The scar was there for years. We learnt a .303 was lethal up to two miles away, and accurate up to one mile. This lump of wood and steel was an unrelenting death machine. Better to learn it now in the safety of our hut than out there in the live environment.

We weren't there long at the College location when we were informed we were to move to a new HQ. They had secured the WW2 hero and Spitfire pilot, Sir Douglas Bader CBE, DSO, DFC to officially open it.

'It must have a very tricky door handle if you need a famous pilot to open it,' I said. Flight Sergeant Gowland had me down for 20 press ups for that one.

Sir Douglas Bader CBE, DSO, DFC was a true hero. He had over 20 kills to his name flying Spitfires and Hurricanes, but with the added complication of having no legs. He lost them showing off in an aerobatic display before the war; his aircraft clipped the ground and he crashed. His log book entry was 'Poor show'. What an understatement.

He was shot down, or collided with another aircraft (it was never confirmed) over France and was captured by the Germans. He was incarcerated in Colditz castle, and the only way to stop him trying to escape was to take his tin legs away. His batman was literally the man under him; he was tasked with carrying Bader everywhere sans legs. A TV documentary after Bader's death made clear said servant wasn't impressed with DB, in fact, he hated his guts. At least he had them. Sir Douglas was a straight speaker, swore like a trooper and was nothing like Kenneth Moore, who portrayed him in the 1956 film, 'Reach for the Sky'. He was a tough cookie, he had to be. Wars aren't won by shrinking violets.

Me inspecting Sir Douglas Bader, 1977. I'm fifth from the left, next to Cadet Evans, the shortest cadet. Anthony Gowland is to Evans's left. (Basingstoke Gazette)

Sir Douglas CBE, DSO, DFC duly turned up with his wife, to inspect this unholy rabble. His wife wasn't called

Julie, she was called Joan, but she seemed very nice nonetheless. The cadets were all lined up on parade, there was a big turnout, including the local press. Sir Douglas managed extremely well on his artificial legs, certainly better than many of the lads who had the real thing.

As he shuffled along the front row, I remember him sidling into my full view, as we were not allowed to move our heads. I still have the picture. I felt like a fraud in front of this man. I wonder what he would be thinking.

SDB: Hmm, not a bad turnout. This cadet looks like a sack of shit tied around the middle.

Cadet Sergeant Paul Edwards (Spud) got Sir Douglas to sign a copy of his autobiography. Spud was young to have completed an autobiography, I hear you say. No, it was Spud's copy of Sir Douglas's autobiography. How did Spud have SDBs autobiography, did he have access to his house? Etc, etc.

The new hut was set in the grounds of The Vyne School, near to the Dove House Unit which was for educationally subnormal pupils. David had attended The Vyne, originally Charles Chute, and Alison had attended Dove House. Sister Alison always had difficulty reading, which was partly or wholly caused by an affliction of her eyes. She was unable to keep focus on one point, especially when stressed; you could observe them rolling in her sockets, always returning to the middle and then to roll to the sides again, over and over. The condition is better recognised now.

The new HQ took longer to cycle to; it was a good four miles or so from home. We used to enjoy 'bike-o-batics' on the journeys across the rough ground between the many roundabouts. We all had racer bikes, five speeds, sometime before BMX and trail bikes became available. We would emulate the Red Arrows display team with our bikes, or at least, pathetically try. It would often be me, Colin, Martin, Purdey, and a few others dependent on who had turned up for parade. The antics would invariably end up with a few crashes or a tumble in the undergrowth. We would pull up on grass, back brake on and skid one way, one after the other. Martin's rear wheel buckled on one such attempt.

'Shit!' he exclaimed. Quite. Then it was a slow ride home as Martin was forced to carry his wounded steed.

There were often unwelcome additions to our number. 'Bigger Boys' (as Kevin and Perry dubbed them), O'Shea and Davey, would sometimes intrude, like vultures or harpies, intent on dismay. Dis wasn't May, it's Heath, I keep telling you, Block'ead. They were older cadets, probably 17 then, but unfortunately they were taller, brasher, bastards in fact. I couldn't escape bullies wherever I went. They would grab a beret off our heads, mostly mine, and throw it around until I was almost in tears.

'Who wrote My Ding a Ling?' shouted O'Shea.

'Chuck Berry!' Cue my titfer sailing through the air like a cloth Frisbee. They would eventually give up and sod off. I wished they would forever. I hated them with a vengeance.

Flight Sergeant Gowland had a little brother, Anthony. He started soon after us. He was always 'Me, sir! Me, sir!' whenever there were questions at lectures. We had lessons in various topics, aircraft recognition, the principles of flight, the structure of the RAF, radio communication, weapons. It was during the height of the Cold War, the Russians were the ever present threat across the East/West German divide. Little Anthony couldn't get enough of it, and loved the sound of his own voice. We took the piss behind his back, but not really to him, as his big bro was the most senior cadet. Little Gowland, or Tony as he liked to be known, became my nemesis. Not only did I despise nepotism, he was an irritating little shit. An irritating little shit who would become a Tornado pilot, no less.

Rafe Stevens I had known since I was 6. He was immortalised on our home cine film for my seventh birthday party. I had lost touch when I went to Harriet Costello, but here he was, a 443 Squadron cadet. Unfortunately, he became great mates with Gowland. That put the end to that friendship. His duplicitousness knew no bounds; he would listen to and encourage our bitching about Gowland and then report back. Tosser.

We would attend parade twice a week, 6pm till 9pm. The only thing I really struggled with was to get a superb shine on my boots. I asked David how he did it in the army. 'Lots of spit,' was the answer. Yes, but how much spit compared to polish? Do you use a spit meter? I rubbed my boots for so long and so hard I wore my forefinger away. At least the subs were small, and no other youth organisation could offer such activities as shooting, flying aircraft before you were old enough to drive, and attendances at working RAF stations. The ATCs motto is Venture: Adventure. Go out and find your thrill. Sitting at home on a PlayStation can never compare. If I had to suffer various indignities with this bunch of fools, so be it; the rewards should be worth it. We were all looking forward to actually shooting these damn rifles and experiencing flight in two-seater aircraft. We didn't have to wait long.

There was a mass of protocol and procedure to learn. Only salute an officer, not a non-commissioned officer, such as a corporal or sergeant. You salute the Queen's commission, not the man. Could the man please take it off? A lot of officers were arseholes, can I salute the commission without the man seeing? Don't salute indoors; don't salute unless you are wearing your hat, the order and timing of the salute, the orientation of the hand, the arm, and the body. It was never ending. Not only that, some twat had spent years making all this bullshit up. The forces must employ special inventors of new bullshit unless the old bullshit wears out.

We didn't mind. We lived for our bikes, now we also lived and breathed aviation. We all had plans to join the RAF, become pilots, to work on planes, whatever. Our dads would take us to air shows and we would be overawed by the skill and spectacle of the Red Arrows, or the majestic lumbering of the Battle of Britain Flight Lancaster. We all dreamed we were Spitfire pilots, like Sir Douglas Bader CBE, DSO, DFC.

Except with legs.

My cousin Robert's dad, Uncle Bob, served on the *HMS Hood* in 1941 in the gunnery section. Along with 20 mates, they went on a 20 pint bender and missed the disembarkation of the ship. They were all disciplined, however, the *Hood* had sailed for Scapa Flow and a few days later was sunk by the *Bismarck*. Only three survived out of over 1400 sailors. Maybe the one other exception that being legless can save your life.

4. Hunting, Shooting, Flying

My first away camp was looming. I had been chosen with a dozen others to attend RAF Coningsby in Lincolnshire for a week. I had never spent a week away from home without my parents before, let alone been to Lincolnshire. Great, Martin was coming. Ah, shit, so is Little Gowland. Both Gowlands in fact, it was Gowland squared.

'You're gonna get toothpasted, Heath!' shrieked O'Shea. He could barely contain his glee. In fact, he couldn't, his glee leaked everywhere.

'Yeah, we're gonna DO you, Heath,' gleed Davey. Yes, I was worried. My teeth would get a right pasting.

'You do realise what they mean, don't you?' enquired Rafe. 'They put toothpaste all over your balls. Apparently it stings like hell.'

I wasn't so worried about the alleged pain; I didn't want those arseholes anywhere near mine. Looking back, it didn't deter me. I must have had balls, albeit toothpaste free.

The only times I had stayed away prior to this was in Martin's garden. A couple of times we slept in a tent, only for his dad to keep shouting out of the bedroom window to be quiet. The only way to relieve yourself was in a bucket. Stevens Junior shone a torch on me as I lay astride our two beds, perfectly silhouetting me against the tent walls as I peed in the bucket. This coincided with Stevens Senior shouting at us for the tenth time. Happy days.

The mental image faded. I was snapped back to reality. 'We're gonna get you Heath,' O'Shea repeated on his way past outside, parade was over, he needed a breath of fag air.

Thankfully, that Irish git wasn't going.

We had wised up to O'Shea and his antics. We would often speed off straight away or wait to see which way he would go, then go in the opposite direction; anything to get away from him and his mates. The route home would take us across the railway, past the cemetery, across the blue footbridge over the ring road, and back into South Ham. The blue footbridge is about 40 feet above a busy dual carriageway, and would often be a stopping off point on the way home to eat some chips. The screwed up paper was let go one night, hitting a car windscreen, nearly giving the driver a heart attack. In the headlights, he must have thought it a rock. As his horn blared, more in alarm then anger, we pedalled off into the night.

The blue bridge was a site of reflection and adventure. Cars would whizz underneath, and we would find different ways to challenge ourselves. Once we dared each other to work our way up the support structure underneath. It was a perilous shuffle on the bum, on a concrete arch barely wider than four feet, 40 feet above the road. We were mental. Probably goes with the territory of being a male teenager.

On TV was a comedy about National Service in the RAF, called 'Get Some In!' Our journeys in the daylight to parade were continuously punctuated by some 'wag' shouting 'Get Some In!' at us. Nobody knew what the phrase meant so it made no sense, beyond someone trying to be funny. Oh, so you recognise we're in RAF uniform? Good. Dickhead. We would sometimes make ourselves into a minor spectacle; on cue, we would hit the blakeys on the road and treat onlookers to a pretty display of sparks. Anything to please.

TREVOR JOHN HEATH

RAF Coningsby Annual Camp August 1977. L – R from rear: Sgt 'Spud' Edwards, Cpl Thomas (Lilley), Cpl Lovegrove, Cdt Davey, Cdt May, Me, Cdt Rolfe, Cdt Stevens R (Monkey Man); Front row, Cdt Gowland, JT, Rev. Batt, Camp Commandant, Flt Lt Bloxham (VR), Flt Sgt Gowland, Cdt Evans. Martin was in the air in a Chipmunk. (MOD Photo)

The full line up for Coningsby: Sergeant Edwards (Spud), Corporal Thomas (Lilley), Corporal Lovegrove (no nickname, already beyond parody), Cadet Rolfe (Purdey), Cadet May, me, Cadet Stevens R (Rafe, 'Monkey man'), Cadet Stevens M (Martin), Cadet Gowland A (Little Shit), Cadet Davey, Flight Sergeant Gowland, Cadet Evans. Also coming were Blockhead and Reverend Batt.

The late Reverend Batt was a local chaplain. He might have been a great bloke, but from my 14-year-old perspective, he was a right miserable bastard. Corporal Thomas was dubbed 'Lilley' after a diffident character in aforesaid TV show. He had a little moustache and specs, and loved the opportunity to shout and exercise his limited authority as a corporal. He was possibly ok underneath. I didn't look underneath as that would be impertinent. I think he never forgave us for giving him such a godawful nom de plume. Lovegrove was Lovegrove – nice enough guy. Rafe was called 'Monkey man' because he had the demeanour of one – all bandy armed and legged. Evans was short and irreverent – unlike Batt who was short tempered and a reverend.

Block'ead was a thoroughly decent cove, but he drove us up the wall. Deaf as a post, in fact I think I've met posts with more acute hearing. You had to try and tell him things five times, each attempt he would turn his better ear with his mouth wide open, sucking for breath against the occlusions in his fag-clogged airways. And I could hit him for the amount of times he called me May – we didn't look at all alike.

I enjoyed ATC as it gave me time to be with Martin and Colin. As they were at Cranbourne School, along with most of my junior school contemporaries, it was opportunity to catch up and learn about their experiences. Colin had started using the word *remedial* to describe thick kids. We shortened this to 'rem' and called anyone we hated 'a rem'. If they were genuinely thought stupid, that would be a descriptive bonus. Most of the rems we encountered were called Barry. It was a running joke, if you were called Barry, we would automatically assume you were a bully, a rem, or both. The BBC programme, 'Waterloo Road' had a bully character called Barry Barry. The writer must have had the same association.

Col was having a hard time with a fat lad called Perry. He was in the Army cadets, a 'pongo'. We saw him a couple of times as we cycled through South Ham, exchanged unpleasantries, and sped off, chased by the overweight, puffing and panting asthmatic wreck. Traversing through South Ham was the equivalent of crossing the Bronx, always danger, and always wayward youths spoiling for a fight. It will be always, probably.

August 1977. Basingstoke Railway Station was our rally point. Amongst the chaos of cases, fussing parents and last minute enquiries of 'Do you have clean handkerchiefs?' we set off on our long trek to Lincolnshire. All I really recall of that trip was that it was long. We had to change trains at Grantham and Sleaford, which broke up the tedium of viewing miles and miles of flat countryside. On eventual arrival at RAF Coningsby, we reported to the guardhouse, as is customary, before lumbering with our luggage to our billet.

We were shown inside a nondescript building, upon entering we had to ascend a staircase to the first floor, to the left, and this was home for the next seven days. The billet room was one of several; other squadron cadets were in the other billets across the landing and next door. The room itself housed a dozen single beds, steel framed, grey paint, grey blankets, and grey lockers. Half the beds were one side of the room and vice versa. I don't know why they had a vice in there, maybe we would turn in our sleep (Boom Tish!). We were shown the showers and given time to unpack. All in all for a front line operational fighter base, it was all a bit quiet.

'It's all a bit quiet, innit?' I said to Martin. He started putting clothes away in his locker, his bed next to mine.

'Yeah,' he agreed. 'Where are these Phantoms, then?' The F4 FGR2 Phantom was then part of the main deterrent fighter bombers operated by the RAF. Housing two powerful Rolls Royce Spey engines, they were ageing but housed formidable ability within their airframes. Their official role was for air defence, close air support, low level strike and tactical reconnaissance.

'Wot you on about?' said Martin. Sorry, explaining for the readers in the 21st century.

'They don't fly at weekends,' Spud told us. 'The pilots use the time to get pissed.'

'Yo!' exclaimed Gowland. 'Sounds like a good plan!' Yeah, right. We're 14. We're on a military airbase. You stupid little shit.

The JT (Junior Technician) was on hand to help us with anything we need. A fat, piggy looking man, with bushy eyebrows, he was creepy. It was dislike at first sight.

'I'm only across the hall, boys.' Yeah, good. Thanks for letting us know. Bye.

We were shown to the NAAFI, i.e. the canteen. RAF food is normally superb, unfortunately, I was still in my extremely fussy period, and didn't appreciate it at all.

'Just chips please.'

'Yo not wahntennythinilse, san?' All the serving staff seemed to be Scottish.

'Only a drink of squash, please.'

At the end of the serving row it would be the same.

'Chepsonli, izz et? Yo not wahntennythinilse, san?'

'No thanks. Were you serving down there as well?'

'No, aye tekth' munny. Yo lads are cuvveredahlwikennywees.'

Fine. I think I got that. I sat down at a table, joined by the others. Most had full platefuls.

'I dunno why you come to camp,' stated Rafe, stuffing mouthfuls of food. Only use of a spade would have been quicker. 'You don't like the journey, you don't like the food, scared of getting 'done'.' He meant being toothpasted.

I was gobsmacked. 'I'm gobsmacked,' I said. There, I told you I was. 'I don't come to camp for the food or the journey, and certainly not *to get done*.' I'm here for the activities, the aircraft.'

Silence.

'...When eventually they appear!'

'Well I'll have the food you don't eat,' scoffed Monkey Man, in both senses of the word.

*

At 10pm, we were all in our bunks, it was lights out. We were all extremely tired, excited, talked out. Except we weren't. As soon as moonlight hit the pillow, the whispering escalated to a full blown commune of joke and storytelling. The laughs would get louder, become more extreme with every funnier story. Every event had to hit fever pitch, and for some reason, the following joke tipped it into hysteria.

'Why is the Red Sea red?'

'Dunno,' (times 11.)

'Because Queen Victoria reigned for two periods.'

Pause. Uproarious laughter. Probably a little bit of wee.

We would all drift off into a lovely, peaceful and satisfied sleep. Only to be awoken by an earthquake.

'Shhhh,' said a torch. What's going on? Torches don't talk. I was coming to in the beam of a torturous torchlight. The bed was shifting.

'I'm just tucking you in, go back to sleep.' It was the JT. He was so close I could hear him breathing heavily. He shone the torch in my face. I couldn't see him directly, but I watched his every move. Eventually he moved to the next bunk, and the next. Martin and I locked gaze. What was he up to? The room was silent, transfixed, all you could hear was his breathing. Eventually, he buggered off.

We all sat up. We had sussed his game. Bloody perv.

Next morning, Gowland senior said the squad next door was going to issue their guys with baseball bats. The JT had obviously been looking for a fiddling opportunity around the block.

Breakfast; nope, nothing was flying. It was quiet as the proverbial mouse. Yesterday, the proverbial mouse squeaked 'a stitch in time saves nine' but was too quiet to hear. It was Sunday, so we had to attend the obligatory church service, led by Rev Batt. He had to justify his jolly up north somehow. Most cadets had probably never attended church on Sunday, although in schools they still sang hymns in assembly. I was an old hand, with being a former choirboy. Not the sort of thing to admit to in this company. After the tone deaf had sacrilegiously ruined a few classic hymns, we were coached off to RAF Cranwell, to use their swimming pool. Cranwell was where the pilots had their basic training, on Jet Provost trainers and Beagle Pup single piston engine aircraft. They used to have Tiger Moths and later Chipmunk aircraft, but the ATC now had these.

The cadets (and the armed forces) are obviously strong on being physically fit. I was still a rotund little fellow; the group photo shows me as the shortest in the line. However, swimming was my bag, man. The game of football later was not. Sunday disappeared in a blur of exertion, anticipation for the week ahead, and trying not to upset anyone, especially the regulars. It must be said (or even written), apart from our own and some other ATC officers, we were treated extremely well by the RAF personnel, who were all friendly, northern and called something like Jock or Mickey.

We were called the Space Cadets.

*

Monday morning. We sat at the breakfast table, munching toast, wiping the sleep out of our eyes. The table suddenly started shaking uncontrollably. Get a hold of yourself, I told the table. The salt and pepper pots became a blur of vibration; an unholy crackling roar seemed to be exploding all around us. All the servicemen and women didn't flinch.

'What the hell was THAT?!' It was, in fact, two Phantoms taking off on the 9,000 foot runway. With reheat, their thrust each was in excess of 20,000lbs. It was then followed by two more and two more. Wahay! This is what we were here for. We caught sight of them out of the window. The reheat flame, the unburnt, reignited turbine gases trailed the aircraft by a further 20 feet, a bright orange and purple colour. *Now* we believed we were on a fighter base.

Every morning, we would have a billet inspection. We had to make bed packs.

'Can I make a jetpack instead, please?' inquired Martin.

A jetpack might have been easier. The idea of bed packs is a truly military one. Fold your sheets and blankets in such a manner to be neat, presentable, and easily transportable. Having to use a ruler to obtain the correct dimensions and achieve crisp corners seemed impossible. We made them in pairs, as cloth doesn't follow the rules. It took ages. We were all assigned other cleaning tasks; sweep the room, dust surfaces, punch May, that sort of thing. We were satisfied all was spick and span, then the Warrant Officer from another squadron would come in, wearing a white glove (long before Michael Jackson), and run a finger along the top of the door frame.

'Oh dear,' he would say, shaking his head, his fingertip grey with traitorous dust. 'Points off.'

That's not fair. Who looks on top of door frames? Robert Wadlow? The WO would open a locker. If a single item was deemed out of place, points off. Bed pack inspection: a corner half an inch too long; bed pack pulled apart. 'Do it again!' It was cruel, unnecessary and standard military bullshit. Welcome to camp! We would have to redo the bed packs that took us an hour in the first place.

'Practice makes perfect, gents,' Flight Sergeant Gowland would smirk.

On parade, we fared just as badly. We had all learned to iron shirts and trousers especially for this trip. We took turns at the ironing board the night before to look smart; only for Evans to wear red socks and get kicked off parade.

'Evans, you dickhead,' we remonstrated when relieved. 'What were you thinking?' Cadet Evans shrugged. He had no excuse. A little guy, freckly, he seemed to be exercising a certain rebelliousness. That doesn't work in the military. Conform or you're out. Evans was tasked with extra cleaning duties as penance. He had cost us vital points in the competition with other billets.

Up to this point, the ever present threat of 'toothpasting' hadn't been realised. Every trip to the showers, and the feeling surfaced that this could be the time. So far, so good.

We were allowed to visit operational areas of the camp. I chose Air Traffic Control; the Radar room seemed interesting.

'Ah, a space cadet!' beamed the guy who was to show me around. The radar room was in near darkness, various operators sat in the orange glow of various monitors. I was told what the little blobs on screen meant. It was ultimately irrelevant, as my eyes became very heavy as the sweeping line went around, and around and around... it was hypnotising. It took all my energy to stay awake. Thanks for that. Yawn.

Much better was Night Flight. We spent a few hours in the company of the aircraft maintenance men for 29 Squadron and 6 Squadron flight line. Unsurprisingly, we were hosted by a hilarious little guy called Jock. He wore his ear defenders on the sides of his head all the time. He looked like a deflated Mickey Mouse. If you could obtain a degree in swearing, Jock and his mates would hold Master's.

'Where you fookers from? Bear-zing-sturk? Never fookin 'eard of it. Where's the fook's that? Ampshire? You all soothern fookers, are yer? You all look a bit pale an' paystee, dunyer? Didn't anywoon tell ye nartho' Watfood is man's coontry, youse lot need to be a bit brawner to tak us on, like.'

It was wonderful. We'd travelled over 200 miles to suffer this kind of abuse. We were being treated like adults, to a point. Mummy and Daddy weren't there to rescue us, whatever the mock crisis. We were learning to stand on our two feet, even if it was hanging off the wing of a Phantom jet, conversing with custodians of the vernacular, or making a flipping bed pack.

Soon after the Phantoms landed, we would swarm all over them. A 57 foot long Mcdonnel Douglas Phantom close up is quite a sight. It's impossible to appreciate the size from an Airfix kit. A two-seater supersonic fighter bomber, the overall impression was of a giant eagle, the nose cone like a bill, the wings and control surfaces like metal feathers. Jock would show us where to look for obvious signs of leak or damage, such as ice or bird strikes. 'Ye can alwees tell from th' smell efets a bairdstrryk,' he said. Spey engines spinning at thousands of rpm would chop up and incinerate small birds within a second. What does it smell like? 'Dis-gustin. Like kay eff see.'

We would walk underneath, crouched down, and walk along the wings, in a few strengthened areas shown by markings on the smooth surface. Martin and I stooped under the jet, removing panels with speed braces and feeling very grown up. Hydraulic oil and fuel dripped everywhere, and judging his moment to avoid drips, Martin ducked under the arrestor hook. He felt a large boot on his backside, firmly rooted into his coccyx. It was Jock, who sternly indicated that you never walk under the hook, lest it crashes down on your head. Martin fought back the tears, all the while confirming his initial instincts that Jock was as thick as two short planks. Jock was a FLM, Flight Line Mechanic, or 'Phlegm'. It was an accurate phonetic acronym, as he was a total gobshite. At one point, I sat astride the jet, feeling like I was on top of the world. Alas, no camera allowed let alone available back then.

After the shrill scream of the ground generators faded, we settled back into the crew quarters for a hot drink with the lads. Martin and a few of the other guys were on this detail, and Jock loaded us with trophies to take home; red cloth and plastic 'remove before flight' lanyards, empty gas canisters used by display parachutists to trail smoke, and 'anti-bite' plates, which were like metal number plates painted with diagonal lines. These were put in places to remind you to duck or avoid injury, lest the pointy bit sticking out on a plane would 'bite' you. A lot of the time was spent reading newspapers.

"Ere, it says here,' said Martin, perusing one of the dailies, 'they've just discovered the rings of Uranus.'

'Best scoot under the covers tonight,' I said, 'or the JT will find yours.'

We proudly took our booty back to the billet, only for Davey to take an instant attraction to my bite plate. He came over and bold as brass, wrestled it from my grasp, i.e., stole it. I was overwhelmed by the audacity, and that he was bigger than me. As I reeled from the assault, I realised it would have been difficult to get it home anyway. A point he sorely rubbed in, trying to assuage his guilt for the blatant robbery. That was it, Davey was on the hate list, never to be removed. Lilley and Lovegrove being older cadets did nothing to help, therefore complicit in the crime. Zere names vould also go on ze list.

*

We were pretty free to negotiate the base on our own, so long as we stayed away from obvious security controlled areas outside of our remit. We visited the Battle of Britain memorial flight, and at close quarters we viewed the magnificent Lancaster bomber. Coningsby started as a Lanc base in 1940, so this old bird had come home, to be wheeled out on special occasions for air shows. The Hurricane and Spitfire were its spiritual and historic guardians. In 30 years, we had progressed from supercharged, Merlin-powered, wood-framed aircraft to the supersonic behemoths of today. We were reminded of that power as Martin and I sauntered back around the hangar and back toward the other side of the airfield. As we traversed the tarmac, a pair of Phantoms began taxiing behind us, making toward the runway. We quickened our pace, as the screaming birds began to catch us up. Eventually, we realised we were not going to outrun them. The crew could obviously see us, canopies were open, but I guess they assumed we knew where to go; which we didn't. They were almost upon us, and we leapt onto the grass beside the taxiway. As we did so, we turned away, closing our eyes, as we were caught in the jet wash; it felt like being in front of a giant hairdryer; hot air enveloped us with an enormous roar. As soon as the danger passed, we gathered our composures and continued on our sojourn back to the billet. From the billet window, Spud had observed a pair of Lightning aircraft parked up across the base; we now had time to observe them. They were completely hollow – no engines, you could see straight through from the engine intakes to the rear nacelles. We were told they were moved around the base on cloudy days 'to fool the Russians'. Whether Russian SS20 missiles in Red Square were cardboard is open to conjecture.

We were finally going to be let loose on the firing range. We had drilled and drilled on range discipline. It was a very tightly controlled environment, understandably. Set quite far away from the rest of the base, at the entry point we could hear loud sharp reports as weapons fired. We were reminded it was a criminal offence to remove live or spent ammunition from the premises. All ammo would be collected at the end. It didn't deter idiots like May.

A line of weapons were laid against sandbags, mostly .303 Lee Enfield rifles, some .22 calibre. I started with a .22, aimed it toward the target 25 yards away, and slowly squeezed the trigger. Pfft! The shot was fired. It felt like an air gun. With the ear defenders on, the loud whip crack sound was reduced to a lowly pop. This was easy, I thought. The sharp, sulphurous smell of cordite filled the nostrils, and on pulling back the rifle bolt, the shell case ejected, spinning to the floor. As these hit the ground, they made a satisfying tinkly noise.

On inspection, I had grouped my rounds well enough to achieve ATC marksman on my first attempt. Well done! Five rounds had to be within the area of a 10p piece. To achieve RAF marksman, the same had to be done with the .303 rifle.

I spent ages cradling the .303. Just raising it above the sandbag, the weight was relatively crippling. I aligned the sights with the image of the man on the target. I held my breath, and pulled the stock well into my soldier. I slowly increased the pressure on the trigger; when will it fire? A little more pressure, hold it steady; don't waver…

BANG! Jesus! The weapon jumped a mile, and I felt as if I had been kicked in the shoulder by a mule. Does anyone kicked by a mule think that it was like firing a .303? The power of this thing was shocking. The recoil, followed by the cordite, made the hairs on my neck and head stand on end. My shoulder ached, and this was round one. I could probably stand more rounds with Giant Haystacks.

Steadily, I fired my full 10 rounds. Each time, the stiff bolt jerked back and ejected the hot shellcase, which found a silent landing on the grass or a tinkly one on the tarmac. I was glad it was over. My shoulder was killing me.

'You should put your beret under your denims, to soften the blow,' advised older and experienced Spud, one rifle range session too late. I'll remember next time.

On inspection, the grouping was not tight enough for RAF marksman. No problem. I still did well. So did Martin and Purdey. Oh, so did Little Shit. Typical.

As we lined up to exit, we had to deposit our collected shell cases into metal containers, and declare we had no live ammunition or empty shell cases on our person. As we exited, and began our return to the billet, May grabbed my griping shoulder.

'Look at this,' he said. He had somehow swiped a couple of empty shell cases. You fool, May, you'll get us all in trouble. He put them away, rapidly, before someone senior saw. Someone senior saw didn't see although it was before him. There was always one who tried to spoil it for the rest. If he had been caught, we would all have been guilty by association and embarrassingly forced to open our pockets. I began to think that Davey was welcome to the bite plate; did they have metal detectors on the gates? I didn't know, but they certainly would nowadays.

That night, I wearily slipped into my bed. Hold on, something's wrong here. I can't get my legs more than halfway down. I heard sniggering, and saw other cadets trying, unsuccessfully, to contain their laughter, including Martin.

'You bastards,' I said. They had performed an apple turnover, also known as an apple pie bed. The sheets were folded over and tucked in halfway down, but outside the bed looks normal. I had to get up and remake my bed. What a cruel, albeit common trick. Let's do it to May.

Martin and some others had acquired a fire bucket. They filled it with cold water and waited for the first cadet to fall asleep. May was the first observed, so they dipped his hand in the water, hoping he would pee the bed. Hey presto! He awoke and told them to eff off.

I drifted off to a fitful sleep. Urgh? Wassat? My hand is all wet! Martin!

Next day, we had to assemble for the group photo. Martin had the call to go Air Experience Flying in the Chipmunk trainer. He sauntered off, and we assembled outside the billet to be immortalised on photo paper. The Camp Commandant joined the line up, so there are two rows, uniformed youths and beer gutted middle-aged men. I look abjectly miserable – I remember the sun in my eyes but I wasn't unhappy. Certainly the week held plenty of fear and anxiety, there were so many new experiences and no respite from everybody and everything.

We convened for lunch in the NAAFI. Martin was back.

'How was it?'

'It was great!' he enthused. 'He asked if I wanted to do aerobatics. I said yeah, next moment we're upside down in a barrel roll...'

'Gosh!'

'...Then he's telling me to brace myself, we go into a steep dive and he pulls it up...'

'Yeah?'

'...Into a loop. I'm struggling to raise my arms, the pressure was horrendous. Horrendous! Afterwards he said we pulled 4G!'

'Didn't you feel sick?'

'Yeah, totally. It was great!' It didn't stop him tucking in now, though.

The call came through. Heath, you're next. Report to the training flight ASAP.

At the training flight ASAP, I was kitted out with my parachute and helmet. The leather headpiece housed the RT (Radio Telephone) which had a dark green rubber face piece. You had to talk into this to communicate with the pilot. The parachute was in case of emergency.

'If you are told, 'Jump jump jump,' do not wait to be told again, acknowledge the pilot, 'I am jumping, sir,' but don't wait, he will be gone!' we were told by the Safety Instructor. The Chipmunk T10 trainer had been used for decades to train pilots, and the pupil was placed in the back behind the instructor. We were shown on a mock up how to release the canopy, slide it back, and how to jump out. All extremely tricky on the ground, as the parachute hanging off one's behind caught up on everything. Against the aircraft's slipstream, it would be even more difficult.

'Don't worry,' said the instructor. If the aircraft is on fire, you'll find a way to get out!' No truer words were said in jest.

Inverting the aircraft and falling out was a tried and tested method.

It was my turn to go. The previous flight had completed, and the red, white and silver Chipmunk, registration WK590 turned and faced the taxiway; the prop was turning and the engine producing that familiar howl bespoke to small aircraft. I stood up and tried to walk; it was redolent of Monkey Man, bent forward, the straps so tight on the parachute it looked to an observer if I had cacked my pants. I slowly ambled with the instructor out to the plane, the engine note louder now I was outside. As we got closer to the fuselage, the slipstream from the prop was a forceful stream of air into my face, and the small elevation of my leg onto the wing was even trickier. There is a small painted strip close to the fuselage that says 'walk here'. It would be a short walk; it was only a metre and a half long. *Not much exercise there*, I thought. The next hurdle, literally, was getting a leg over into the cockpit. The stream from the prop was intent on throwing me off the plane altogether. One leg in, on the seat, then the other, followed by the careful lowering of the bum onto the seat, cushioned by the chute. My god, it was cosy. Cramped might be a better word.

The instrument display was right in your face. Anyone would think it was picking a fight. The rpm needle was wavering as the engine idled, I could make out the artificial horizon, the compass in between my legs, great, my arse is facing south. Also, the slip and turn indicator, the airspeed indicator, the altimeter... yep, we had learnt all about these in class. It was a barrage of grey and glass. The instructor connected my RT. Then he connected my safety harness, pulling the straps so tight I could hardly breathe. The canopy slid shut, and the engine noise attenuated. Next I heard the crackling voice of the instructor through my headpiece.

'Can you hear me back there?'

'Yes sir!' I answered meekly. The straps were so tight I

could hardly talk. The sound over the intercom was intermixed with the engine noise, so it was extremely dalek-like. Where's Dave Langley? We could have a Skaro-based conversation in here.

'Ok, ready to go? We're off.'

In the rear seat, the controls are duplicated from the front. I saw levers move, ah, that's the throttle, that's the mix lever (for the fuel mixture); the Gypsy major engine screamed in agreement and moved the plane forward. The view forward was of the pilot's head, as on the tail wheel, we were at the wrong angle for me to see anything. As we bumped along and lined up on the runway, the RT crackled into life. Brief exchanges with the control tower, and we were cleared for take-off. The throttle went all the way forward, the revs shot up and the engine note became a constant pitch. The nose came down as we lifted off the tail, and the outside strips of green either side of the runway sped past the canopy view. Within seconds, we were rising through the air. The ground fell away, and we were flying, the two of us in this little construction of aluminium and fabric. The view was breath taking; in an airliner, you can only see out of a small window, here, you had a view all around the aircraft, obscured only by the wings. We ascended to approx. 2,000 feet, and the instructor asked if I wanted to take control. It was really tough to understand above the engine noise. I answered into my mask, the rubber smell made me feel queasy. I switched the RT to 'on'.

'I have control, sir.' I took the control column. The aircraft yawed slightly, rolled and pitched in slow movements. I corrected the movement with the column. I hadn't as yet found the rudder; I was transfixed on the horizon. The instructor turned to talk to me. I think he was telling me to look around outside the cabin to be aware of other traffic, but as his voice became raised it became an unintelligible garble. I gave him the control back, as I couldn't tell what he was saying, and he was shouting at me. He must have been aware afterwards that I was a little overwhelmed at flying the plane myself, so he pootered it around the sky, pointing out local landmarks on the ground. I imagined what I would do if I had to escape – yes, I could pull that canopy back and get on the wing, yes I could jump out. The ground was a long way down, but it looked like great fun to jump out. As the plane was turned into a tight bank, the world slipped sideways, and I could feel the increasing g-force on my body. It pushed me into my seat, the earth was on its side and I realised how important it was to be tightly strapped in. The occupants and the airframe were one. We moved together in three dimensions and anywhere we wanted to go.

All too soon, after 20 minutes, he brought us down to land. The speed seemed to increase the closer we got to the runway; suddenly we were on the runway and began the slow taxi back to the training office. I thanked the pilot, and once released from the harness by the ground instructor, slowly raised myself up to get out. Exit was just as hard as entry. I monkey walked back into the hut and took off the helmet. I was exhausted. It had been exhilarating, and adrenalin had pumped throughout.

We were all going through the same process, and becoming enlightened by our new experiences. It was my turn to impart my news.

'So, did you do aerobatics?' asked Little Shit.

'No, I didn't fancy becoming a puddle on the floor.'

'Aaah, you wimp! I'm going to if he asks me...'

'Yeah, it's borin', otherwise,' added Rafe. Hardly boring, but bravado knows no bounds.

'I did four barrel rolls,' added Purdey. 'The pilot was loving it, I was almost about to say that's enough and he threw it into another one!'

Each event was followed by the garrulous youth babbling away for hours. The elder cadets were quieter. They had seen it all before, been there, and done that. Spud was always smiling, and had a happy disposition. Gowland senior was always serious, straight down the line. Good bloke, but I always wished he would lighten up a little. He would berate Little Shit for calling him Keith. 'Flight Sergeant on parade,' he would correct. Little Shit was always so keen to impress, if not the officers, it would be his peers. He always had to be at the forefront, the centre of attention. I despised the attention seeking; the ambition was apparent but perhaps praiseworthy. It meant he got on.

Martin recalls a cadet who openly displayed his ability to fart on cue. By process of elimination, it could only have been Lovegrove. He remembers us circling his bed whilst a half-naked cadet raised his rear in the air, showing off his petomane ability. He also thought he was probably gay. Sorry if it wasn't you, Lovegrove. But it sounds pretty funny even I can't recall it first-hand.

*

18.8.77. My log records this day was for 'all day map reading exercise.' I believe it should have read 'walking for miles and miles in mud, shit and pouring rain.' We were off orienteering. I thought this meant visiting Chinatown, but no, we had to get from A to B to C with the aid of two feet, a map and a compass. 'But there's no place on this map called A or B,' I told Spud. He happily whacked me around the head.

'I guess this blue bit is the 'C',' I ventured, pointing to The Wash on the map. He went to whack me again, I swerved and he took May's beret off.

'Oh, sorry, May!' said Spud. 'I was aiming for Heath but your head was in the way!'

We had to convene in a big hall to collect our denims (overalls) and waterproof clothing. It was chucking it down outside, dark and bloody miserable. We arrived from our squad from breakfast in dribs and drabs. Some more drab than others. As I went over to find our guys in the milling ensemble of 100 or so cadets, May was keen to impart some urgent news.

"Ere, I pulled up Evan's waterproof for a laugh, and I found he had his dick in his hand! The dirty sod was playing with himself!' May could hardly stop laughing; his face was always in a state of perpetual amusement.

Evans didn't confirm or deny such scurrilous information. Therefore it seemed to be true, he really was a little wanker.

We collected our denims, our huge waterproof that weighed a ton and seemed to be one size fits all, i.e. huge. It had a hood and it would keep the rain out, anyway. The NCOs (non-commissioned officers) gathered us in teams, showed us briefly where we going on the ordnance survey map, played with their silver compasses and we were off.

I had no idea where we going, how long it would take, or even what was the point? I could understand a class about map reading, which we had covered back at base. I had yet to truly learn the benefits of working within a team, or the fact that all individuals have to pull their weight. I was to trudge along, get tired, wet and completely fed up; probably because I felt excluded from the decision making process, the seniors led, instructed and decided where we went. We walked for hours, across fields, woods, county lanes, squelching in the mud. The rain was relentless, it seemed to find every surface that wasn't covered and ran down into places that were. I was cold, my feet ached. Vision was restricted by the hood. Are we there yet?

Gowland Junior handed me the water bottle. 'Your turn,' he helpfully told me. Yes it was but I wish it wasn't. It was bloody heavy, on a strap that after a while cut into your shoulder. What are we carrying this for? Stick your tongue out if you're thirsty! I whinged, moaned, and whinged again. After hours of torture, we arrived at Point B. Lunch! On a muddy hillside in some woods, we were proffered some weak squash, a packet of crisps and a pork pie. Who wants my pork pie? Martin had it. He bit into it, grimaced and was almost sick. He had a mouthful of jelly, he wasn't keen on it. It found an exit.

We carried on after 'lunch' to a few more meeting points. By now it was raining so much, that birds were devolving back into fish. Shiny puddles rippled as drop after drop pelted down. The typewriter rain pinged off the top of our hoods, and all I wanted was a hot shower. I'm in a never ending shower, and I want more? Eventually, after a long hard day on the hoof, we wearily entered the billet block. Our leaden legs barely made the stairs, followed by the disrobing ceremony in the laundry room. This was a narrow utility area between billets, and it stank of wet laundry and gorgonzola cheese. It was probably Evans's socks. We hung up our wet clothes and took a moment or five to recover. Flight Sergeant Gowland sat down and addressed a few of us. Was he going to post us?

'Well, gentlemen; it's official. They are confirming war.'

My heart skipped a beat, ran off around the block, and finally came back again.

'What? With the Russians?' I said. He was so sombre; I thought he meant there were forces about to attack each other across the east/west divide of Germany.

He looked at me as if I was mad. 'No, with next door. We are officially at war with their squad.'

You wally, you really had me going. There's me imagining imminent nuclear Armageddon and he's talking about earning a few points more on room inspection and drill in healthy competition.

Back to the billet, strip off clothes, get into those hot showers... hold on, what's going on here? Senior cadets wielding toothpaste... oh, no, they're not, are they? They were. We had to subject ourselves to the sadists as they squirted different red and white cream all over our lower bodies. Rafe joined in with the instigators, so did Little Shit, as his mate. It was humiliating. One by one, cadets exited toward the showers, dripping toothpaste as they held towels close to their bodies. I was subjected to the cold treatment, it didn't hurt, but it was messy. I was about to get cleaned off, and I was accosted by Little Shit, we were the last two in the billet. He came close.

'Heaf, you're always moanin'!' He paused. His face dropped. 'I hear what you say about me, about what you call me...'

Wham. He punched me in the chin. My ears started ringing. Wha, what? Did he just hit me? We stared at each other. I walked away, to my shower. I cleaned off the muck of the day; my chin was hurting, but not too much. It was a light punch, an almost unstoppable emotional reaction from him. He got his wish. I stopped moaning. I certainly didn't engage with Rafe. I had had it with both of them. Cheeky bastard. How dare he hit me?

Cadets were comparing notes on the caustic nature of toothpaste brands. 'Oh, that Macleans really stings! Colgate does nothing, though!'

No, well, it's meant to keep your breath fresh. I guess there were a few in the squadron with minty balls that night.

As we drifted off to sleep, the rain still lashing the windows, my thoughts turned to the next couple of days. Our adventure was nearly over, we would soon be home. I wanted to go home, now; I wanted to get away from obsequious oafs and paedophiliac lower rankers. Little Shit was the biggest little ranker of them all. That night, the JT did his rounds again. A dozen pair of eyes followed his every move. Why would a grown man tuck in young lads unless he had unclean intentions? He made my flesh creep. The last day, just before we left, a cadet let his bike tyres down. I hope he wasn't too deflated by us leaving.

5. Rising Up

The world was changing. Jimmy Carter was the new President of the USA, the Queen was celebrating 25 years as Monarch, and Elvis had just died aged 42. And just after the week away at camp, we were thrust into the local spotlight at the Basingstoke Show. This used to be an annual summer event, which hosted a show jumping competition at its centre. All the local businesses used to turn out and flog their wares, set on the Basingstoke common near to my school. Our base was a large tent, within which we were fed and watered, as well as a respite from the weather. As it was September, it was always steaming hot, and we were obliged to keep berets on at all times. This meant the sweat used to build up under it, giving one's hair a Turkish bath. The cadets were stationed by the horse jumping fences, and had to pick up the fallen beams when the horses charged into them. This they did quite often, which also unseated the rider on many occasions. We could handle picking up the fences, although they were extremely heavy; what we weren't told to do was grab the reins of errant horses, which would run around as their hapless jockey, resplendent in red coat, would struggle to get up after headbutting a six-foot barrier. We would look at each, silently questioning whether we should attend horse or rider, ultimately deciding: no. The St John's Ambulance men, bless 'em, resembled a fleet of Private Godfreys from 'Dad's Army'. By the time they would reach you, you'd be dead. The PA announcer would try and make light of it, sometimes a little bit of panic would enter his voice. 'Would someone please like to grab that horse before it runs onto the A30...?!' A member of the public would normally oblige.

It was a long, hard, hot, physical day, but it was great fun. Lunch was a bread roll and tomato soup, beef burgers and Battenberg cake. May dunked his cake into his soup.

'Urrgh, May, what are you doing?' laughed Purdey. May cackled and carried on doing it. I wasn't as yet keen on beef burgers so I donated mine to the braying mob, i.e. Adey May, and who had both as well as his own. At debrief, back at base, Blockhead asked who was it who didn't like burgers, as they had tried to cater for all. I put my hand up.

'Ah, yes, Cadet May.'

'Heath, sir.'

'Sorry, I meant Cadet Heath. And who was it who was dunking their cake in their soup?'

'Cadet May, sir!' went the call.

'It wasn't, it was Heath!' deflected May. In Blockhead's confusion and deaf state, it went down in folklore that I was the cake dunker of 1977. Woe betide anyone who let me speak the truth.

At school, I had a difficult year. All my report books seemed to state, 'Trevor is not making the requisite effort, could do much better.' Five years is a long time to sustain interest, let alone maintain strong work. However, I got the message, and started to put more time into my studies. It's possible it had begun to slacken because of the joint pressures of ATC and school orchestra; one would eventually have to give. Playing in the orchestra was enormous fun, as I had started as a lowly third violin, but now was in the first violins and my sound was cutting through. I had progressed up the grades faster than Miss Mason could measure, and was now working towards Grade Four. If there wasn't a local festival to play, it would be rehearsing at lunchtimes and some evenings for end of term concerts. We would have really good visiting piano players, and Mr Murray Brown, my third year form tutor, was extremely good. He was also a bit of a misanthrope at times; Lucas Murphy screamed, 'Jew Test!' at the end of one day in our form room, and about six of us dived after the coin he threw, including me.

'You, you, you, detention,' declared Murray Brown. What? For diving after a half penny piece? He was one of a few teachers that came with us on a skating trip to Southampton. He was late back to the coach, and his collar was covered in lipstick. He was extremely embarrassed and tried to get it off.

'Never hurry a Murray,' said Shaun Roe, wittily. That became our catchphrase for him, after a famous Murray mints advert. Our form room was in the new music block. Murray Brown disappeared into the store cupboard one morning, and Shaun pushed a table across the door, just as a joke. MB wasn't impressed and ended up kicking the door, causing the table to damage it. Once he had furiously fought his way out, it was big trouble for Shaun. Bloody Murray Brown, what sort of teacher goes mental like that?

Being a bit of a mentalist was a contagion that spread through creative types. Miss Mason could be an absolute nightmare; a seething gorgon of spitefulness and ego. Between playing, we would all be playing our own little bits and pieces, which was cacophonous and irritating. As she raised her baton, if she wouldn't receive instant attention, she would throw a strop. If the playing was out of time, she would throw a strop. If someone was late, she would throw a strop. In fact, I think the picture I am painting is not of the most patient person in school. The concerts would make up for it. The best two we had were playing the 1812 Overture, complete with awesome kettle drums recreating cannon fire; and Gershwin's Rhapsody in Blue, with MB at the piano. We were a damn good orchestra at that time; standing ovations and first prizes at competition. Miss Mason gave talk about us having a recording session; unfortunately, it was all just talk, nothing transpired. A shame, as we would have risen to the occasion.

It was also that year I started having migraines. I recognised what it was as Martin had them, and it fit the description perfectly. The first was at a sunny lunchtime; I thought it was the Sun's afterimage still burning on my eyelids; unfortunately it was the start of a migraine with halo. The vision in centre of the eye went very weird, and after a while, I couldn't see anything but flashing lights and a jumbled up view of objects. When the vision began to settle down, came the headache. Oh wow, not just a few pangs but a throbbing, persistent pain that intensified and made me feel sick. The only remedy is sitting quietly in a darkened room; well, that and beheading. I settled for the former. It was an indication of the growing pressure of a teenage boy, exams, puberty, growing up; my body was experiencing changes, my sight was getting worse, and I had to juggle all while suffering the adolescent rantings of a neurotic music teacher.

I enjoyed most of my lessons. Physics was always fun; trying to see how a house fly can fly with its wings singed off by a Bunsen burner is pretty educational. The answer is, it doesn't. It can hop pretty well, though. Those with wool blazers were reasonably safe, acrylic blazers, oh oh – they would go up in flames in an instant. It would be best not to stand near pupils with a sociopathic tendency, e.g. Potter. Graham Jennings and Ian Dorricot were my mates in physics. Graham used to eat two Mars bars a day, without fail. They certainly made him work, rest and play. Surprisingly, he was skinny as a rake. Maths was the only bugbear. I had been put down one class after my first year exam result of 51%. I was always good at Maths, and was in the full 'O' Level stream for my other subjects, but because I made no effort to revise for that flipping exam, I was put into a class full of disruptive elements. My attention would sometimes be distracted by other things, most notably Karen 'Double D' Desborough. She sat next to me for a while and it was hard to focus on the board when she was there. Her cleavage would often cast me into shadow. Natural talent would prevail; I made the effort and got upgraded back to the 'O' Level stream for the fourth year. Now I would have to catch up.

On September 16th, 1977, Marc Bolan was killed as the Mini he was being driven in by his girlfriend, hit a tree. Less T. Rex, more tree wrecked. The Yorkshire Ripper was still at large, murdering young women, the new Space Shuttle achieved its first free flight, and Concorde began the first supersonic service between London and New York. At ATC, we had a succession of guest speakers, one of whom was a Concorde Flight Engineer.

This chap was very entertaining. He explained that on the ground, he couldn't get his fingers behind his flight panel, but at 60,000 feet and at Mach 2, he could get his whole arm behind it. The fuselage expanded that much at that height. At the end of his lecture, he set a quiz question, which I got right after shooting up my hand. I won a Concorde flight plan map, showing the areas where it was allowed to go supersonic. It fetched nearly 20 quid on eBay 30 years later, not bad. After it was over, I set my fellow cadets a question.

'What is white and travels at twice the speed of sound?'

'Er, Concorde?'

'No, May when the tuck shop is open!'

May was terrible. Double entendres were designed for him. I think Finbarr Saunders from Viz was invented from direct observation of the fat sod. If there could be a sexual interpretation of what someone said, May would start giggling. Unfortunately, that would set Colin off, then me. When the speaker was deadly serious, it became a true struggle to maintain dignity.

One week, we had a Dutchman who had fought in the resistance during WW2. We learnt a new word, *quisling*. A quisling was an informer, a collaborator. He spat the word out as if he were chewing on a lump of excrement. He talked for maybe 40 minutes of how his compatriots were rounded up after conspiring to upset Nazi operations. He paused. A hand went up.

'What happened to them, sir?' Evans asked.

'Oh, they were shot,' he stated matter-of-factly. It was a sobering lesson and we all departed that night a lot quieter than usual.

Another night would be First Aid practice. Silky Wilky presented us with Sussie Annie – a resuscitation practice doll. Of course, to May, this was a blow up sex doll. He was purple in moments as soon as Silky started blowing in her mouth. Compressions on the ample proportions of the life-size mannequin had him almost passing out, his inhaler working overtime.

'Some of you I'm sure find this hilarious,' Silky correctly stated. My eyes met May's – big mistake. Keep serious! Keep serious! 'But this could make the difference between life and death.' You're right, Silky, I'm gonna kill May, if he doesn't die suppressing his laughter first.

We all had a go on Sussie Annie. It was hard work.

'If you do it correctly, you will break a few ribs,' advised Silky. Blimey. It always looks easier when someone does it on the telly.

Wilky arranged for us to have a tour of the Police Station. It was probably equal deterrent as much as education – showing us where we might end if we were naughty boys. The cells were very basic, and we heard a few horror stories. It was always interesting to visit establishment buildings; it felt as if we were being kept in the loop. For a chunky old boy, Wilky could still shift. We had a snowball fight one evening after heavy snow, and he raced after me. He eventually caught me and deposited a few pounds of ice down my neck. That evening was given over completely to the activity outside, which showed the instructors had a great sense of humour. Time just fell away, we were all having a great laugh, and no one wanted to start lectures that night.

We received a radio. Not a beach one, but a whopping great thing that required a 20 foot aerial. We learnt how to set the frequency and the correct way to conduct communications. In the days of mobile phones, it seems passé, then, it was very exciting. The only problem being, we would only communicate with about two people, both of whom were civilian instructors with mobile units in their cars. We were Hotel Papa Alpha One; they were Hotel Papa Alpha Mike One and Mike Two. Brevity was not allowed, oh no; to correctly call them, it would be:

'This is Hotel Papa Alpha One calling Hotel Papa Alpha Mike One, are you receiving, over?'

Eventually they would answer:

'This is Hotel Papa Alpha One Mike One to Hotel Papa Alpha One, receiving you loud and clear, strength 5, over!'

And so on. No chat about the weather or the sports results, just bland, uninteresting bollocks. This would continue until the instructor arrived at HQ, counting down the minutes until his ETA. Scintillating. Colin eventually got himself a CB set, Citizens Band radio, spurred on by the success of the film, 'Convoy!' That was still bland, uninteresting bollocks but with complete strangers instead. Martin and I both bought Air Band radios. With these, you could listen to aircraft messaging the ground, and also the Police Network. 'Speedbird' was the call sign for a Concorde. We would spend hours listening in between the static, trying to make out where the aircraft was or a local incident with the cops. Occasionally a taxi would break into the flow with a massively loud transmission that would almost take your ear off.

We learnt the phonetic alphabet and Morse code, so we could converse either way on the ATC radio. Martin rigged up a beeper box from an old tobacco tin, a speaker and a battery, so we could practise. We got very adept at communicating in Morse, to the point where we would say 'dit dah dit' and so on to spell out words verbally, such as 'rem'. In the arcane world of a teenager, a new way to communicate surreptitiously would always be welcome. Text speak? Pah! We were there 30 years earlier. We enjoyed looking toward May, and ditdahing about the Tango Whisky Alpha Tango.

A revolution happened in the UK in the mid-seventies. It was a quiet sedition and suddenly we were overrun. McDonald's opened their first restaurant in Woolwich, London, in 1974. I visited a restaurant with Mum in 1977 and had my first burger. I enjoyed it but it was strange, as I had never really tried beef until then. After that, I got a real taste for it; my taste buds had been reborn, and I started to eat other hitherto rejected foods. I was losing my fussiness. Consequently, and I suspect completely related, I grew taller and slimmer. It was a protracted process, but it was happening. I noticed Martin was suddenly shorter than me? What happened there? Has he taken his boots off?

Somebody else was rising, but not in height. Little Shit and Rafe were promoted to Corporals. Oh no, how could they? The Gruesome Twosome in charge? It didn't really matter, all they could do was drill us around the parade square and take on more delegation duties. At least it officially separated us more as cadets, they could do their corporally thing with their corporally mates. Go on, get over there and *separate*.

Straight after Coningsby, we had an AEF (Air Experience Flight) event come up at our local airfield, Hamble. Basingstoke is part of the Hampshire and Isle of Wight wing. Cadets would apply for such events and would get lucky (or not) based on the number of applicants. Colin, Martin and I all were picked for the Hamble trip. It was always a crack of dawn start. Mum would wake me up before the Sun had got his nightshirt off, around 0430. We would be deposited at HQ and it was always flipping freezing. Aboard a waiting minibus and as the sun slowly rose in the sky, we would rub the dust from our eyes and get excited about the day. The facilities at Hamble were perfunctory but adequate; it was effectively a large hut on the edge of the airfield, which housed a waiting area and a mock up cockpit to practise entry and exit. Those who had not attended camp were having their first Chipmunk flight, such as Colin. It was a lot of waiting around for your turn, which allowed the butterflies to multiply in our empty stomachs. Closer to flight time, we would be strapped tightly into our parachutes. That was it, no going to the loo now; not unless you wanted to risk accidental circumcision. One's trouser legs would be pulled up to shin height, as the crotch strap lifted everything, including ones voice two octaves. The engine note of the approaching aircraft would get louder, until we saw the plane out of the hut window. We would then, in turn, walk the crab/monkey walk out to the stationary Chipmunk, passing our compatriot, mirror image style, walking the crab/monkey walk into the hut. Same as before, RT connected, straps tightened until asphyxiation, canopy shut.

Once airborne, the instructor asked me if I had flown before.

'Have you flown in a Chipmunk before?'

'Yes sir. One month ago.'

'Very good. Did you want to take control?'

'Yes sir.'

He showed me the controls in more depth than last time. He would say, 'I am moving the column to the left, ailerons go up port wing, down on starboard, port wing goes down,' which sure enough it did. 'This is the rolling motion. I pull the control column toward me to ascend, forward to descend, this is the pitching motion. Watch the rudder pedals…'

I did. They moved in and out. The nose of the aircraft moved sideways.

'…Rudder to the left, nose moves to the left, and vice versa. This is the yaw motion. Now, you have a go, you have control...'

'I have control, sir,' I correctly stated, although the reality was I grabbed the control column and hung on for dear life.

'Make sure you look all around you, watch out for other aircraft. Keep the wings level with the horizon, the nose steady, correct any movements, and try to keep on the heading we are presently on.'

It was a little tricky; the altimeter showed slow inclination upward, and gusts would tip the trim of the aircraft constantly. It wasn't a battle, but a constant series of corrections to maintain height and course.

'Let's try a turn; to starboard, control column to the right, with a little bit of rudder to avoid slipping out of the turn, that's it; keep the column there... nose up... ok, straighten up...'

It was awesome. The light in the cockpit would dance around as we paraded the heavens, the view for miles and miles. We flew over *HMS Victory* in Portsmouth, a small toy next to a blue grey sea. The view was becoming a little hazy as we flew over the coast. We had been instructed to operate our life jacket if we had to bail out, but only *after* exiting the aircraft. It was nice to know it had a whistle and a self-inflating tube – as if hitting the water you would have any puff. Life expectancy in the sea during summer was around a few hours. In winter, it can be as low as 20 minutes. Best not to bail out unless absolutely necessary...

All too soon, we turned for base and were coming into land. I really enjoyed it this time, as I knew what was going on and could understand the pilot. As with all things, the experience of doing it makes it easier the next time. It was still a relief when we landed safely. No matter how many times you fly, especially in small aircraft, terra firma is literally life affirming. With airscrew turning in a blur of speed, I climbed out of WK 630 after my 24 minute flight, and walked the familiar bent over monkey walk back to the hut. Now I could eat my sandwiches; confident that I wouldn't be seeing them again.

We had another venture to Hamble in January 1978, in which I flew again in WK630 for a further 20 minutes. I had now spent an hour in the air with Chipmunks, and every time it was exciting and great fun. The very nature of flight does not allow complacency or lack of concentration.

Doing the monkey walk: AEF in a de Havilland Chipmunk, Hamble Jan 1978. (Trevor Heath archive.)

A few of us were chosen to take part in a Guard of Honour parade. It was to be in May at RAF Odiham, representing Hampshire and Isle of Wight wing. We would have to learn to drill with rifles, and were issued with special webbing and gaiters.

The gaiters were a nightmare. They were strapped around the ankles and had to hold the trousers just so; the webbing belt sat around the tunic and were almost impossible to hold in position. Finally, the strap of the rifle was to match the look of the rest of the kit – in white. We were instructed to purchase blanco – no, I had never heard of it – and whiten the kit ourselves. This powder had been used since 1880 by the military to colour cotton webbing, we could now buy it in a paint form. Where could we get it? Oh, God – Staffords. Off to see Ivor and Neville.

'Can we buy blanco here?'

'I'm sure you can buy who you want, love,' cooed Ivor. Shiver.

We had special practice on parade nights to learn how to properly drill with rifles. Normally, we would be wheeled all over the parade ground (i.e. the car park) by the Flight Sergeant or a Sergeant. For this, Blockhead wasn't taking any chances. He employed the services of a professional RAF drill instructor to bring us up to speed. Could he shout? YES HE COULD. AT EVERY OPPORTUNITY. YOU 'ORRIBLE LITTLE CADET!

Once we had been issued with a rifle for the evening, it didn't leave our side until we were exhausted. Slope arms, order arms, trail arms, present arms. Now I know why they call it the army, all they do is tire their arms out. I hoped all this lugging around of a weapon would build muscles, instead the rifle laughed at them. The .303 weighs 8.8lbs (4kgs) and after a while it became a dead weight; a dead weight that's 44 inches long, unwieldy and very uncomfortable. If we messed up, we would have to hold the weapon above our heads until told to stop; it was absolute torture. It certainly tightened up our concentration, as well as the biceps. Drop the weapon, oh dear; run around the parade square until told to stop. I didn't need the gym aged 15, I was crazily active in the ATC.

LEE ENFIELD: Call yourself a man? I've been wielded

by experts, mate.

ME: I'm sorry, I won't be talked to like this by my rifle; you're fired.

The Lee Enfield .303 rifle has been around since 1895, and around 17 million of them have been produced. If only its ergonomics was matched to its ubiquity. We actually enjoyed being shouted at by this maniac, because doing it wrong increased the chances of accidental injury. Drop the weapon from height onto your compatriots' foot or head would not be popular. The worst thing was the blanco. It rubbed off and stained the clothing, as well as needing redoing virtually every week. It felt like you were painting your clothes, because effectively, you were. When it ran out, it meant a trip to Staffords. Could you get it for me, Mum?

Martin and I were struggling to get a brilliant shine on our boots. We spent hours 'spooning' the bobbles on the toecap area. This involved heating up a large spoon and applying it to the leather, aiming to smooth it out. It didn't work. Hours upon hours of applying layer after layer of polish, and we couldn't achieve the desired effect. Martin had a brainwave – why don't we paint it on? We can't do that, I said. Nothing to do with principle, we'd get found out. Martin pressed on regardless. He proudly showed me gleaming boots, the toecap so shiny, that magpies were trying to take off with them. He had painted them with black gloss enamel paint, procured to use on Airfix kits. He topped it off with clear lacquer, so it hardened and was virtually impenetrable. It also meant that aside from keeping them clean, no further polishing was required. Fantastic! I did the same with mine. Voila! Shiny boots! It took a steady hand to achieve a straight line across. We just hoped that no one would suspect. He's always trouble, that no one.

The 1970s was truly the start of the digital age. In the 1973 Bond movie, 'Live and Let Die', I saw Roger Moore with his LED digital watch and believed my life would not be complete without one. When eventually they hit the market, Mum and Dad bought me one for my birthday, probably 1976. It was around £25 and I loved it. The downside was, you couldn't view the time in direct sunlight, and viewing the time drained the battery. 'Don't hit the view button more than four times a day,' was the manufacturer's helpful advice. Brilliant. Suffice to say, LED watches were a flash in the pan, quickly superseded by LCD devices, which revolutionised electronics as we knew it. Around early '78, I felt my life would not be complete without a girlfriend; the analogy is complete, as this would prove to be more trouble than its worth and a major disappointment.

I was very good friends with Cheryl. That would have been fine, but for all the matchmaking pushed upon us by our young peers, which resulted in inflammatory messages scribbled on blackboards, such as 'Trevor loves Cheryl Barton' or worse. We were just friends, and any attempts by outside influences to change that to suit their impressions would not change that. Unfortunately, the taunts wound me up. Mick Steele made one too many quips and I slapped him across the face. I don't know why I did it, as my hand was millimetres from his cheek, I regretted it. Mick went pink, more in shock than pain, and when he regained his balance, paid me back by booting my shins and ankles with his Doc Martens. I retreated from the class room, and rued the fact I had lost a mate over a stupid reaction to a stupid jibe. I needn't have worried, as we both apologised to each other at the end of the day, and it was forgotten. It showed I was touchy about the subject of Cheryl and me as an item, which we weren't. As much as I tried, because it would have been convenient, I didn't fancy Cheryl. I realise now I have always been adept at befriending women, and can establish deep friendships without romance muddying the waters; at that age, I couldn't handle the continual association, so I started to ignore Cheryl. It was subtle at first, but she soon noticed. I would walk ahead of her, try to disengage, effectively being a bit cruel. It left her in tears. I felt terrible, but I had to show the world we were not together. Communication skills are not fully formed at age 14. We basically ignored each other until we left school. It was 22 years before I was able to apologise properly.

Tracy, on the other hand, piqued my interest. She flirted around Art Class, her twizzly long hair in the boys' faces, perfume wafting around like a fragrant Pepe Le Pew. She loved the attention and had the lot of them virtually eating out of her hand. I deliberately feigned disinterest, which sparked one of her acolytes attempt to disinvest me of my heartfelt desires. I gave nothing away on such gentle probing, designed to make me drop my guard and confess my undying lust. No chance, mate. I was flattered that she wanted to know, though. I had virtually zero self-confidence, and when pushed to chat with a girl who I was attracted to, my mouth spouted nonsense in complete dislocation from my brain. Better not to engage. Keep cool. Forget about it.

But I couldn't. Hormones do not see sense. Somehow I cracked a complex code of information and obtained her address. I did what any self-respecting suitor would do when tongue tied discourse dismissed success – I sent her a love letter. Reams of flattery and desires flowed from my pen and expressed themselves on the page. Open heart surgery could not have been more exposing. As soon as the envelope dropped into the post box, I regretted it. I hated myself. Why have I made such an idiot of myself? She'll laugh at me. I'll never do this again. God, what a buffoon. My self-recriminations only ended when she called me. What? You were flattered and pleased to receive my letter? In retrospect, why wouldn't she be? I sang her praises louder than an Archbishop at a Royal wedding. She invited me to the pictures; we went to see 'Sergeant Pepper's Lonely Hearts Club Band' featuring the Bee Gees. It was tosh but she liked it. I liked it because I was with a pretty girl. I cycled with her to her dad's place at Ellisfield, her parents were divorced or separated. I started babysitting with her. We would listen to records, all the really awful K-Tel compilations included. 'I lost my heart to a Starship Trooper,' indeed. All the time, there was no real intimacy. She treated me like a sycophantic lackey. I guess she liked the attention, the flattery. She actually already had a boyfriend; strange relationship. He was a mate of a mate, known as Lofty Lighthouse, because, surprise surprise, he was quite tall. I can't remember his real name. He appeared out of nowhere one day outside the Newman Wing, one of the main school buildings.

'You stay away from Tracy, Heath, or I'll have you!'

'Calm down, Lofty. She can see who she likes, that goes for me, too.'

'I'm warning you, stay away!'

With his empty threat complete, he faded into the background. I don't know what he was worried about. She didn't seem that interested in me; and yet, she wanted to do stuff together. Perhaps it was all a ploy to make him jealous. She seemed to want me for something, but not what I craved from her. I would be mesmerised by her femininity, it ferociously fired pheromones, pinging off the furniture and colliding back into me. She seemed unperturbed. Perhaps she was a witch. She was certainly bewitching me.

'I love your eyes, Trace. Fantastic colour. What are they? (Cue gaze into eyes.) Hazel. What are mine?'

She waved her hand, dismissively. 'Bluey grey, wishy washy, like the sea. The sea makes me sick.'

I laughed off such slights. But it was obvious she had no romantic intention whatsoever. I would stay late with her babysitting, which resulted in a very early morning cycle ride home. It was around three miles. I arrived home about two in the morning on one occasion. Dad was at the top of the stairs.

'Trevor. What time do you call this?'

I attempted to surmount the stairs to bed, tired, disappointed.

'Sorry, Dad, I didn't mean to…'

I didn't finish. Dad pushed me roughly down the stairs. He had never been so violent or uncaring for my safety. I hurt myself at the bottom. He launched a trade about coming home so late, and that it won't happen again. No, Dad. I was angry at him for his anger, and his reaction. I guess he thought I was up to no good. Chance would be a fine thing. Not only was I getting nowhere with Tracy, I was getting into trouble with Dad for staying out so late.

I didn't have to refuse any further requests for babysitting. She didn't ask me again. It was all over before it had even begun. I was unceremoniously dumped with a note in my desk. I was devastated. It was for the best. She was a time wasting, self-interested cow. But I couldn't see that then. I withdrew. Best not to try with the opposite sex, at all. Too much trouble, too much hurt. We never spoke again. It would be a long time before I would recover my self-esteem or indeed, any confidence. I was an untrendy, boringly dressed aviation obsessive with a poor haircut and glasses. My cheekbones had yet to cut through the baby fat. I was getting taller, slimmer, but it was still a year away before the height dissipated the weight into a more acceptable aesthetic; or at least, acceptable to me. I was embarrassed; embarrassed for opening my heart, laying myself wide open to abuse. It left me feeling vulnerable. I didn't like it. I could close off my feelings of anger to irritants like Gowland, or the school bullyboys, who meant nothing to me except someone to avoid. This was different; it cut to the bone, to the core. Melancholia casts a long shadow.

Interestingly, I was definitely getting fitter. Whether it was all the cycling, and the activities with the cadets, but at school, I was getting more able at sports. At cross country running, I was quite a way from last; I even beat Duncan Hall, who was a lanky get and was quite surprised by my late burst of energy to beat him over the line.

'Well done, Trevor,' he said between gasps for oxygen. He shook my hand. I was impressed with myself, and with his magnanimity.

My school work was getting better again, as I started to make the effort. I was back in the top class for maths, and sat next to a late starter to our school, Simon Maroney. Simon was a member of the BAAB club (blind as a bat), and wore heavy glasses, primarily to correct a lazy eye. He was quite disruptive when he wanted to be; he suddenly wrote 'sabotage' across my workings out on a complex problem. Mr Vic was our maths teacher. He was alright but often got up our nose. That was our staple joke. Here's another staple joke, Maroney, your whole maths text book stapled together with about 100 of the metal buggers. Somehow, I was cutting through this buffoonery and obtaining better grades. I had missed out on additional maths, however. Dave Langley and Simon Coates sailed into the algebraic ocean of calculus toward their future accountancy careers; I could barely count my blessings as I had escaped Karen 'Double D' Desborough and her twin mountains of distraction.

*

14.05.78. The day of the Guard of Honour, for the Hants and IOW Ceremonial Review. We were coached into RAF Odiham with cadets from other squadrons. Odiham is a few miles from Basingstoke, the nearest RAF base, and it was a joy not to have travel a long distance for a change. When we arrived, we were left to kick our heels for a while before proceedings began; not literally, as most had to preserve the shine on our boots. One cadet from another squadron had noticed my and Martin's pristine toecaps.

'Ere, 'ow did you get a shine like that on yer boots, like?'

Martin and I exchanged nervous glances. The cadet, unprompted and unwantedly got down closer for a better look. He touched Martin's boot.

'Hey, this is painted on! They've painted their effin' boots!'

Shhh! You idiot! Don't tell everybody! The damn fool started a wildfire of cynical mockery that engulfed the coach. We couldn't wait to get off. Little Shit thought it hilarious. Thankfully, the officers didn't hear.

Guard of honour, RAF Odiham May 1978. Martin is on the left, Anthony Gowland on the right. Mr Bourne is in the middle. Spud is at the back to the right. (Martin Stevens Archive)

Keen to get on with it, and to divert attention away from our lacquered lace-ups, we began an impromptu kit review with other cadets, straightening webbing belts, berets, and tunics. The gaiters were particularly troublesome, forever spinning around, riding up and generally attempting to spoil the ensemble. Eventually, we were marched into the briefing room, given our instructions for the day, and marched out to a huge hangar that normally housed the Puma helicopters. RAF Odiham was host to both 33 and 230

Squadrons, still with the odd 72 Squadron Westland Wessex amidst the Pumas.

There were a lot of cadets there, and the reviewing officer was Air Commodore MJE Swiney OBE RAF; the big cheese himself. Flags were waved, the ground subject to the assault of a few hundred pairs of blakeys, parents and assembled throng looked on proudly. Everyone was to be seated by 1350 hours, the Mayor of Basingstoke to arrive at 1355, and we were marched on at 1400. Oh yes, there were speeches. Unfortunately for some, they went on for rather a long time. After prayers, inspection, and presentation of awards, we had been standing there for nearly an hour.

Crunch. What was that? We can't turn our heads. We are on parade, in full public view. Crash. What is going on? From the corner of my eye, I saw one cadet fall straight forward, landing on his chin. Ouch. He didn't move. I can't believe he didn't break his jaw. Officers were milling all over the place, picking up collapsing faintees who couldn't stand still without causing a fuss. Whoops, there goes another; falling backwards this time after an initial fairly imperceptible wobble, caught by his cadet colleagues. I didn't see that on the itinerary: 14:45 – first cadet bites tongue off after impacting hangar floor; 14:47 – cadet loses toe after rifle from fainting colleague lands on it. They were dropping like flies, as if attacked by Lilliputian lumberjacks in a cadet forest. Thankfully, none of the GOH befell the low blood pressure curse.

Warrant Officer Ledger had given us a tip; if you felt a little light headed, or a leg had gone to sleep, gently rock onto the balls of the feet, or give a little sway; not enough for anyone to notice, but just enough to keep adequate circulation. It worked well. Someone should have told the others. Maybe they did, and they were just peenywally.

Our rifle drill went perfectly, our marching was impeccable. We finished the day tired, our hands and clothes covered in white blanco dust, and desperate to remove our still shining boots. It goes to show that training by rote can achieve perfection; that and a lot of shouting.

6. Flying Low

Images of a burned face on a 40 foot screen are quite shocking. The RAF used that shock tactic on a promotional campaign to raise money for the RAF Association Benevolent Fund. In conjunction with footage from the film, 'Reach For The Sky' and our mate, Douggie Bader (Sir Douglas to you), adverts were screened in cinemas to jolt the general public into reaching deep into their pockets for the fallen heroes of the RAF. After being guilt tripped into the need to donate, willing volunteers were on hand to collect the cash – the ATC.

We were asked if we wanted to attend Cinema Duty, usually it was half a dozen cadets going around with collection tins. It was always embarrassing performing public duties in full uniform; you couldn't exactly melt into the background in full regalia. It seemed like a fun idea, and hopefully, we would get to see a film or two for free.

May, Colin, Martin, myself, Little Shit, Purdey and Monkey Man arrived at the Odeon, Basingstoke, and reported to the box office. The film showing was 'Slap Shot', a violent X-rated comedy, which meant you had to be 18 to view. We were each given a collecting tin, and waited behind the main entrance doors to the cinema before the promo film was shown. As the lights came down, we came in and stood at the back as the film started.

The promo was quite hard hitting; images of burns victims and paraplegics were shown being wheeled around hospital corridors and grounds, and you could see the audience wriggling uneasily in their seats. As young lads, we were equally uncomfortable with the imagery, and in true adolescent fashion, when confronted with socially difficult situations, we found it all quite funny. To make matters worse regarding socially acceptable behaviour, there had recently been a spate of disabled jokes doing the rounds. Sample: What is the definition of cruelty? Fixing a kick start on an invalid carriage. It may read as especially cruel now, but it is a part of growing up, to accept those that are different, not to mock, and ultimately, to help. We were halfway there, at least.

As soon as the film ended, and just prior to the main feature, the lights came up. Colin jangled his tin. I looked at him. He winced, knowing it was a clichéd introduction but it made people turn, see us and reach into their pockets. Some were especially generous – green and even blue notes were going in the tins. For the advantage of those born after 1980, green notes were one pound and blueys were fivers; and a pound was still quite a bit in 1978.

Generosity exhausted, we hoisted the bristling tins back to the main office, and emptied the contents onto the low tables. As soon as a member of staff turned their backs or went out, coins were finding their ways into cadet pockets. Martin observed Cadet May counting, 'One for them, one for me, one for them, one for me…' Very soon, his pockets were bulging to the point he could hardly walk without igniting his underpants. He found his way out to the concession stand, whereupon he bought half a dozen Mars bars and a vat of Coke. His trousers sighed in relief as a mountain of coppers found their way back to a cash tin.

A few of us noticed a fiver had gone missing. Unlikely as it was, if it had been planted as a loyalty test, it would be best to put it back on the table. Gowland and I insisted on it; eyes went around the room. Eventually, Colin declared, 'Doh, oh alright then,' and grumpily retrieved the offending note from his pocket.

The rest of us, after being thanked for our assistance, melted back into the auditorium. The lights were down. We quietly sat down on convenient seats, removed our berets, and enjoyed the delight of illegally watching our first X-rated film in the cinema, all aged 14 and 15. We had never heard such language on screen, as TV was still heavily edited then. We didn't exactly learn any new words, though.

There were a lot of bands I was enjoying hearing on the radio, and a few singles that Adey May lent me to listen to. Ian Dury and the Blockheads, Devo, The Knack, Blondie, The Jam – new wave music was my thing. Colin was getting heavily into Elvis Costello; we would listen to his first two albums on his cassette ghetto blaster in his bedroom. Martin had a young lad living next door who was called Christopher Jones. He wore black NHS specs and Elvis Costello looked like the adult version of Chris. He was a sickly child, and suffered from what I think was osteoporosis. We dubbed him Crisp Bones in tribute. Crisp's diminutive stature contrasted completely with that of his dad; Mr Jones was a heavily overweight chap, perhaps accurately described as 'lardy'. Mr and Mrs Jones indulged their only son; he had developed an obsession with cars, so they rigged up a windscreen wiper on the shed window and attached two pieces of string. When it rained, Crisp would go into the shed and happily wipe his window for hours. The shed also bore a car number plate. Amazingly, Chris turned out alright.

One of the best punk songs of the era was Jilted John – man, we loved that one. God help anyone called Gordon, he would forever be dubbed a moron. It helped if the name of someone you knew would scan, hence the parade night taunts of, 'Adey, you're a moron,' and the like. As said before, Adey's taste in music was quite avant garde. He got us all into Kraftwerk, lending me the Autobahn album. Martin got into it, too. Radioactivity and Trans –Europe Express were way ahead of their time, but it was the first music I listened to in another language that I found appealing.

In the wider world, we were still living with a Labour government under Jim Callaghan, Maggie Thatcher was leader of the opposition, the Yorkshire Ripper had claimed his tenth victim, and the first IVF baby was born, Louise Brown. There was a punk band around at the time called Peter and the test tube babies. Fantastic name. If only success came from imagination or shock factor alone.

Mum took me to see 'Evita', the Lloyd Webber musical in the West End. I had never been to a musical before; I couldn't believe how loud it was. It was wonderful seeing and hearing a bone fide star such as David Essex. He was brilliant. A couple of the songs from the show made the national singles chart, so there was a genuine pop crossover audience enthralled by this predominantly classically inspired music. Theatre and pop hooks – a winning combination. I enjoyed playing in the school orchestra, but began a desire to sing rock and pop, and the violin was not the instrument for it. I was studying toward Grade V on the violin, but I was losing the passion; I wanted to play the electric guitar.

There was inevitably going to be a clash over schedules for extra practice for orchestra and parade nights for ATC. As we progressed toward performance evenings, Miss Mason would demand attendance after school to rehearse. One performance coincided with a parade evening. I didn't feel my inclusion amongst a dozen violin players made me particularly important, so I decided to inform Miss Mason that I would not be attending this time. Oh dear. She started by listening sweetly, and then, as if with a flick of a switch, became a monstrous, fire breathing dragon.

'If you think, Trevor Heath, I have spent months preparing everybody for this show for people not to turn up then you and they will have another thing coming it's not acceptable I am God blah blahblahblah blah...' The words became a blur of noise, the tone was coruscating. Every third or fourth word, the opening syllable was emphasised and spat out with unreasonable vindictiveness. She sloped off, leaving me moist-eyed and very upset. As she had regaled me in full public view in the music block, quite a few pupils had witnessed it. I was asked if I was alright. I wasn't and shed a few blubbing tears. I was asked if the Air Cadets would kick me out. No, I said, but that wasn't the point. All of these extra-curricular activities were voluntary. There should not be attendance by force of personality. I hated Miss Mason even more after this. It spelt the death knell for my orchestra involvement; death by *violins*.

At every concert, we had to be seated and the leader of the orchestra would enter, sit down, and we would then commence. The leader was invariably the best violin player in the first violins. Seated at one of the penultimate concerts we performed at Harriet, a new leader came in; it was a girl who was not only a year below me, but she was at Grade 4. At that time, I had passed Grade 5. I was incensed; angry that I had been passed over by an inferior player, and also that I didn't know we had a new leader until that moment. After spending nearly five years in the orchestra, and one of the senior players, I thought it only right I should have been informed, let alone be missing a promotion.

Soon after, I let Miss Mason know my tuition status. She was quite surprised; as I had private tutelage independent of the school, she had not been aware. It didn't matter. I was affronted and that was not to change. In the last year, she invited me to join the Area Youth Orchestra. That was quite an honour, and could have led to a career playing classical music. I declined; it would clash with ATC, and I felt at that time, a career in the RAF beckoned. Apart from that, I wanted to spite the old cow.

Martin, Colin and I all identified with being an Air Cadet. We weren't pupils at our school, or members of our families. We had found our vocation. Or so we thought. Only one of us was destined to join the RAF.

*

01.09.78. Off again to RAF Odiham, for a site visit. We had been semi-promised a flight in a Puma, the troop carrying choppers based there. It was a very exciting prospect; none of us had flown in a helicopter before. The Aerospatiale A330 Puma is a four-bladed, twin-engined medium transport/utility helicopter, dubbed the HC Mk 1 for the RAF. Odiham was the first operational base for them in the UK, at 33 Squadron, since 1971. Able to carry 16 fully laden troops, their top speed was around 160mph, not exactly zippy, but fast enough. The RAF would eventually order 48 of them for transport duties, and there were plenty of them over the skies of Hampshire every day. After a brief introduction to one in the hangar, we were told we would be off for a flight. Fantastic.

Close up to Puma XW226 on the flight pan, the rotor blades hung down in a mechanical evocation of sleep. Technicians removed covers, began checking oil levels, a hive of activity sparked it into life. Generators whined, and we were invited to step aboard. Entering through the side door, we were confronted by side by side canvas seats, which were even more uncomfortable than they looked. We all had a lap strap, no lateral straps across the body. We faced the windows along the fuselage and I was opposite the door. It wasn't just us cadets; we were sharing this AEF flight with a few grizzled US Vietnam veterans. It was to be a joyride to and over London. Even more fantastic! Martin flew in another Puma which didn't go over London.

One of the Yanks sat on my right, resplendent in olive drab and helmet, and Cadet Evans sat on my left. The Yanks were Chinook pilots on a liaison visit. The RAF were looking to replace the Pumas with Chinooks, so I guess they were getting an insight from the septics on operational details. We could hear aircraft close to us starting up, the rotors gaining speed and increasing in volume; the familiar air beating sound of powerful motors turning blades was all encompassing. Soon, our engines sprang into life, and as the rotors increased in velocity, the whole cabin started shaking from side to side. It felt like we were in a giant cradle being rocked by an unseen giant on speed. The noise was unbelievable; to converse in the cabin, you had to really shout in the ear of the people next to you. The Pumas alongside us slowly ascended, one by one, until they were hovering about 20 feet up. Here they remained, implacable, for a few minutes; then, without a change in noise, we felt ourselves gently rising, the view in the window changing; we were above the airfield now, and could no longer see the tarmac. We hovered on this amazingly stable platform for a minute or two, and then one by one, the Pumas moved off. We were last in the line, the ground sloped to the left as our nose went down and we surged forward and upward. The speed increasing, our view of the surrounding countryside sped past as we headed east toward the Big Smoke. The turbines and rotor gear whined constantly, it was a veritable racket but these beasts were made for war, not comfort. I could see the railway lines below, little tracks winding their way across the model floor, tiny cars wending their way around a huge carpet of green. It's always a wonder when you fly, and where do all the swimming pools come from? It was a bit of a murky day; the horizon was cloaked in grey. Still, it was good enough visibility to see the ground clearly. Before too long, we were approaching the outskirts of London, and we tracked the Thames until we were over the city. We were probably about 2,000 feet up; there are strict limits as to how low over London you can fly, but I tried to gauge the height compared to my recent experiences in Chipmunks.

As we swung over the Thames, I could make out familiar landmarks; as I gazed wondrously out of the relatively small windows, one of the crew moved toward the door. Suddenly, he wrenched it open; he was getting us all a better view! Light, cold air and even more noise filled the cabin. Holy shit. The Houses of Parliament filled the door as if it were a framed portrait.

I turned to the American visitor to my right; he leaned in to hear.

'Houses of Parliament!' I bellowed.

'Bucking-ham Palass?' he replied, quizzically.

'No, the Houses of Parliament,' I reiterated, slower and louder.

'Oh,' he said, not understanding at all, disappointed it wasn't the Queen's pad.

The aircraft rolled, and as we were turning, another amazing building filled the door. I jabbed my finger toward the Christopher Wren designed construction, and turned to the Yank.

'Saint Paul's Cathedral!' I shouted, with all my might.

'Bucking-ham Palass?' enquired the Yank.

By now, I thought he was taking the piss. I didn't realise all Americans were dumb, even clever ones like pilots.

We clattered over the city, taking in the white and grey skyline, feeling completely removed from the hustle and bustle of the activities on the ground. It was a great way to see the sights, no queues up here. And then, as if ordered especially for my companion on my right, Buck House hove into view.

I leaned in one more time, engaged the Yank, and pointed at the sprawling building at the end of The Mall.

'Buckingham Palace,' I said, as loudly and as clearly as I could. *That should make him happy*, I thought.

'What?' he said.

'Bucking. Ham. Palace,' I repeated.

'What? I can't hear what you're saying,' he said flatly. Dumbass Yank. I gave up.

Soon, we turned and headed for home. The door was heaved shut. It had been disconcerting when it was first opened, but after a while, it became normal. It was certainly warmer when he shut it, though. The journey back was calm and uneventful. We were nearly back at Odiham, when suddenly, we started going down. What? Where are we? We're in a bloody field? What's going on?

It transpired one of the vets wanted a go. Really? A quick kerfuffle in the cockpit, and we had a septic at the controls. Woah! We lifted off again, without use of the clutch this time. Jerky, side by side, this guy was getting a feel of the controls. Don't you realise you need L plates in this country? And passengers aren't allowed! We ascended at a fast rate of knots, and when we had gained around 1,000 feet, he started to throw us around. The view of the field out of the windows suddenly became looking down on the field – we were at right angles to the ground in a really tight turn. I could feel the g-forces increasing and was thrust into my seat. Evans raised his fist and looked at me, indicating it was tough to raise his arm. He beamed his toothy grin. 'Woh,' he said, enjoying the Newtonian effect. Next minute, we're flipped over the other way, empty sky filled the windows. This continued for a few minutes, I was starting to feel a little uneasy, and then it was all over. We descended, the RAF pilot took back his baby, and we continued on for the last couple of miles back to base.

As we exited the cabin, the pungent smell of jet fuel still filling our nostrils, the whine of the ground generator welcomed our return to earth. Our bodies had been assaulted by extreme decibel levels and forces of gravity, our senses filled with aesthetic beauty and harsh mechanical brutality. Deaf, shaken and only slightly stirred, we had one hour and ten minutes in the company of our favourite armed force and mode of transport; just another day in the corps.

*

There was a constant stream of cadets joining 443 Squadron. Every month, one or two would join and we would get to know them over time. The biggest leveller was parade drill; if you were slow to learn, it was a good indication of how you would be with other lessons and tasks. One of the funniest characters would be Peter Denham. Tall, awkward, his beret permanently trying to escape his head, he was a major source of merriment and ribbing from the rest of us. He would puff out his ample chest whilst standing to attention, like a pigeon. This would earn him the soubriquet of Budgie. The funniest thing I have ever witnessed was when he cycled up to the side of the parade hut at the start of the evening, stopped, and keeled straight over on his side. He had been unable to extricate his feet from the pedal toe clips, but he didn't ask for help, or say a word; he just silently went over until he crashed, painfully, on the tarmac. His drill consisted of tick-tocking for ages; most of us might have done it once or twice, Budgie just couldn't coordinate himself. Spud would often be in hysterics, trying to bark out orders whilst this puffed out clown kept kicking the heels of his fellow cadets and trying the patience of all around him. He was like a younger version of Corporal Jones from 'Dad's Army' – turning the wrong way, always half a step behind.

Cadet Simmons was just plain ugly. He looked like he had been wearing a stocking over his face for a robbery and someone had taken a cast of it and left him like it. Alright bloke, though. Roberts looked like a pixie. Dudley was a little bloke as well, quiet but he was very able. Chris Tipler became a good mate. And then there was Andy Ritchie.

Andy was a year younger, skinny, rosy-cheeked, and had a problem keeping his arms straight as his elbows didn't appear to lock. He marched like C3PO after running out of oil. However, what truly set him apart was the hyperactivity in his bowels. He was truly a one man sewage plant. Vesuvius would have a problem keeping up with the amount of sulphurous emanations from this lad's rear end. Saddam Hussein could have used him as a biological weapon. We only had to stand on parade for 10 minutes at the start and end of a parade night, but if there was a toxic guff that silently engulfed us, it would be from two sources only. A sample from the air would most likely reveal a toxicity content of

10% May, 90% Ritchie. It was awful; something had obviously died in Ritchie's guts and the world was to know of it. I swear the area around him turned green. Certainly cadets in breathing range did. Thankfully, his other forte was telling jokes, which was much more socially acceptable. Purdey and Ritchie were our main sources of new humour; now we would say something was a viral hit. It used to be down to these two telling everyone they met the same joke ad infinitum.

Corporal Howard, as with other NCOs, would occasionally instruct us for lessons in aircraft recognition, weapon technology, and other interesting topical information. He was always very straight and serious. Many of us would have a laugh, but I always wanted to learn. Howard surprised me one night by saying he thought I was very intelligent. I know I was reasonably so, but I took it as praise indeed from certain individuals. Whether it was true was immaterial. Constantly berated for being poor at sport and being four-eyed, a positive statement would always be welcome. Praise has a better effect on the soul.

Our favourite CI (Civilian Instructor) was Mr Downing. A middle-aged Northerner with thinning hair, resplendent in his sports jacket and tie, he always brought unbridled enthusiasm for everything. For this, we knew him as Overgrown Schoolboy. Nice chap.

This group were to be chosen to attend RAF St Athan camp this year. As I went the previous year, I couldn't complain, but it was a pain that both Martin and Colin were going, and I wasn't. The full line up: Mr Downing, Flt Lt Bloxham, W/O Ledger, Flt Sgt Edwards, Cadet Denham, Cpl Howard, Cadet Rolfe, Cadet Stevens R, Cadet Simmons, Cadet Bell, Cadet Evans, Cadet Stevens M, Cadet Tipler.

RAF St Athan Annual Camp 1978. L-R from rear: Mr Downing ('Overgrown Schoolboy'), Flt Lt Bloxham (VR), W/O Ledger; Middle row: Flt Sgt Edwards, Cdt Denham, Cpl Howard, Cdt Rolfe, Cdt Stevens R; front row: Cdt Simmons, Cdt Bell, Cdt Stevens M, Cdt Tipler.

After that, in September, we had to attend this year's Basingstoke Show. As usual, we arrived earlier than the public, to have time to help set up horse jumps and move kit. There was a static display for the Army, which had figures high up on scaffolding. I was still trying to survive not wearing my glasses all the time, and I could see what looked like guys in camouflage gear hanging off gantries across the site.

'Look at those bigheads up there,' I said to Colin and Martin. They nearly wet themselves. I couldn't tell from a distance with my terrible short sightedness that they were cardboard cut outs. They spent the day telling everyone of my myopic mistake, to add to my embarrassment. The show was bigger this year, spread across the weekend, and we attended both days. There were some wonderful stalls selling memorabilia. I had my eye on a steel Air Raid warden's helmet. In the end, Purdey bought it; I think it was a fiver. I settled for a WW2 army bayonet – a lethal spike of steel held in a scabbard. Today you would probably be locked up for openly selling it let alone having it in a public place. Dad liked it, as it prompted many memories from his post-war activities in the Army. I don't mean he went around stabbing people, more the association with weapon training. The weekend was blazingly hot, and we toiled heavily replacing the wooden beams back onto the horse jumps as the show jumpers repeatedly crashed into them. The difference from last year was that I ate my burgers this time.

The other major change was that we were issued with a new uniform. Out went the separate collar shirts, tunics and itchy trousers; in came woolly pulleys, normal shirts and better trousers. The casual look was in, and it was supremely comfortable. Bye bye fifties, welcome to the late seventies.

Well, almost. The most popular film of the summer was Grease, featuring John Travolta and Olivia Newton-John. The music was everywhere, on the radio, the TV, the PA at the show, the fun fair in the memorial park; it was literally inescapable. And Colin had a girlfriend.

Col had been seeing blonde, brown-eyed Tessa over the summer. He would go out walking her dogs with her. It meant he was less available than usual. He even took her to see Grease twice. She was 16, Col joked she was a cradle snatcher as he was still 15. It all ended in tears, literally; he took the mickey out of her and she punched him in the crown jewels. Young love indeed. We were comparing notes sometime later, and Gowland overheard us talking about Tracy.

'Tracy Woolford? My mate's going out with her; shagging her rotten, by all accounts!'

Oh my god; if it wasn't bad enough hearing slanderous news through the grapevine anyway, and completely unverifiable, but to hear that from *Little Shit*? The world had just ended.

*

09.09.78. We had a new event in the calendar; the Farnborough Air Show. September that year was very busy for us cadets. I had been to Greenham Common air shows with Colin, and they were always spectacular, but Farnborough is something else. The morning was spent poring over the aircraft lining the runway for the static display, and meandering through the large marquees hassling companies for freebies. We didn't care what they gave out; it was a tacit competition to obtain more than anybody else. Boeing tossed out bees on the hour; little bug-eyed furry toys with a Boeing tag twice as large as the stick on toy itself. There were some fantastic displays, simulators and mock ups of fighter jets, all the things that enthused us. We were a pain in the arse, I thought. Cadging little monkeys. I came back with a bag full of stickers, toys and photos. The piece de la resistance was a Mcdonnell-Douglas press release pack full of glossy photos of fighter aircraft; that was a truly prized gizzit, named after the phrase we uttered at every stand: Gizzit here.

The main attraction of Farnborough Air Show, unless you are with a corporate entity, is the exciting air displays. Due to terrible crashes in recent years, air shows have been sanitised and subject to health and safety issues, such as limiting certain manoeuvres away from the crowds. In 1978, when the Red Arrows appeared in their Gnat aircraft, they announced their arrival over the crowd at minimum height, around 150 feet or less; Jaguar fighters would scream low overhead, the sound woefully trailing behind until the ear shattering impact would burst every eardrum in the vicinity. Harriers would hover, fly backwards and roar off to return at close to the speed of sound, and any ounce of hearing left in your cranium would be drubbed out by sheer decibel assault. I would return home, as we all would, deaf, dehydrated and with a sunburnt face, having had a wonderful afternoon craning our necks toward the skies. Our contribution was receiving those from others; collecting for the RAF Benevolent Fund. I was happy to help toward such a deserving cause, but I didn't want to forever associate the collection tin with public events. It was a release when we able to be let loose and explore on our own. However, we were in the public eye, in uniform, and instructed to be on our best behaviour at all times. I don't recall any incriminating events on that occasion; more's the pity.

*

16.09.78. This was the date we attended RAF Abingdon at Home. We were just plane crazy. See what I did there? All the usual suspects were in attendance, the large RAF bombers, the fast jets, and large transport aircraft as Abingdon was the home of the Logistics arm of the RAF, the Transport Command. The Vickers Vulcan was always and still is a very impressive-looking aircraft, a nuclear bomb holding delta winged colossus. No surprise it always carries the signature epithet, 'mighty', as in 'The Mighty Vulcan.' A Star Trek fan might think they were heralding the arrival of Leonard Nimoy. What made this particular event a little different was the number of unusual aircraft we saw that day.

One of those was the Campbell Cricket autogyro. This tiny aircraft houses one pilot, and the motor turns a prop, which pulls the craft forward. The free main rotor turns due to the forward motion through the air, which provides the requisite lift. If the motor stops, you don't stay in the air very long.

We were watching British Airways Tristar Captain, John Kitchin, buzz up and down in the BA Campbell Cricket. He regally waved as the little plane passed above the crowds, sounding like an overexcited lawnmower. As he brought it into land, we were right against the fence and had a perfect view. As it passed right before me, about 50 feet up, the motor noise stopped. The nose went down as the craft pitched forward, the main rotors lazily spinning and approaching the ground rapidly. It skewed to the right, the nose wheel badoinged into the grass, causing a large bounce, and a big 'woo' emerged from the crowd. Next moment, the body of the aircraft hit the ground on its right side. Ouch. Bet that hurt. Officials started running toward the stricken Cricket, and after a few seconds, the pilot emerged, unscathed, still waving. He was alright. For a while, he wandered up and down the area where the rotors had impacted the ground. The undercarriage had been damaged, it actually snapped off the right main gear. After about five minutes, Ken disappeared into the crowd, still waving. I guess the show must go on. How embarrassing. We didn't know if it was his fault or a mechanical fault.

One of the main papers, I think 'The Daily Mirror' had a write up about it which was half speculation and half total guff. I wrote to the editor and told him so. I received a reply saying as I was 'obviously such an expert' I should volunteer for the subsequent inquiry. I didn't feel qualified for that, but when they write 'the pilot vanished into the astonished crowd' when in reality he had wandered about for 10 minutes, I felt I had to set the record straight.

Recently, I found an article from Flight Magazine dated 04.11.78. Apparently, after a six minute display, the propeller started to vibrate severely. The ignition was switched off, ceasing propwash over the rudder. In other words, in a gusty crosswind, he had switched off his steering controls. Twat. Directional control was lost because of the low airspeed and low height.

*

We were back at school after the summer holidays. This was the final year, the build up to 'O' Levels, the big one. I had maintained my position in the top classes for all subjects, and was destined to take Ordinary Level exams in nine subjects. Some of us were given the opportunity to take certain subjects early, as I was with English Language GCE. The results were always published on the notice board, so in the melee to check your own results, your peers would have the opportunity to check yours too. Perhaps that's why they are called peers, because they peer over your shoulder to mock your achievements. I remember on the occasion of the English result, Simon Coates saw mine and said, quizzically, 'Eh?'

'What's wrong with it?' I said. No, not 'Eh', it was A. Oh. No, not O, A. A? A? Eh?

I indeed had achieved Grade A for my English Language. Result! It was more relief than anything else; one down, eight to go.

The final year of school was a strange one for me. I had started to feel light headed before morning assembly, and was eventually excused attending. It was a stress related psychological condition, but at the time, Doctor Hamber said my 'cardiovascular system was developing.' He alluded to school children of my age 'always throwing up all over the place,' which was nice. It was more a feeling of being trapped in assembly, claustrophobia, unable to escape due to the imperative of standing or sitting still between rows of yobby kids, amongst them my many enemies. Over the course of four years, I considered many of the pupils to be my friends, but I would also never even aim to get on with the bully boys, it was just avoid at all opportunity. Getting out of assemblies was a suitable opportunity. The day seemed to settle in after that.

We were given a series of educational films in our final year. I think the aim was to deter us from alcohol, drugs and sex for life. Well, one out of three ain't bad. The drugs film was particularly harrowing; it featured footage from a post mortem on a drug overdose victim. That certainly got the adolescents throwing up over the curtains. Interestingly, we were feeling more grown up by being treated like grown-ups. One female teacher who sat in with us on the sex education film, which concentrated on contraception primarily, correctly stated we were all ok talking about sex, regardless of (in)activity, but when the subject of love arose, we became bashful. Never a truer a word was spoken; we all instantly turned red and the room temperature rose by five degrees.

Boys mature at a slower rate than girls; fact. Sitting on the cusp of 16, we were all giggly schoolboys, some of the girls were virtually *wimmin*. Sharon Davies in our form, 5T, was seeing a man called Alan. He was all of 17, but to us, he was from a different dimension. Muscular, tall and well built, he would turn up before the end of the day in his black leather jacket, contrasting completely with the little boys decked out in their maroon blazers. We would get out of his way in the same fashion as a spider scuttles from an unknown source of vibration in its web. He once accosted Guy Berger, just because he could. Guy had refashioned himself as a bit of a tough guy; we had never fallen out, but he had just stopped communicating. This sullen, intense young man just capitulated instantly to the elder threat. Girls loved tough guys. Little did they realise, or even realise now, the tough guys are the ones most handy with their fists, and not always contained to altercations with blokes. Not that Alan was like that, I never knew him; but that was the archetype.

The closing last months of school would herald a period of massive change in my life, and of my friends. The decisions we would make on our exam choices, our performance in those exams, whether we chose to further our education, or start work, would alter the course of our lives forever. Institutionalised in education for 10 years, we suddenly had to start to wake up the real, wider world. For a while now, I had felt that I wanted to pursue a role working with aircraft. My sight being so bad precluded a role as a pilot, my absolute preferred choice, but my experiences on RAF camps showed there were exciting and interesting jobs to do. And yet… I also had a real yearning to do art. From a young age, I adored drawing from comics and copying artwork. My scrap book at school was chock full of wacky inventions and humorous prose. My top subject was English. Even my English teacher recommended I took a career in writing or made it a serious hobby. But I was also good at sciences, particularly, physics and maths. I was ok at languages, studying both French and Latin. I had taken Latin as a second language, over German or Spanish, because in the second year I had a mad inspiration to go into the medical profession. Think again! So, regardless of my burgeoning desire to draw, I could not see how to sustain a career in it. Unfortunately, I didn't excel in art, so that put paid to that dream anyway. In 1978/1979, it was almost incumbent upon us boys to go into engineering or manufacturing, because that was the source of most employment. With the correct coercion, I could have been persuaded to drive toward a more artistic path, but there were two distinct reasons why I didn't at that stage.

Mum had told me that if I wanted to pursue the university route, she and Dad would provide for me to go. I didn't doubt they would, but after witnessing the commercial sacrifices they went through to provide for Jackie at Cambridge, I didn't feel comfortable asking them to do so. Mum earned a good salary as Senior Lecturer at Basingstoke Tech, but Dad was now driving vehicles for the local hospital which paid bugger all. It was always argument city in our house, and I think most of that was caused by money, not that I remember or heard all the discussions. Mum tried to get us to move to a larger house, but it all fell through 'cause Dad didn't want to move; perhaps because he felt uncomfortable with the increased debt. It certainly became easier for them just after I left school, because the mortgage was paid off and they started to travel more.

The second reason was more to do with the total inadequacy of Careers Advice at school. My adult view of this taints the actual experience, as I was almost resolutely determined by this stage to aim for an Engineering

Apprenticeship, primarily with the RAF. So, I entered the room to meet the Careers Advisor. She was a heavily pregnant woman (I've yet to meet a heavily pregnant man), of around late twenties. Great career advice love, go into social services and get knocked up. Bob's your uncle. Anyway, instead of actually looking at my skills at offering alternate paths of destiny, it was, 'Yep, you've made your mind up, follow that path.' I had no concept of what I could do in life. I was studying for nine 'O' Levels. What about pushing the envelope, asking if I had considered a job as a Top Judge or a Senior Policeman? Show me a path to get there? No, of course not. We know these jobs are the domain of the public schoolboy, the old Etonian, part of the Old Boys Network. That sort of job wouldn't be within the grasp of someone like *you*. It makes me angry just thinking about it. The lack of vision I was subjected to by apathy on her or her department's behalf; we were allotted maybe 15 minutes to determine our fate, ostensibly forever. It was woeful. I bounced out of the meeting happy, glad that the Careers Advisor agreed I was following a sensible course of action for me. The reality was, given a greater depth of understanding about what was out there to aim for, I probably would have opted for the university route. I would have been unsure about what job to do, but it would have given me time to work it out. Unfortunately for me, I was destined to aim for a work placement that although was completely sound in employment prospects, and completely respectable, it was not going to be particularly enjoyable. In fact, I was going to be fucking miserable.

The other subject within my study portfolio was geography. I had given up history in order to take geography, and that had been a tough choice. I enjoyed learning about geology, glaciers, volcanoes and the physical aspects of the world. Now, we seemed to be learning about the next North American town, where it was, what river basin it sat in and what they produced from their local resources. Was that it, because that was all it seemed? The problem was, all these places blurred into one mass of non-connected data. I couldn't see how the subject was structured, and most importantly, what to learn for an exam. It didn't help that the two biggest distractions were Miss Andrew, our teacher. She had a bust that in comparison to Karen Desborough was like the Alps against the Himalayas. They were both impressive in their own place, but Miss Andrew? Look at the norks on that! I spent every lesson transfixed, as were my friends, my eyes only meeting my written words when they threatened to spill over onto the desk. I didn't notice that she wasn't a great teacher; I didn't care. Look at those norks!

There was one further earth shattering event that shook me to the core before the close of the summer. At the close of parade one evening, Bloxham had an announcement to make.

'I am glad to inform you all we have decided to promote a few of you this evening…'

We all look at each other, lined up in our rows, standing easy but feeling anything but. Who? Who? Spit it out, Blockhead!

'…Would you please come forward Cadet Stevens…'

Martin, pleasantly shocked, came to attention and smartly marched up to Bloxham.

'Well done, Corporal,' Blockhead said, shaking his hand.

Martin regained his position but not quite his composure. He was made up, in both senses of the word.

'Step forward Cadet Bell…'

Colin duly went forward to collect his badge. This must be it! We joined together, trained together, achieved together. They're going to make us all corporals! I readied myself; my heart started pumping even more.

'And finally, please step forward Cadet…'

I was virtually already moving...

'May!'

The world stopped. My hearing went. I sort of saw that Fat Bastard smiling and smartly marching up to Blockhead in front of me. I could feel myself breathing but I wasn't there. I had transcended to another dimension. If I was there, it would only have ended in murder.

Parade was over and so was my world. I congratulated my friends and fought back from showing my disappointment. But I still couldn't believe they picked May over me. Why May? Did Blockhead get us mixed up again, as he did always? Surely not. The others in the promotion discussion must have discussed the merits of us all. Did Little Shit have an influence, being one of our direct peers? Had I queered my pitch by hating him?

It didn't matter. What was done was done. What I couldn't understand was that being truly objective, Adey May had been fairly inconsistent in attending parade, whereas I only missed it if I was ill; Adey often turned up in his civvies, which I never did; I applied myself well to all tasks and we were all at the same level, first class cadets, working toward our leading cadet badges. I don't know if they genuinely felt May was better than me, but based on the fact Martin, Colin and I were fairly inseparable, maybe that was a deliberate tactic to break that bond. As we cycled home that dark night, past the spooky graveyard, I was pretty inconsolable. Colin tried to commiserate, but he was understandably drunk on his success. I had learnt life was perplexing, unjust and just damn annoying. Some questions will never be answered. I hated Blockhead even more, the nicotine-stained leathery old git. What should have inspired me to perform did the opposite; I felt demoralised, demotivated, and moreover, embarrassed. For that, I could not forgive.

7. Sweet Sixteen

'If you go up today, you'll probably puke all over the place. I don't recommend it.' So said Spud the day we visited RAF Lyneham, 02.11.78. It was a dirty, grey, November day. We had been semi-promised a flight in a Hercules transport aircraft, but the weather was too bad and they weren't going to take us up. We had to settle for a tour of the base, which incorporated a visit to the dog section. This wasn't a reference to WRAFS, the serving RAF wimmin, but the Alsatians used by the RAF regiment to protect the grounds. If I had wanted to see them I would have gone to Crufts. Thankfully, we did get to jump aboard a Herky bird, albeit only on the ground in the hangar. We entered via the cargo ramp and had a poke around the cargo netted hull. Not much to see really. More interesting was the flight simulator. This was a very expensive piece of kit, a mock up cockpit suspended on hydraulic rams to duplicate exactly the experience of flight. Back then, the images provided to the cockpit were provided by a small camera that moved around a large model housed in its own room. It seems ridiculously quaint now, but prior to the advent of digital technology, it was the only way to do it. Not only that, it looked pretty good in the cockpit window.

Four days later I received my Leading Cadet badge. For this, we had to sit an exam based on our in house training in various subjects. I was now able to educate other cadets in lessons. I enjoyed this very much. One new cadet was being disruptive and troublesome, and after the umpteenth time of reproaching him, I gave up the liberal strategy and went for corporal punishment; I turned from the blackboard and threw my piece of chalk at him from 10 feet away. It hit him square between the eyes. It not only shut him up for the rest of the evening, it impressed the others so much, they shut up as well.

Maybe I was still angry from being passed over for Corporal. Maybe I was getting meaner. Maybe that was a good thing; we were being effectively groomed by the Government to become trained assassins. Perhaps I had been too soft and that was the reason for May pitching above me. I had always been a happy and smiling individual. Now I had become more withdrawn, circumspect, a little more serious. There was a lot to contend with in the coming year; our final school exams, the prospect of employment, massive changes in life circumstances. We were all maturing, well, Adey May excepted. I was definitely looking forward to getting out of school, probably to join the RAF, see the world. No more exams after that. Hah! What a joke. Life really was taken as it came, planning was short term at that age. Definitely, my two years in the ATC had prepared me for virtually anything. And it wasn't over yet.

The winter of 1978-79 was the third coldest of the 20th century. We had widespread snowfall, and there were huge snowdrifts. Martin, Col and I went out on a beautiful, crisp blue day over the holidays, and spent the whole day larking about. The Brighton Hill roundabout underpasses had drifts almost as tall as we were. Martin dived in headfirst. It was hilarious; he ended up with his feet sticking out, unable to move. We had to dig him out before he suffocated. We all made snow angels, and I took some pictures of us against our imprints in the snow. As the light faded at the end of the day, shadows cast on the ground were multiple shades of pink and blue. I painted what I could see in art class, which went down well with my art teacher for observation. We were all wrapped up in our snorkel jackets, hoods around our heads with faux fur lining the front of the hood. Cheap, nasty nylon coats, but they did the job.

We found some steep banks next to factories on the nearby industrial estate, and slid down backwards in our coats. We would do that for hours. When you have no money, you really do have to make your own entertainment. We were still carefree, young, unencumbered by issues of responsibility. Why does it have to end?

*

27.01.79. A visit to RAF Odiham for shooting. I fired 28 rounds on the .303 that day, but it could all have ended in tragedy. We had been told, multiple times, that if the weapon jammed or there was any problem, to make sure the weapon is aimed down the range and you raised your hand. One cadet had an issue, his rifle had jammed. The instructor, whom I had never seen before, went to assist. Purdey and I couldn't believe our eyes; the instructor was struggling so much to release the bolt, he had the weapon aimed toward us as we were to his right. I felt distinctly uncomfortable, panicked even; do I risk being shouted at for getting up, out of the line of fire, or rebuking this officer for being a total effing idiot? I did what we all did; shut up and wait for the fool to either clear the jam or kill us with incompetency. I guess he didn't kill us as I don't think heaven have typewriters.

Afterwards, Purdey and I were telling everybody who hadn't seen what had transpired. I felt lucky I only had an aching shoulder. It was still freezing, and snow lay on the ground outside the range. As we had been firing, a Chipmunk flew low overhead. I could have shot it out of the sky; with a rifle in my hand, I had a choice; a choice to be lawful and sensible, or a choice to be murderous and evil. It is existentialism Jim, but not as we know it. Life is our hands, we have the power alone to change certain events concerning ourselves. Never had I felt it so much at that moment. I was glad I was a good guy.

The actress Rosamund Pike was born the very same day.

We were stuck in a terrible rut in the UK. It became

known as the Winter of Discontent, public sector workers were going on strike right, left and centre. Rubbish was overflowing in the streets as bin men were on strike, graves were undug, and the dead weren't buried. Jim Callaghan, the Labour Prime Minister, was famously quoted as saying, 'Crisis? What crisis?' That was the end of his career.

Three days after nearly being shot on the range, mine began. I was promoted to Corporal on 30.01.79. I should have been happy; after all, I had been promoted, and not that long after the others. It had come too late. We had joined up together and we had been splintered by the fractured timing of the promotions. It should have been us three together. Now it was only me.

I started to think about what I wanted from the Air Cadets, going forward. The biggest and most exciting challenges were still ahead of us if we wanted them. Spud was a qualified glider pilot, so that would be the next available goal; there was annual camp, there was international camp in Germany or Cyprus, and there was a flying scholarship if you were a) good enough, or b) a jammy bastard. They didn't hand out too many of those. I had a medical for the Gliding course with my Doctor on the 12th February. I was classed fit to fly.

Mopeds. Moooove Funky moped. The comedian, Jasper Carrot had a hit with a novelty song called 'Funky Moped'. When you were sixteen, with a provisional licence, you could ride one with an engine capacity not exceeding 50cc. I was coming up to 16 on the 2nd March. Wahay, exciting stuff!

Except – I didn't have one, nor the means to afford one. Brother David did. He had bought a step through Honda PC50 three years earlier, which he now no longer used due to the fact he had a car. I had enjoyed starting the thing up in the garden, and put-putting around, albeit for 10 yards. Now he was bequeathing it to me. It certainly wasn't a cool machine; top speed 35mph and visually it carried the aesthetic of a beefed up ladies' bike, but it was motorised and my entrance to the adult world.

Mum had a surprise for me. She had ordered me a black leather motorcycle jacket. It was lovely, but I told her it had to go back. I couldn't possibly wear that jacket on a step through 50, I would look ridiculous. Less rebel without a cause, more rebel without a decent motorcycle. I hated to hurt her feelings, and I was quite gracious, but Mum had always bought my clothes. I was almost 16 and I had to buy my own now. Well, I let her buy my motorbike garb. She bought me a Belstaff waxed cotton jacket that was extremely practical and stylish. Coupled with a green open-faced helmet, gauntlets and boots, I was almost good to go.

First, though: training. There was a nationally organised programme called the Star Rider course. Bronze Star was the introduction to the motorcycle and its controls. The Silver Star was to teach proper safety, and to riding test level. The earliest you could take your motorcycle driving test was 17, so all I needed now was the Bronze Star. In 1979, training was not compulsory.

It was a Saturday morning at a coned off area of road in Brighton Hill. They supplied the bike, which was a 50cc moped with a clutch. The PC50 had an auto clutch, so all you had to do was put it into gear and twist the throttle. Getting used to using a motorbike clutch was probably the hardest skill to learn in driving any vehicle. The instructor would straddle the front wheel, and after showing how to mix throttle and clutch, invite you to have a go. I don't know how many times I stalled the bike but it was probably 15 minutes before I could mix it well enough not to. Eventually, I was riding up and down with complete confidence, utilising the indicators properly (which weren't on the PC50) and correct use of hand signals (essential for the PC50). In effect, I was now ready to ride any moped but the main achievement was control of the vehicle and experience of powered mobility; the PC50 was more like a lazy boy pushbike than a true motorbike, so you had to control and indicate with your arms; tricky turning right, as to control the throttle and hold your arm up signalling right could end in disaster. It wasn't cool, but pedalling would move the bike forward while the throttle was closed.

The moped du jour was the Yamaha FS1-E. Known as the 'Fizzy'. It was probably the most popular moped of the era, late 70s/early 80s. It looked like a proper motorbike, although scaled down, but with a top speed of around 55mph it was a jet fighter compared to my Wright flyer. Who had one? Purdey was the first. He proudly showed me his yellow machine at his home prior to being old enough to actually ride it. It was a model pre-August 1977, as after this date, all models were restricted to 31mph. Therefore, derestricted models became highly sought after. His parents were better off; they did live in Kempshott, after all. All mopeds sounded like a hyperactive wasp caught in a tin can, as they mostly had 2-stroke, high revving engines. The only saving grace of the PC50 was that it was a 4-stroke; it sounded quieter, smoother, had better fuel consumption and removed the need to add additional oil. Unfortunately it was effing slow.

*

02.03.79. Sixteen today! I can legally ride my moped. Er, no, not quite yet. I have to go to school. This meant, as usual, catching a bus. I don't know how we all caught buses in those days, I mean, they didn't issue big enough nets. Activity was soon to ramp up. Our final exams were looming in May and June, so we had to finish our courses let alone revise toward the exams. I had submitted applications to different companies for an Engineering Apprenticeship, as well as to the RAF. Cadet Ritchie's dad and brother both worked for Dan Air Engineering at Lasham Airfield, eight miles from home, so because of Andy, I applied there for an Airframe and Engines apprenticeship, and to British Airways at Heathrow. Although I was sure the BA job would have wonderful training, the thought of working at Heathrow was daunting, because without suitable transport would mean living on site in their YMCA. I needed a job, for which I needed five good 'O' Level passes at grade C or above, including maths, English and physics. I was pretty confident that was going to happen, as I already had the English pass.

Next day, Saturday morning, unencumbered by age restriction or school attendance, I donned my helmet, jacket and gloves, and fired up the PC50. This entailed pedalling with gear engaged on the stand until it fired; bounce off the stand, twist the throttle, and off we go! No hang on, better open the back gate – Jesus, that was close. *Put-put-put* down the side alley, bounce off the kerb, twist the throttle… speed increasing, maybe 6mph. Stop. I'm at the end of the garage block, about to turn left onto the MAIN ROAD. Well, Mansfield road, my home street, but it was the public highway for the first time. Look left, right, left again, and… we're off! Wow, I'm doing 20, 25 – I'm going uphill effortlessly. No turning pedals as on my pushbike. This is great fun! The wind whistled past my closeted ears, and as I reached the top of the road, carefully turning right, I pulled over to the kerb, and bumped up it. I pop popped onto the porch in front of Martin's home, and killed the engine. Die, you 1.8hp bastard! No, I turned it off with the key. That was it; all six tenths of a mile to Martin's house, my first journey; time to show it off.

Colin wanted to have a go. 'Trev, Trev, let me have a go, Trev, Trev, Trev.' Colin and Martin had a mate at school called Henry who repeated statements over and over, which could be really funny and also extremely annoying. I rode with Martin and Colin on their bikes to close by where we had the Star rider training, and attempted to instruct Colin on the simple operation of the PC50. With all the mechanical control of a total buffoon, he twisted open the throttle fully, was unable to close it, and ended up in a ditch.

'Colin!!'

'It's alright, Trev, I'm ok,' he said, dusting himself down.

'Sod you, is the bike alright??'

The RAF careers invited me to their Reading office to take their entrance exam. *Oh, how nice to be invited*, I thought. *Do I get tea and biscuits?* The NCO who met me and the other candidates was the same guy who had given us a lecture at ATC. He was quite an engaging guy with a dry wit. The tests were not quite so funny. Hours of multiple choice questions, most of them English, physics and maths based. I hadn't yet completed the full 'O' Level syllabus for physics, and was unsure of some of the questions on supported beams. There were also quite a few questions on general maintenance of vehicles and oil types. I thought, I want an Apprenticeship to learn about these things, how was I supposed to know them already?

I even had the medical. What does that entail? I enquired. 'The medic puts a spoon under your bollocks and asks you to cough.' Righto. Sure enough, he did inspect the crown jewels but didn't use a spoon. He was probably stirring his tea with it. Urine sample, family medical history, tests for colour blindness, it was extensive. I passed with flying colours, probably because I could see them. At least I passed something, and not just water.

Eventually, I was offered the role of Direct Entry Adult Technician, or DEAT. The problem was, it could be Airframes, Engines, Weapons, Avionics, but one role, not two. I wanted a dual role apprenticeship, Airframes and Engines. The DEAT training was a year, whilst the full apprenticeship was three. It seemed half-arsed and not what I wanted. Imagine it written down in abbreviated form, direct entry adult technician Heath; or DEATH.

'Well, I think the Apprenticeship role is a little beyond you,' said the Careers guy. If he was basing that only on a test score, which covered subject content I hadn't been taught yet, I only had one answer for him: fuck you, fuck the tests and fuck the RAF. I never went back.

*

I had had my heart set on an RAF career. It didn't take too long to set my focus on a commercial-based one instead. There were multiple companies I had yet to learn about, let alone contact. For now, I pursued the ones that came back to me with positive responses.

For BA, I had to take entrance tests at their Hounslow test centre. I took the coach from Basingstoke bus station to Heathrow, from which I and multiple other candidates were bussed to the test location. Lined up in rows, we sat more hours of tests. I felt these went much better and I was more confident, but the sheer number of applicants was daunting. How am I going to compete with this lot? This was one day's quota and there must have been sixty or more. That day was memorable because I recall buying a few LPs after I got back to Basingstoke. I bought the Kraftwerk 'Autobahn' album, 'Parallel Lines' by Blondie and 'Armed Forces' by Elvis Costello.

Ian Goodyear went home at school lunchtimes, and on Radio 1 chart days, would come into Latin class after lunch to tell us what the new Number 1 was. The top three one week were 'Oliver's Army', Elvis Costello, Gloria Gaynor's 'I Will Survive' and 'Tragedy' by the Bee Gees. I was longing for Elvis to be number 1, I thought it was a great song. I went home with Goodyear a couple of times, and he turned me onto Tubeway Army just before Gary Numan went massive. Happy days.

I had done well enough in my tests to get an interview at BA. I saw a woman with veiny legs and a guy who asked non-sequitur questions that perhaps were designed to throw me. He didn't need to try as I was completely thrown by the whole experience. He flashed me a picture of an aircraft cockpit. 'Do you know which aircraft this is?'

'Yes. It's a Concorde,' I correctly stated.

'You're right,' he said. 'What tells you that?'

I pointed out the distinctive control columns, the four engine throttle levers, and the angled cockpit glass. I didn't point out I had a photo of the Concorde cockpit on my bedroom wall.

In the end, I was offered a place on the reserve list. Good, but not quite good enough to secure a place. I was quite relieved. I didn't fancy sharing accommodation with other young lads at aged 16. The only reference I had for YMCAs was via the Village People hit song. I certainly didn't fancy being propositioned by gays or having to dress as a cowboy.

That left my application with Dan Air Engineering. I didn't know much about Dan Air but I knew they were an airline. The Engineering maintenance base was at Lasham Airfield, sited halfway between Basingstoke and Alton on a windy country road. It was a major hurdle getting there on my PC50, as some of the hills were quite a challenge for its tiny motor. I had to offer additional human power, i.e. pedal like mad to assist on the larger hills. A little run of eight miles took about half an hour. Once there, I had to negotiate my way around the airfield on the perimeter track, past the main runway, and into the industrial complex. I reported to security, a little hut some way from the hangars. Opposite was a static Dakota aircraft in Dan Air London livery. The DC3 was Dan Air's first aircraft, now mothballed as a museum. I met Ted Snelling, the apprentice instructor, and Norman Mullen, the head of training. Ted was an engaging little guy of around 40, slicked back black hair with a deep, sonorous voice. He gave off the air of a spiv or an ageing Teddy boy. He also had a wonderful deadpan wit. Norman was older, with greying brown hair and was a little portly. He had a very gruff voice and a gruff Northern manner; not a man you wanted to mess with. Along with a few others, I took the requisite tests and had an interview with both of them.

'I see you're in the Air Cadets?' asked Ted.

'Yes,' I said. 'I'm a Corporal.'

'Oh,' said Ted. 'When I left I was a Flight Sergeant.' Bastard. I was going to get to know Ted very well. He loved to play one-upmanship games.

I was quite astounded when they offered me a four year Engineering Technician Apprenticeship, subject to achieving my qualifications. I would also have to attend Farnborough Tech College once a week, which in the short term, meant further entrance tests. This was for my ONC (Ordinary National Certificate) in Aeronautical Engineering, but renamed the BTEC as it was specifically covering Technical subjects. Stick that in your pipe and smoke it, Royal Air Force! Beyond me, indeed.

I accepted their offer. The start date would be September, so before then, I had the 'simple' matter of taking and passing all of my 'O' Levels.

Well, of course it wasn't. It was going to take a lot of hard work. Dave and Simon took their maths exam early, because they were clever swots. Against them I felt like a Trevor clot. We started to have previous test papers in class, to prepare for the actual exams, and I was doing ok. For English literature, we were covering 'Julius Caesar', Shakespeare's famous play. We had a school trip to view a production at the Hexagon theatre in Reading. The assassination of Caesar (sorry about the plot spoiler) was extremely bloody and all I could think about was the stage cleaning operation after curtain fall every day. However, Shakespeare performed well opens up nuances and better understanding of the prose, so it certainly helped.

I was pretty good at mimicry and showing off, but during school acting which focussed on performing plays, I never engaged with it. More fun was when we could perform little skits in English. I recall Lucas Murphy, Neil Henderson and I pretending to be a dissolute rock band in one little class performance. We got a few good laughs. Neil and his twin brother Alistair were natural performers. They later appeared in a cereal commercial but I never saw them on TV again after that. They were absolutely identical; not many people could tell them apart. I once accosted Alistair in the corridor thinking it was Neil, wondering why he had left the class I had just been in. This was in the first year before I had met Alistair.

I was also quite inventive in music, when I had the opportunity. Even back at King's Furlong, I had impressed Mr Jenkins by my simple arrangement of a few bars of the 2001 theme, 'Also sprach Zarathustra', performed with Colin on the chime blocks. At Harriet, with Shaun Roe on 'spooky laugh and announcements' and Dave Langley on piano, we performed a three-minute piece as a potential jingle for a radio station. With amazing prescience, we had Shaun announce 'This is Radio 3' at the end of it, capped with a Vincent Price cackle that could have come straight off of 'Thriller', predating that by three years.

*

Revising for my exams was hard. It wasn't just the task of trying to take in all the information, which was a major task in itself. Home life was full of the sound of my parents shouting. It seemed to be the only way they communicated these days. I don't know why as the house was just my parents and sister Alison, now, so it wasn't as if we were overcrowded. Pressure of work was the most likely cause. To blot it all out, I had David's old record player he had given me, on which I played my albums over and over. With music playing just loud enough to mask the voices, I could concentrate on the subjects I had to cover. I gave myself six months preparation on all subjects, but really knuckled down about one month before. I wasn't sure it would be enough. Latin, particularly, was the hardest subject. It wasn't only the verbs and sentence structures, it was the damned literature that was so frickin' hard. As we joked for years, Latin is a dead language, it killed the Romans and now it's killing us.

Pages and pages of translation to memorise; I didn't think I'd do it. In the end, I didn't. I must have learnt about one third of it.

*

07.05.79. May bank holiday. Jackie's fiancé, Gary, was a self-employed builder. He asked if I wanted to help him one day. How much will I get; a fiver? You're on! It was a blazing hot spring day with a beautiful blue sky. We turned up at a nice detached bungalow, where Gary was building an extension. I helped to chop bricks with a trowel, lay bricks, and generally broke my back in the scorching heat. I loved it. Within half an hour I had slashed my finger, and had to politely request from the owners use of their kitchen tap and a plaster. The blood was trickling down my brick dust smothered hands until I was nicely taped up. Back to work. Mixing cement, carrying loads, I was totally unused to physical labouring and it knackered me out. When we stopped for lunch, Gary didn't bother washing his hands so neither did I. Cheese rolls with added mortar. Mmm, nice.

What was great about that day was how fast it went. When you're busy, and interested, time flies. Unfortunately, the opposite is also true. At the end, he handed over the precious blue note. I went straight out and bought 'Strangers in the Night', a double live album from heavy metallers, UFO. I was getting into rock music in a big way, when I could afford it.

Brother David had a paper round as a teenager. I went with him once. It seemed a lot of hard work for little reward, but it does instil a work ethic. I didn't have a job until the offer from Dan Air, but I was always helpful at home. I loved to run the hoover around, help wash the cars, and begrudgingly would help with the washing up. I could work the chip pan well, a major achievement in the kitchen. At Harriet, a major omission was the complete lack of domestic training. We had no lessons at all in sewing, ironing, cooking or any other useful skill. Martin and Colin at Cranbourne had domestic science, in which they did have those sorts of lessons. Maybe because Harriet had always been a girls' school and they hadn't quite woken up to the modern world.

Martin had turned 16 in December '78, and he had set about obtaining a moped. Blockhead had one for sale. That sounded intriguing. What was it like? It was a Honda C50, bronze and white, basically a real old fart's machine. It didn't matter, it was cheap, available, and Martin's parents bought it for him. So, now I had one; and then there were two.

I turned up at ATC for the first time on my step through machine and ran the gamut of the standard piss taking and interest from my fellow cadets. Why didn't I get a Fizzy? Er, this was free. How fast does it go, apart from backwards? Whose Granny did you mug? Yes, yes, heard them all before. It all seemed so normal to have to justify your every decision or even your next breath. At that age, you are in the constant arena of judgement from your peers. Very few cadets were old enough to have a car. Spud had a gold-coloured Vauxhall Viva, but he was 19 and practically a man. Going home, I would ride along with my fellow cyclists and we would always be wary crossing the main part of South Ham. One evening, about 9:15 and very dark, the call went up that someone was throwing stones at us. Emboldened by numbers, the half a dozen of us chased elusive figures across the next two streets. Suddenly, there was a standoff. Half a brick was thrown with force and it just missed the front of my bike as it skipped along the road. I could just make out the perpetrator in the dark from the streetlight; it was Paul Benton. Benton was a blonde-haired head case from school. I had many a run in with him. I didn't fancy another. We wisely retreated. He had obviously been spooked, his mates had scarpered. Cornered, he did what any rat would do, he lashed out. We left him alone.

Mopeds were great fun and extremely practical machines; mine had a fuel economy of over 200 miles to the gallon. However, like any machine, it is only as good as the person controlling it. Cycling home from a parade night about a year before, Colin, Martin and I were in standard formation at speed going down Station Road, a long hill just north of the railway station. A guy on a moped was coming the other way, at speed, and suddenly he was waving his arm about, supposedly for us to get out of the way. I looked back at Martin; what's wrong with that guy? We were all on our side of the road. The moped rider came straight across our path to cut the corner turning right, colliding with Martin. There was an almighty bang. Colin and I shot past, unscathed, and immediately stopped. We started cycling back uphill to the collision zone. Martin was on the ground, as were both bike and moped.

'My fucking bike!' the guy screamed at the top of his lungs. Colin and I cringed. This guy sounds like a nutter. He's performed like a nutter; we just wanted to see if our mate was alright. As we got closer, the guy had an apparent change of heart and started checking Martin was ok.

'You alright mate, yeah? No 'arm done, yeah? Your arm is it? Duzzit 'urt, yeah?' He grabbed Martin's arm and waggled it; if it hadn't been broken in the crash he was risking snapping it now from over enthusiasm. Martin's bike had taken a real blow. Thankfully, residents came out of their houses and witnessed what happened. Martin had a check-up at the hospital, and was fine except for bruising. The mad fool on the moped was fined and endorsed for driving without due care and attention. It was always Martin that seemed to pick a fight with vehicles. Aged about 10, he had been hit by a car on the Winchester road and run over. He must have been made of rubber. We all seemed to attract the attention of nutters, though. Maybe there was something in the Loddon Valley water.

It was a full moon. It had eaten far too much cheese. It was another ride home from cadets, me and Martin on our mopeds, the rest on their pushbikes. We were halfway, and rode past the cemetery, gravestones eerily lit in the moonshine. Just as we approached the blue footbridge, there were figures already on it. We couldn't quite make them out until we were upon them. They blocked our path. I recognised the main one – it was Roger Berry; my old nemesis. Chris Tipler knew him, as he was quite notorious in the neighbourhood. I wanted to ride on, but I couldn't just leave the others. Berry was unpredictable and volatile. It was best to not provoke him. We didn't know if he had a knife or a weapon, or if he would use one. We all knew who he was. Berry started chatting to Chris. The other two of Berry's mates left. Chris whispered to Martin and I, 'Do you know who this is? I don't want to worry you, but this is Roger Berry and he has a reputation for being a bit of a juvenile delinquent.'

No shit Sherlock. We said, we knew. I popped my moped on the stand. Berry manoeuvred himself to sit on it. He didn't ask. I was instantly alarmed. He sat on it and continued chatting nonchalantly. He pretended be interested in the ATC. I knew what he was up to but felt powerless to stop him.

'Oh, let me remember how to start one of these things,' he said. He felt down to the engage switch, clicked it into gear, turned on the ignition and pedalled furiously. Before I could even start to protest, he had it started, he bounced it off the stand, and he rode it straight off back toward the cemetery. Oh my god. I had just let Roger Berry steal my moped. How could I be so stupid? I shouldn't have got off of it. It wouldn't have mattered; he would have probably hit me. I ran after my departed machine. I could still hear it; the motor was cutting out. I arrived 100 yards down the path to see Berry exclaim, 'Shit!' and furiously pedalling trying to get it to restart. As I caught him up, I grabbed the handlebars.

'Er, can I have my bike back now please?' I demanded, politely but firmly. Amazingly, he instantly gave it back. He had been thwarted, his plan backfired but thankfully the bike didn't. What he didn't know was that when I placed it on the stand, I had turned the fuel tap to 'off'. In that position, he only had one minute's worth of fuel.

In life, there is sometimes a cycle of events, pun fully intended. Berry and I had gone full circle. Both times he had tried to steal my bike; both times I had beaten him. Thankfully, I never saw him again.

There were some superb records that came out in 1979. I loved 'Jimmy Jimmy' by The Undertones. John Peel was the first mainstream DJ to play them with 'Teenage Kicks' but this was the first time I had heard them. The other wonderful track was 'Strange Town' by The Jam. They had been around since 1976 but after 'Strange Town' they became my favourite band. It's hard to understand exactly what about one particular artist or band interests you against another, but with The Jam it was the sound, the aggression. I had never really liked The Sex Pistols as they came across as vile individuals. I don't feel that way now, but I certainly wasn't interested in the nasty aspects of punk, such as gobbing. Sid Vicious had just died, after allegedly killing his girlfriend, Nancy Spungen, and him committing suicide. The Pistols had a great sound and energy, but The Jam also had the tunes. Weller came across as a right hard bastard. From what I have read down the years, that seems to be the case. I was not alone, as The Jam were to become one of the most popular bands of the post punk era. There's something about a Rickenbacker guitar through a Vox AC30 amp turned up full.

May 1979. He was still a fat bastard. No, not that one, the merry merry month of. Unfortunately, it wasn't, as our exams were about to start. It was two exams each day, completely different subjects. Monday might be maths in the morning and French in the afternoon. Many subjects had two exams, such as maths, Latin and French. It would have been beneficial to have these exams the same day, but no, that wasn't the case. Each exam was around three hours long, and we were either lined up in rows of desks in the main school hall or the Sports Hall. In subsequent years, I have read or heard media reports that schools wished to change the time of year for exams as it is too hot in the summer to sit for them. Well, for us, it was absolutely stifling. With the mental pressure of the exam, sitting in an airless room just made it unbearable. But we got through it, so future generations should suffer too!

We were instructed that there would be no talking, whether we could or could not use a calculator, to ask a question to raise your hand. For one maths exam we could use a calculator, for another, we couldn't. We couldn't attempt the physics paper without one. During the paper handing out session, Shaun Roe turned around to me and flashed me a message on his calculator; 'hello' made from numerals and inverted. I smiled at him. We were probably the first generation to use calculators, so the full range of possible words was explored at various times; shell, shell oil, sod off I'm trying to concentrate, etc.

I was happy with the maths papers. I had organised my time well enough to attack the easier answered questions first, and to go back and work on the harder ones. I took all the time allotted and the time just fell away. At the end of these exams, my hand always ached from writing so much.

I had no confidence in the Latin papers. The literature questions were surely going to be too hard. Astoundingly, the third I had learnt came up in the paper. Talk about lucky. Or fortunatus spurius.

My English Literature exam was entertaining. I felt I had written reams of text, and counted back my sheets, about eight sheets of A4. I glanced at a girl to my right; she had written about 13. Christ. Hopefully it would be measured predominantly on quality and not just quantity.

I got a little confused in my French oral. It was only maybe 10 minutes of speaking French with the female examiner, but she started talking about school dinners. I thought she was on about being in a restaurant, so I asked for the menu, which she seemed bemused by. Overall, I felt it went just about alright. The main French exam was fine also, for when I couldn't remember the words for parking, I translated it as leaving my car by the pavement. There's always a way if you remember *something*.

Chemistry was just a complete disaster. I think I got my name right. I might not have though; I didn't know the chemical symbol for Numpty. Physics was harder than the test papers we had been working through, and one or two questions covered subjects we had not learnt. It was worse when you compared notes later with your friends; some said one thing, others said another. In the end, you can only trust your own instincts and hope it was right; too late to change now.

Pink Floyd released their fantastic track 'Another Brick in the Wall', with the refrain, 'we don't need no education.' Classic. It incorporates what I believe is one of, if not *the* best, guitar solo ever. As kids about to leave school, we adopted it as our anthem. Unfortunately, we did need an education, and we needed qualifications. Maggie Thatcher had just been voted in as the first female Prime Minister, and there would be 18 years of Tory rule to follow. Times were going to be tough.

I was going to miss many aspects of school life, but there were certain things I would not miss; being thrown in the sandpit on my birthday, irascible coffee breath teachers, bullies, prefect duty. Both Simon C and Shaun Roe had eloquently persuaded me to perform prefect duties for them they didn't fancy doing; well actually, they gave me cold, hard cash but who's arguing semantics? It was a big mistake; just telling other kids they can't walk down a certain corridor at lunchtime was often full scale war. I had to extricate one girl intent on kicking me in the nuts just because she didn't like being told what to do; another pair of blonde identical twins will forever be dubbed The Loudmouth Twins for the arguing they did about a simple instruction. I think the teachers couldn't care less about the insurrection; they had their peace and quiet in their fag-laden staff room. Not all females were horrendous, though. I was having a people watch at lunchtime and my eyes rested on a lovely face and form, a third year with a striking prettiness and determined eyebrows. She was slim and graceful and I found I couldn't take my eyes off of her. She saw me looking and instead of us breaking gaze, she smiled beatifically. I smiled back. It was a nice moment, it existed for that time but there was no intent on a follow up, she was a fourteen-year-old. She was also obviously comfortable with being looked at. She was Elizabeth Hurley.

I was due to start my Gliding Course at RAF Upavon, and it was proving difficult to obtain a proper starting date. It would entail a few residential weekends on Salisbury Plain, and weather permitting, should take about four full weekends of flying before being able to fly solo. Martin attended one or two weekends before I started, and he gave me the background and what to expect. Just as I was coming to an end of school life, thinking I would leave the bully boys behind, Martin told me about Jacko.

Jacko, or Staff Cadet Jakubowski, was the main cadet in charge at RAF Upavon. He was a 19-year-old gliding instructor and had made Martin's first weekend a nightmare. Jacko had come back to the billet late, pissed, and basically terrorised everybody. Great; it would be something to really look forward to. At least Martin knew where to go, which was to be beneficial on my first trip.

'Oh, and there's Tony.'

'Tony?'

'Yeah, he can be a bit of a git as well.'

'Wonderful.'

'Don't let that put you off. The actual gliding is superb.'

I wasn't put off. I was full of trepidation, but that was normal.

It was going to be the experience of a lifetime.

8. Going Solo

01.06.79. Martin, Purdey and I caught the bus to Salisbury. Laden with our bags, we had to change at Salisbury bus station to catch the connecting bus to be dropped close to RAF Upavon. By the time we arrived on that warm Friday evening, it was already dark. The road leading up to the airfield was flanked by huge trees and was unlit. We could hear an owl calling in the distance, cicadas chirped, the countryside was awash with noise. Wind swished through the fully leafed trees, a high frequency barrage to add to the rural soundscape. We were spooking each other as we dragged our cases, to the point where it all became too much, and we ended up sprinting the last half a mile to the gate.

From the gatehouse, Martin led us to the transit billet, where we would be housed for the weekend. Upavon can truly be called the birthplace of the RAF. It was used for pilot training for many years, and was now home to the 622 Squadron VGS (Volunteer Gliding School) as well as the Army Wyvern Gliding School. Not that we worried about that now. We found the food machine, bought some drinks and crisps, and aimed to settle into our billet. I took a top bunk, Martin took the one below.

It wasn't long before I met Jacko. He turned up late, around 10pm, just as we were settling into sleep. He had had a few, and reeked of booze. He wasn't very tall, had thin, dark hair and a reedy moustache. His eyes were glazed and he was unsure on his feet.

'Who've we got here then, Stevens?' he slurred.

Martin tried to introduce us courteously and

professionally.

Jacko came up to my eyeline as I lay on my bed.

'He looks like a coont. Are you a coont?'

I tried not to laugh. I wasn't sure if he was serious or just messing with me.

'No, I'm not, Jacko.'

'Jacko? Jacko? My name, cadet, is Flight Sergeant Jakubowski to *you*.' He wobbled again. 'You are a coont, aren't ya?'

Phil and Martin were stifling their laughs. Jacko staggered in their direction. 'And you can stop laffin an all!' He saw Phil. 'And oo are you? Another cooont?'

The smell of alcohol was overwhelming. He must have drunk a barrel. He grabbed a broom and tried to shove it up my behind. I squirmed and writhed but he was persistent.

'You laff at me you coonts and I'll shove this broom up yer arse!' I thought at one point he might succeed. He persisted for ages in his attempt but eventually gave up. We were all laughing too much to properly defend ourselves. Eventually, he departed to sleep in his own billet.

'Cor, he's a bit of a wanker, inne?' understated Phil.

'Yeah,' I agreed. 'Less Jakubowski, more Jerkaforeskin.'

We found that very funny. That was the name that stuck.

In the morning, the sun blazed through the windows and we made our way to the mess for breakfast. Staff cadets were arriving in the morning who obviously lived locally enough to do so. We met Tony, similar age to Jacko, who had a bossy manner but seemed alright. He was a smoker and that gave him a rough edge to his voice. Jacko and Tony, apart from being instructors, would drive the Land Rovers to transport the gliders, and us, around the base. God help you if you referred to a Land Rover as a jeep. The first morning was a true baptism of fire and introduction to life with these crazy guys. We had to prepare the vehicles so first stop was the maintenance hangar.

Ostensibly, the airfield was exactly that; a very large field. At one end were the hangars with the aircraft, at the other was a border to the next set of fields. From the usual take off point, to the left were fields and then the main road; beyond and around it was all MOD land. The feeling was that you really were in the middle of nowhere.

In the hangar were the two Land Rovers we were to become very accustomed to. They had room for two in the front and perhaps six in the back under the tarpaulin.

'Right,' said Tony. 'We use the acronym, POWER to check the vehicles before use. That stands for Petrol, Oil, Water, Electrolyte, Rubber. If it's a diesel, we don't put petrol in because that would be very fucking stupid. We check the oil level, the water level, and the electrolyte level of the battery and top up as necessary. Finally, we check the rubber on the tyres.'

'Why do the tyres need a rubber on them? Will they get pregnant?' Martin tried to be a smart ass but that sort of thing didn't wash with Tony.

'How tall are you?' He said to Martin.

Martin looked dumbfounded and a little concerned.

'Why?' smiled Martin, nervously.

'Answer the fuckin' question,' said Tony, pulling out some tow rope.

'About five foot seven?' Martin said, unsure of the actual answer.

'Lie down,' said Tony.

'What?' Martin said, unsure of what Tony was getting at.

Tony didn't ask again. He used a judo move and pulled

Martin to the concrete floor. Then he started counting out lengths of rope using Martin as a measuring device.

'How tall are you?' he said to me. Here we go. Both of us were on the floor as human rulers.

It was becoming apparent that to get on some physicality was often called for. This was our world back in 1979. It didn't endear us to these elder guys but I have to admit they got the job done.

Within a short time, Tony had his tow rope sorted. Tony and Jacko wanted to check the airfield for obstructions before we towed the gliders out.

'Get in the back,' instructed Tony. We leapt in and Tony slammed his foot on the accelerator, necessitating a firm grip on the cabin sides. We bounced out onto the grass, which had just been cut. As he revved the engine past an acceptable level and crashed the gears, bits of grass came in through the back, semi choking us. We were bouncing all over the place and couldn't have been going faster than 30mph.

'Rabbits!' exclaimed Tony, as he turned the wheel violently left and right to chase them. The view forward was restricted but I could see two terrified bobtails leaping away, rapidly changing direction with Tony wrenching the wheel in pursuit. We were thrown left to right, up and down, it was a real challenge to stay upright and even on board.

'Oh, they got away,' Tony said, disappointedly, and as quickly as he had changed course, he reverted back to straight driving and normal over revving.

Satisfied the airfield was clear, we started to move kit.

We had two types of glider; the Slingsby Sedbergh T21, which was a dual seat side by side, and the Slingsby Cadet T31 tandem seater, also known as the Mark 3. Both were wooden with fabric skins, both designed in the forties, and painted in the standard red, white and grey livery of RAF trainers. They were also both open cockpit gliders, and resembled small barges with wings. We operated left hand circuits of the airfield, launching side by side with the Army gliding club on our right, who operated right hand circuits. They had more modern K13 gliders with full canopies. They also had parachutes; we were told we couldn't have them as we didn't fly high enough to warrant them.

At the launch point, sited a third of the airfield's length, was a large red and white chequered mobile control tower, in which launch signals were flashed by beacon to the winch operator. The winch operator sat in a converted tractor with a motorised barrel, around which were the launch cables. The winch was sited at the bottom of the airfield. He had a handy emergency release; a large axe in case the mechanism jammed or the cable could not release from the glider. All the Rover drivers and the launch operator were staff cadets. Jacko was a little different as he was also a qualified gliding instructor. The fact he was also a pisshead was probably irrelevant.

It was a beautiful sunny day, with a light breeze. We hitched up the gliders on their trailers to the Rovers, and towed them out to the launch point. The control tower was like a caravan with a glass roof, so inside it was more an office and it got bloody hot. There was a simple box-like construction of aluminium that was the lamp control, with a three-way switch. Take up slack was a slow pulse of the lamp signalling to the winch operator to remove slack in the cable once hitched to the glider; all out was a faster pulse, that meant open the throttle to winch faster and lift the glider into the launch; stop stop stop – hmm, let me remember what that meant. This produced a continuous light that told the operator to cease all winching. Coincident with the light was an audible sound, so even if you were looking away from the lamp at the launch site, you would hear the beeps and react accordingly. The winch operator was quite some distance, because some launches could be as high as 1,500 feet, so that length of cable had to be free to allow that height, let alone what had wrapped around the cable.

The gliding instructors were a real mix of backgrounds and personalities. Some were old school ex-RAF, some civilian instructors. It came across in their manner which was likely to be which. All I saw at first was a disparate bunch of guys dressed in one piece denim flight suits. As a first timer, as was Phil Rolfe, we had to help out on the ground with other cadets before we even had a sniff of an actual flight. We both observed Martin in action before we even did that.

Martin in a Mk 3 Glider, RAF Upavon 1979. Cadet Instructor Griffin and Mills are in the denims. (Trevor Heath Archive)

There was so much information to take in it was overwhelming. Ever see a wind sock trailing away in the wind at an airfield? It's not there to flap colourfully in the breeze. It shows the wind strength and crucially, the direction it's coming from. No need for fancy equipment here. Gliders always take off into wind and aim to land into wind, as do powered aircraft, but it's even more critical for a glider; if the airflow stops over the wings, you drop like a brick, without recourse to a motor to bring more thrust. The prevailing wind would dictate the direction of take-off and therefore the set-up of the equipment; a bit like flipping a coin for direction of play in a sports match but without the element of chance. The wind sock was high enough to be viewed from every point of the airfield, in a nice bold yellow colour.

Martin launching a Mk3, RAF Upavon 1979 (Trevor Heath Archive)

The gliders were manoeuvred manually off their trailers with a cadet on at least one wingtip and normally two pushing the body. Care had to be taken as the fuselage and wings had large areas of stretched fabric, and it would have been easy to pierce it with just your fingers. Overall, they were pretty sturdy wooden craft, and surprisingly heavy, 176kg unladen.

Free from the trailer, one wing was rested on the ground with the glider facing the winch, or turned 90 degrees with the wing down toward the winch.

A staff cadet would arrive from the winch direction, towing perhaps four cables. A cadet would unhitch them and pull one forward when instructed to connect a cable. This would only happen when both cadet and instructor were seated and strapped in, ready to go. There was a checklist against which the safety aspects were covered, the acronym was CBSITCB. This was also printed on checker tape and stuck on the front of the cockpit. The cockpit itself was extremely basic; an ASI (Air speed Indicator) and an altimeter to check height, a piece of string on top of the nose was the slip and turn indicator; the control column, to move the ailerons (wings up and down) and elevators (nose and tail up and down); rudder controls operated by the feet (left or right steering); a yellow knob to the left of the control panel to release the cable; and a lever on the left side of the cockpit to operate the spoilers on the wings. It wasn't exactly the Space Shuttle.

I observed a glider launch, Martin at the wingtip. The instructor, sat in the back, cadet in the front; the instructor verbally worked through the basic checklist.

'Canopy – we don't have a canopy, we have a windshield (checks windshield is fully attached).

'Ballast – not applicable, Straps (both instructor check their respective harnesses are tight and secure).

'Instruments (taps altimeter, makes sure glass is intact).

'Trim – we do not use trim.

'Controls – can we have wings level, please?' This is the instruction for Martin to lift the wings level. As he does so, the instructor cycles the control column, moves the column to the left and right, visually observes correct movement of ailerons, elevators, and rudder. It actually looks like he's stirring a soup cauldron.

'Controls are fully free and in the correct sense (this means right aileron goes up as the control column is moved right and vice versa, and elevator goes up when column pulled back).

'Brakes – we do not have brakes, we have spoilers.' He then pulls the spoiler lever, and the spoiler plates lift up from the top of the wing.

'Spoilers fully extended and in line?' he asks the wingtip cadet, who replies... Martin, what do you reply?'

'Spoilers fully extended and in line, sir.' And the same when closed.

'Cable on!' Another cadet drags the cable across the grass, and bearing in mind it could be almost half a mile long, it takes a bit of effort. The cadet asks the instructor to open and close the release.

'Cable on, sir!'

'Ok,' said the instructor, 'all clear above and behind?' Martin checks the sky around the glider for anyone landing.

'All clear above and behind, sir,' is the appropriate response.

'Ok, take up slack!'

The control room then starts the lamp flashing to the winch operator. Very quickly, the cable starts to snake and writhe through the grass; in the early morning, it would flick up dew into a spray. Cadets soon learn to keep clear of the cable as it tightens. As the cable suddenly goes straight, the glider starts to be pulled straight and move forward. The wingtip cadet has to hold the wings level at the tip and run with the craft as far as he can. As the craft picks up speed, the instructor yells, 'All out!'

The lamp is flashed faster, the glider picks up more speed, and the cadet running is forced to let go. After 10 yards or so, the air over the wings is enough to allow the control surfaces to be effective, and if a wing drops then very quickly it can be corrected back to level; the glider whistles into the air – my god, it's going like a bat out of hell and at an extremely steep angle. The wind against airframe and cable produces a whooshing sound, and as the glider starts to level off, the noise subsides. Peering into the sky, the nose dips and the cable is released, where it falls quickly back to the ground, closer to the winch than us.

Martin walks back to me at the launch point. 'And that's all there is to it,' he says, echoing the famous Bruce Forsyth line from the Generation Game. Before long, we are all active in various stages of the operation, launch after launch. Gliders complete their circuits and soar overhead, whooshing air and flaring above us, readying to land. As soon as they are down, two of us are in the Rovers to retrieve them. We load them back onto the trailers and back to the launch point. It was hard, physical, but enjoyable work. Each flight was usually no more than three or four minutes, dependent on launch height achieved.

The time came for my first flight. Jerkaforeskin was going to take me up. Oh, God, does it have to be macho Jacko? I am strapped into the front seat. It feels like some sort of demented fairground ride. The seat is flat wood and very uncomfortable. Just getting in, your knees hit the wooden sides. I was always covered in bruises after gliding. Which glider is it? *WT901*. Be good to me, *901*. The pace is casual; nothing is hurried when gliding. Safety is paramount. My heart is pounding. Jacko goes through the launch checks. No going back. I look forward, I see the instruments and the angled instrument panel, above which is the small Perspex windshield. The slip and turn indicator is on the nose. Before us is just grass. The winch is so far away, I can't see it. Instructors chat just feet away, it's a wordless noise as I concentrate on the impending flight. I feel as if I am strapped to a large firework and someone is going to light the blue touch paper at any moment.

Jacko calls for wings level. The small movement makes me feel queasy. The birds are singing but there are no trees.

Noise carries a very long way on an open airfield. Jacko calls for clearance.

'Aircraft landing, sir,' is the reply. We can't turn to see against the straps. I hear the whoosh of air as a glider comes over our heads. I hear the instructor talking to the cadet as he is 40 feet above us. He is calm but clear; the craft descends and lands to our left, away from our intended path.

Jacko asks again, this time we are clear. 'Take up slack,' he states, and the cable quickly tugs at our front. I am jerked back in my seat as the nose pulls up and forward. I hear Jacko shout, 'All out!' behind me and we start to really move. The cadet on our left is running, running and then disappears. We are in the launch; the wind whistles through the struts and we are almost lying on our backs; the nose is pointing to the sky and all I can see is blue. From the sides of the cockpit I can hardly see the ground falling away. The control column has a mind of its own, duplicating the motions Jacko is applying behind me. Below us, the tension in the cable increases, making a groaning noise, as if being tortured. We sway left, right, a gentle sashaying as we increase in height. The altimeter shows we are climbing, 500 feet, 550 feet, 600 feet... the speed is fairly constant, 45 knots. As we climb higher, the cable pulls us into an arc, and the nose starts to come down. As it does, I can see over the nose and the airfield comes into view. Wow. I can see for miles. My glasses suddenly start bouncing on my nose. The wind has got under them and they are threatening to lift off. I clutch them to my face in panic. The air is really rushing past my ears now, over the top and sides of the cockpit. Jacko pushes the stick forward, releasing the tension on the cable. He pulls the release knob and there is a solid 'thunk' from below us as it releases the heavy cable. We slow down, the wind subsides, we settle into steady flight. It is beautiful, peaceful, calming. The launch was terrifying, now it was getting easier; but we are still over 1,000 feet up, with no canopy; it felt extraordinarily exposed and dangerous.

We turned left for the crosswind leg. The left wing dipped as Jacko moved the column, I stared down the wing at the fields as they seemed to rotate around us. Soon again, as we descended, we turned left for the downwind leg. The wind was behind us now, speed fairly constant at 35 knots; to our right, I could see over to the main road and beyond; to our left were the buildings on the base, grey tarmac areas standing out proudly against the predominant green. We passed the control tower, another glider was launching, a small red and white toy slowly making its way down the billiard table. Around 350 feet, we turned in for the last crosswind leg, and we started to put on speed for the approach, which meant dipping the nose and descending faster. We turned sharply left for the approach, speed back up to 40 knots. Jacko engaged the spoilers to lose lift and height; it was if we were falling out of the sky, my stomach was somewhere above me. A few seconds later, height optimised, we made ready as the ground came up to meet us, the green whizzing past the sides of the cockpit. The nose wheel engaged with the ground, and we rumbled along for ages, bumping, until the noise stopped. We came to a halt; the wing went down and thumped the ground. All was quiet; the Rover was almost upon us, the engine note started to fill the all too transient calm.

Jacko leapt out of his straps.

'Come on, time to push,' he said, as if I was in labour. We pushed the crate back on the trailer, leapt into the yellow Rover, and back to the launch point. That was me done for the day. It was all of three minutes. Time had stretched and it had seemed much longer. I was initiated. The work was to begin on the actual training.

In the evening, after we had settled the kit for the night back in the hangar, Martin, Phil and I amused ourselves in the TV room. There was a drink and crisps vending machine, so we were quite happy with a can of Coke and old episodes of 'Batman'. It had been a long day. The elder cadets disappeared as they were old enough to frequent the pubs. It was going to be quite different the next time we came.

The Sunday flying embedded the procedures in my mind. Unfortunately, I was not to fly again that weekend. Demand was high and availability of aircraft was low. The Army group next to us occasionally brought their K13s into a beat up of the field; they had a top speed of around 120mph, and they would dive low over the field on the approach, shoot along seemingly flat and then pull up, wingover (rotate 180 degrees) so they were then diving again, before pulling up the nose to land. It was very impressive. Quite a few of our instructors took up the offer to ride with them when they could. Jacko had a go; he had his tongue up the rears of the other instructors. To us, he was the Flight Sergeant, to them, he was an eager boy, reverential and compliant. He was alright when he was sober.

I began to spot dangerous behaviour in other cadets. Instructor Mills, a frizzy-haired beer-gutted guy in his late thirties, was quite funny. He had a strong Hampshire accent, and was the most laid back of the team. When he saw one cadet wrap himself in the cable, which made it easier to pull, he gently lent his advice.

'Don't wrap yourself in the cable, son. If that guy at the winch turns it on you're going to go shooting down that airfield minus your knackers.'

The cadet spun himself sheepishly out of the python-like cable, and had a quick fumble to ensure he was still intact. Another poor practice was allowing a wing to drop just before releasing grip whilst running alongside. I was now a corporal and had no hesitation in instructing other cadets when I saw such transgressions, even though I was a novice myself.

I had to revise for my geography exam. With the next few weekends being busy with gliding, I was not going to fit in enough time for it. So be it; I was not going to get a second chance at this. Even though we were heading into summer, the weather and other obstacles would get in the way of a linear training path.

The next time we went down to Upavon, on 17.06.79, I had another weekend with just one flight. This time, it was a trip in the Sedbergh side-by-side trainer, again with my mate, Jacko. As it is a larger cockpit, although cramped together, it felt even more unsafe than the tandem trainer, as it felt more open. As the cable was grinding below us on the launch, nose in the sky, one of the wings lurched upward. It was a sunny day and the warm air was rising fast.

'Hey, we've got a thermal!' enthused Jacko.

As we neared the top of the launch, facing the hangars this time due to wind direction, I felt a real sense of panic. The ground was a long way down; we were open to the elements, and glider WB994 seemed all over the place. I grabbed my duplicate column.

'I have control, sir!' I told Jacko.

'No, no, let go of the stick, there's a good boy,' said Jacko. I complied. In my fractious state, I wanted to control this thing; he didn't seem to be in control to me. Of course, he was in full control; I just couldn't contain my panic and wanted to get out – a bit tricky at over 1,000 feet.

As soon as he could, Jacko released the cable and went hunting for the elusive thermal. He soon found it, and banked the glider into a tight left, and then a tight right turn.

'Wahay, we're going up!' he exclaimed. What a strange sensation in a glider. I could feel upward motion, and the sun was going around us, but the altimeter didn't move; we were defying gravity and staying at virtually the same height for ages. After an eternity of probably 40 seconds, Jacko lost the lift. We continued on our circuit.

We rumbled to a halt on the grass. Jacko had asked me if I was alright but I hadn't got my head around this flying lark yet. To obtain the equivalent of your sea legs on a ship, it can take a little while. It would take a few more flights, but it was going to come.

Jacko could hardly contain himself; he wanted to go back up again. He went up with another cadet, caught a succession of thermals and was gone for over half an hour. When he returned, he was pretty frozen as he had reached 4,000 feet. If it was 20 degrees on the ground, it would be around 12 degrees up there, factor in the wind chill – brrr.

There was a new character in our midst. Cadet Melbourne was a friendly chap from Totton, near Southampton. He was another one with a Hampshire yokel-sounding accent. I don't recall his first name but we nicknamed him Sid anyway; after Sydney, Australia. He hated that. His green denims had a woven name tag on the front. His first meeting with Jacko and Tony was memorable.

'Why have you got Melbourne written on your denims? Are you Australian or summat?' said Jacko.

'No. I'm from Totton,' said Melbourne.

'Then why have you got fuckin' Melbourne on your tit then?' added Tony.

'That's my name, Melbourne.'

'Well that's a pretty stupid fuckin' name,' spat Tony. 'Is that your first name or your last name?'

The grilling never stopped. It was continuous piss taking from the moment we got up to the moment we left the site. We went for lunch together in the canteen. Melbourne had a favourite joke which he told everyone when he met them.

"Ave you 'eard the one abowoot the balokeoo went into a purrb and orrrdurred a point o' piss an a shit poie?'

'No?'

'This baloke, roight. Ee went into a purrb, and orrrdurred a point o' piss an a shit poie...'

Yes, I think we got that bit. This was recanted as he

stuffed his pie, peas and chips...

"Ee drank dowoon is point o' piss, then he ate 'is shit poie. Luvverly, 'ee said. Then he threw up alloover the place. Some baloke asked him, "Didn't yew enjoyeeyoor point o' piss an' shit poie?" An' 'ee said, "Yeah, but theyurrs a bloke o'oertheyurrpeckin is nose!'"

The first time I heard it, it seemed mildly amusing. After 10 renditions it sort of lost the negligible-to-start-with appeal. Sid liked embellishing his joke with the actions as he devoured his lunch and orange squash.

Another staff cadet was Simon. He was blonde, angular, a spitting image of actor Mackenzie Crook, before we knew who he was, of course. He was also the last to get a joke; nice guy, thick as shit. There was Cadet Moffat, a gentle giant, academically very clever, but he seemed to be living in an alternate dimension to the rest of us. Quiet, he hardly said a word, but when he did, it was usually about half an hour after the preceding conversation. We called him Muppet. It seemed to fit.

There were two other guys and I can't remember their names. One was a sergeant, with a bright ginger thatch of hair and incongruously thick, black eyebrows. He reminded me of Ken Dodd's Diddymen. We got on very well although his name escapes me, but I think his first name was Trevor, also. Hi, Trevor Also. He spoke very well, which made a pleasant change from the strangulated vowels uttered by the locals. The other chap I have pictured with Martin, Rolfe and Melbourne outside the hangar, but I cannot recall his name. He was dark haired and a little squat, and I'm pretty sure he worked the winch most of the time. Ooarree be the winch troll. In between launches, there wasn't much time to chat, but we came together at meal times and caught up. It was either launch or lunch for him.

Gliding would usually end mid-afternoon on the Sunday, giving everyone time to return to their normal lives. I was getting quite frustrated with the lack of flying I was receiving, two weekends and only two flights. Other cadets well into their training would have flight after flight, especially when leading up to solo. Still, it was another tiring but entertaining weekend, and we had to get two buses back home. Thankfully, we were soon to get a lift to and fro with a member of our squadron; Spud, already a glider pilot, was to study for his instructor qualification. It meant we could travel with him in his Vauxhall Viva, yippee!

The following weekend we arrived to find there was no gliding on at all. Before emails and the internet, communication was a trifle more hit and miss. It was a long trek down to Upavon to discover this. Martin didn't go that weekend, and I have pictures of me, Rolfe and Melbourne against a backdrop of Wessex helicopters parked up on our gliding strip. It was a weekend of RAF exercises, and in the coming weeks we would see an escalation of activities around the base. We peered in and around the choppers, sitting sentinel on the grass, their rotors snoozing beneath the overcast sky.

A couple of guys in camouflage gear walked up to us. I thought they were going to tell us off for taking pictures.

'Hey, has one of you guys got a camera?' asked a dark Scottish voice.

'Yes, I have,' I volunteered, showing off my cheap but dependable Agfa automatic with poxy 110 film.

'Could we borrow it? Or even you take pictures for us?' This guy had a face and neck which was a mass of boils. He was one ugly son of a bitch. I think his head was held together with pus.

'Sure. What do you want to take pictures of?'

'Well we're on the refuelling flight. We're going to be the first crew to refuel a Chinook before we start getting them in the RAF. One's coming in later.'

Anyone seen a Chinook? Refuelling Flight RAF Upavon, 1979. (Trevor Heath Archive)

Cool. The only thing was, they needed a new film because the one in the camera was mine. We leapt in a vehicle and went off camp to a shop to get a film. We returned, and waited for the Chinook to arrive. And arrive it did.

What a sight, what a sound; a huge twin-rotored helicopter, the CH-47C was to be converted to the RAF standard HC-1, and at just under 100 feet long, it was an unbelievably impressive sight as it slowly came into land, right in front of us. Dust, grass and dirt were thrown our way as the giant eggbeaters bore down their huge thrust. It hovered for a while; the throb of the engines was terrifying and exhilarating. I clicked away with my camera at the olive drab Olympian, before it descended and shut down. The noise was gone and the refuelling team wasted no time posing in the loading ramp and beside it, whilst the crew conversed with other assorted assembled RAF throng. I felt like a VIP as the official photographer; pity I was wearing a very old brown jumper and brown cords. Within a very short time, half an hour or so, the chopper was off. The refuelling wasn't going to happen, not here at least, but Jock and his boys had their precious snaps. I handed over their film. I believe my fee was a can of Coke.

The official photographer for a day, RAF Upavon 1979.
(Trevor Heath Archive)

It was literally the bright lights of Broadway to tumbleweed in the space of an hour.

The only recompense was, we were now given a house. The transit billet Nicolson, no more, we were now based in a respectable proper building with a cooker, separate rooms and decent beds. We still had our sleeping bags with us though. That evening, I grew increasingly tired of Melbourne and Rolfe's yammerings and tried to sleep in another room. They kept talking for hours. In the end, fatigued and bleary-eyed, I came in and berated them for the noise. 'Will you please just shut up?'

They did; for about a minute. Then it started again. Oh dear. Was I ever going to sleep away at this camp? Various cadets would come in and disappear again. Where did they go? I wonder. Jacko would always turn up, as would Tony, and then go out again, probably to a club somewhere. At sixteen, it was a bit boring in the evening, as we were too young to drink, drive or indulge in mindless vandalism lest we got thrown in the guard room cell. And yet here we were flying aeroplanes in the daytime. Bizarre.

We all woke up late. I knocked on Trevor's door. I heard his curtain go across, the obvious realisation it was daylight, and heard the loud exclamation, 'Bloody Hell!' He was either concerned about us starting late or he was a vampire. The door opened to reveal a ginger boy with wild eyes and an urgent manner. I guess he wasn't a vampire as his pale skin was intact.

Muppet slept with his teddy. He was like a big kid; a big kid who was sitting his 'A' levels. We all liked him. He never said anything to upset anybody, he just never said anything. His life was in slow motion. He was a real sight in the Mark 3 cockpit, his height ensured he towered above the diminutive instructors; as the craft flew above you with him at the controls, the drag from his torso I'm sure slowed it down by about five knots.

The elder cadets were attending discos on Saturday nights. We found this out when Spud starting driving us to Upavon. It was a joy driving with Paul, he was a really smiley blonde guy; although he was older and our superior, he was down to earth and kept us informed about what was going on. The approach to Upavon was good fun, as the roads were mostly empty and hilly, so Spud would thrash the hell out of his Viva to give us a bouncy and undulating country thrill. It also meant we left home later and got back earlier on a Sunday.

The car radio would dominate our journey. 'Ring My Bell' by Anita Ward was everywhere, as was 'Sunday Girl' by Blondie, one of my favourite tracks on the 'Parallel Lines' album. The absolute hit of the summer was unquestionably 'Are Friends Electric?' by Tubeway Army. When I hear that record, I'm bouncing in a Vauxhall Viva with Spud, breathing in the smell of freshly cut grass and turning somersaults in a wooden glider. Oh, yes, that bit is yet to come.

9. Summertime Blues

Mainland Britain was quite a dangerous place in 1979. The IRA was blowing up politicians with car bombs, notably MP Airey Neave in the House of Commons in London earlier in the year. Although we were mere cadets, attending any event in uniform, or being on military bases, carried a risk in itself. This was part and parcel of the psychological warfare intrinsic to the Irish terrorist campaign. Although I no longer wanted to join the regulars, the more an alien aggressor wanted to attack me or my establishment, the more I felt aligned with it. I might have actively disliked certain individuals, but they were my comrades in arms; they would have my back, and I certainly would have had theirs. Not that we were in any way actively political, except May came out with some total bullshit about being a Communist. Instead of sensibly backing down and accept pretentiousness, he laboured the point, so I really had a go at him. We were in the middle of the Cold War years with Russia, nuclear threat was a constant worry, and here's our supposed mate lining up with Moscow.

The last weeks of school were fragmented; I only attended revision classes or exams, so there was a lot of space between the last day and the start of my apprenticeship in September. I went in on my moped a couple of times, which was fun. It all felt like a major damp squib; there was no great party or letting off steam. Alice Cooper didn't turn up in leather keks and heavy makeup, screaming 'School's out!' The vast majority of my good friends were going on to Sixth Form College, so would be together for the next two years. I was going forward into the unknown, with people I didn't know. Perhaps that was why ATC still held its appeal, as I had continuity there for a bit longer.

I'm pretty sure the last exam I sat was geography. I hadn't understood the subject structure and found it nigh on impossible to revise effectively. I felt it went really badly. However, the rest seemed to have gone reasonably well, so the last time I went out of the school, I could only think about going forward. There were no grand goodbyes; people finished on different days dependent on their schedules. I couldn't wait to be free of school. Bon voyage to all the arseholes. Until the next set came into view.

Anyway, my good mates I would keep in contact with. What I didn't realise is that many people come back into your life at the most unexpected times. The longer you go on, the more it happens.

So, my focus now, was a summer of leisure and flying. I had been chosen to go to camp again, this time to RAF Leeming in Yorkshire, and a whole new brace of characters to contend with. As Martin and Colin had gone to St Athan, a dead boring week it transpired, they wouldn't be going this year. It was a new scenario for me in July and August that year, as I was totally free of school and work. I was technically unemployed until September, so I drew unemployment benefit for those weeks. It wasn't much, but it kept me ticking over and paid for my moped petrol.

I was still very uncool in my dress sense, my haircut and my overall outlook. I used to get my hair cut at Carey's in the town centre. It was true production line hair cutting as if we were sheep being sheared. There was a line of four or five stylists and although you could choose your preference, you were normally allotted your turn by raffle ticket. It was therefore literally a lottery if you had a decent trim or a follicle butchering. The floor was always awash with dozens of multi-coloured scalps, and the same young lad with the broom sweeping it up. The guy taking the money, I presume Mr Carey himself, sat by a desk in an immaculate suit. I don't know why the desk had a nice suit but there you are. My cut was one up from a pudding bowl – they didn't actually use a bowl. I had no idea whatsoever about how to even choose a style, let alone what might suit. Short will do. Thanks.

Similarly, with clothing, so long as it was functional I was happy. Martin, Colin and I went to a party in Bounty road, opposite the cricket ground. Martin and Colin had a slow dance with real life girls, but I sat in a chair stroking some black Labrador. My top was a zip up Honda cardigan, hardly cutting edge Carnabetian attire. I needed my eyes opened to my sartorial shortfalls, which didn't come from my immediate mates, as they were discovering these issues for themselves.

I went home and started putting pen to paper. I wrote reams of lyrics for songs I would eventually write, when I could learn the guitar; Sister Jackie had taught me three or four chords on an acoustic guitar, but I never really applied myself until then. I made a conscious decision, I was going to buy an electric guitar and learn how to play, to back myself singing. I couldn't yet afford one, but I gave up the violin in preparation to start a new and exciting instrument. Watching The Damned on Top of the Pops, I thought, *If this bunch of fools can do it, so can I.*

Somebody had rigged up a rope swing from a tree near the blue bridge. You could sit astride a log attached to the long rope, and swing out over the steep bank which led to the main road. Martin, Colin and I had a great time on it. May was there on one occasion with us. On my turn, I was really enjoying swaying out as far as I could, which meant walking up the bank astride the log to the highest point and leaping off. I was spinning, spinning, enjoying the height and the adrenalin rush, but then Martin, the little devil, spun me around toward the tree trunk. You can always rely on your mates to try and kill you. Fearing I would hit the trunk and break my face, I eased my rear off the log and let go – still about six feet up. I landed heavily on my left wrist and winded myself. I could hear them all laughing their heads off as the log dangerously swished past my head. Ow, that really, really hurt. I ambled my way to the footpath, and dusted myself down. I thought my arm might be broken. I saw flashing lights and my hearing started to fade; I was sure I was passing out. May immediately placed me in the recovery position. Within seconds, the feeling subsided. Unfortunately, the pain didn't. Who would have known it? May could be useful after all. Colin was spectacularly unsympathetic, refusing to believe my injury was as bad as I could tell it was. I cycled home, as we were on our bikes, and Dad suggested we go and check it out. I was given an x-ray but it wasn't broken, my wrist was badly sprained. I couldn't sleep the aching was so bad. It took weeks before it stopped hurting, but thankfully I still had full movement in my arm.

*

30.06.79. At last, some proper glider training was going to start, not just air experience flight. I was to fly with Instructor Pidgeon, who was middle aged and fat. We dubbed him Walter; as you do.

'So, what's your first name?' said Walter.

'Trevor, sir.'

'Kevin?'

'No, Trevor, sir.'

'Ah, Trevor. Ok. Right, Kevin, we're going to…'

'My name is Trevor, sir.'

'What? What did I say?'

'You called me Kevin again, sir.'

'Oh, sorry, Trevor. Once we're up, I'm going to demonstrate the controls and what they do, then I'm going to let you have a go, Ok? Good lad, Kevin.'

Sure enough, after the launch, Walter showed me the movements of pitch, yaw and roll. I couldn't turn to see the instructor, but being right behind I could hear him very well. The major problem was communicating to the rear, as you had to turn left or right and shout.

'Right Kevin,' started Walter from the rear seat of *XE800*. 'Let's start with the control column. I push it forward and we accelerate, but we also lose height faster. It should be positioned so we maintain a constant speed of around 35 knots. Any slower and we risk stalling, so don't go below this speed. I pull the column back, we raise the nose and slow down. I move the column to the left, the left wing goes down, and same to the right. If I push on the pedals, to the left we yaw left…'

As he did, the nose moved left and I had a huge blast of air in my right ear.

'…And if I yaw right,' followed by a blast in my left ear. 'Then back to straight and level.' The noise instantly subsided. 'Now you try, Kevin.'

Well, as Kevin wasn't here, I thought I'd try instead. I took the column, wacked the wing over to the left, and then to the right. It responded instantly, which took me by surprise. I tried the yaw. This was better; driving myself I felt in control. Concentration removed the fear.

'Good,' said Walter. 'Let's try a turn to the left, move the left wing down but with a little left rudder.'

I turned the glider downwind. I enjoyed making the turn as deep and banked over as I could.

'No, we're not Spitfire pilots,' Walter chided. 'Not too steep.' Bah. I was enjoying myself, you old goat. The problem was, a lot of height is lost in a turn, especially on a steep one. A couple more turns to practise, and before I knew it, we were coming into land. A three-minute flight is a short time to train.

'Good,' said Walter as we pushed the glider onto the trainer. 'I'll explain the launch procedure this time.'

On the instruction, 'All out,' the glider picks up speed and due to low airflow over the wings, the column is rested centrally and forward, as there is no control over the structure until the airspeed is above a certain amount. At about 100 feet, the pilot slowly pulls the column back against the tension of the cable, to gain maximum height. Too far, and the aircraft will 'hunt', a pitching oscillation that increases unless the tension is reduced. If the speed going up is too fast, the pilot wags the tail, i.e. yaws left and right as an instruction to the winch operator to slow down. If the cable breaks, as it can often do, you have to be ready to act immediately or the aircraft can stall, i.e. pitch down and crash. The procedure changes dependent on height and wind direction. There was a lot to take in, and it had to be learnt in the air, not just from the manual.

Walter went through the launch procedure as we waited for the next available slot. In flight, he demonstrated what he was doing so that I might have a go next time. I was now getting used to this rocket ship on rails ascent into the wide blue yonder, and wanted to instantly acquire this skill and knowledge to fly, but it was more like rainwater slowly seeping into layers of clothing than leaping into a swimming pool, an accumulation of little bits of information and putting them altogether. The first flight was more akin to a dunking in the middle of the ocean.

When it was my turn to take over the launch, the wing dropped violently. I pushed the column over to correct it, which worked just before the wing hit the ground. Then we were in the climb. As told, I pulled the column back to gain maximum attitude and height. Slowly, the nose started to bob up and down. I could tell easily when we were rolling, and corrected that immediately, but this was sneaky, the bobbing started slowly and as we came to the top of the ascent, we were really bouncing up and down.

'Ease off the elevators a little, Kevin, as we are hunting!' shouted Walter. I did so, and the oscillating stopped. It had started subtly and almost before I knew it had become violent. *Next time I'll know*, I thought. It was feeling your way, minute by minute. Each new section of the syllabus had its own inherent danger signals attached. I dipped the nose, and pulled the release knob three times. As always, on the first tug, the cable detached. The second two pulls are to make sure nothing was left dangling, otherwise we would be flying around looking like a goldfish doing a number two. Worse, the cable left attached could snag on the ground and cause a crash.

After three flights, it was lunchtime. That was all my flying done with Walter. I was then going on to fly six more flights with Mills. Good old Mills. He wore large sunglasses that looked like Elvis cast offs and he had a thatch of black wiry hair. He was always unshaven and was a real fat slob. Still, not all of us can be perfect like him. Our first flight was a cable break, which took me completely by surprise. We had only just pitched up and we were suddenly going nose over. Thank God for the tight straps, negative G almost made my brain eject through the top of my head as Mills pushed the nose down to avoid a stall. We were only 100 feet up, so he brought it down in a straight line. It was a tremendous view of the field being so low and nose down, and the cable on its drogue fell away in front of us.

'Shit,' exclaimed Mills. 'I didn't mean for that to happen that was a genuine cable break.' Cable break flight, one minute duration.

Around the base, on Salisbury Plain, all hell was breaking loose. Paratroopers were jumping in droves from Hercules transporters, and large artillery fire was increasing in intensity and volume on the surrounding hills. Exercises were going on across the plain, and we were right in the middle of it in our little gliders. Smoke mushroomed into the air miles away, and as the big guns fired, there would be huge booming explosions that shook the ground.

As we sat in *XA238*, as usual awaiting a launch slot, Mills let go an enormous fart exactly coincident with an explosion on the horizon, shaking the glider. I felt the vibration of Mills' fart through the wooden structure at the same time.

'Fackin'ell,' Mills exclaimed. I have no idea to this day if he was referring to the intensity of the neighbourly barrage or that he almost ripped himself a second anus.

The following day, on the Sunday, I had four more flights with Mills in *XN238*. Martin was getting plenty of flights in too, but he was way ahead on his training, having started earlier. We were all progressing at different rates, as much of the time it was pot luck as to how many flights you would get in a weekend.

At lunch, Jacko was talking to Spud about some girls they had met the night before. He apparently asked one girl if she had ever had a strapadicktomy. We all thought that was really funny. When Simon arrived with his plate of food, Jacko thought he'd mention it too.

'Yeah, well I said I'd had an appendectomy, so I asked her if she had a strapadicktomy,' said Jacko, expecting a similar mirthful reaction from Simon.

Simon continued to eat, looking nonplussed.

'Say it slowly,' said Jacko, attempting to enmesh the slipping gears in Simon's misfiring brain. 'Strap – a – dick – to – me.'

Simon was still stoic, confused, and obviously hungry.

'He's too busy masticulating his mandibles,' said Spud, as he poured orange squash down his throat. He instantly laughed at the absurdity of what he just uttered, and almost choked as squash came out of his nose. His pale eyelashes fluttered furiously as he grabbed his throat, and began smiling as he realised he wasn't going to die.

'Oh I get it,' said Simon, still devouring peas. 'Strap a dick to me... yeah, very funny.'

*

We had learnt to parade around a drill square, now we were parading around the skies. However, all the flying training in the world has one most important aspect: learning how to land. With these gliders, we would line up straight on the final leg, adjust the height with the spoilers to not land too far down the field, and attempt to slowly lower the aircraft onto its belly wheel directly beneath us. Watching other cadets bounce their gliders hopelessly down the field indicated how tricky it could be to perfect. As you fly the circuit, the height gives the impression you are barely moving, but as soon as you approach the ground, at around 45mph, you 'round out', i.e. pull the stick back just enough to keep the nose level, and the whizzing past of the grass either side of the cockpit accentuates the speed. Martin was instructed to imagine he had to cut off the heads off as many daisies as he could, which takes a gentle pulling back of the column every few seconds to maintain steady flight. Mills showed me this manoeuvre but I couldn't get it right; I'd either soar upward and overcook it, resulting in a loud bang as the wheel hit the ground, or I would just hit the ground far too soon and kill the flight. Still, it was early days. I had yet to start 'Recovery from unusual attitudes'; I was a teenager – that would take another four years at least.

The weather that month of July was slightly warmer than average, reaching 30 degrees at the end of the month. All we knew was that it got bloody hot. We would wear shorts under our denims but we couldn't exactly dress casually, so it was never really comfortable. Once in the air, the airflow and altitude kept you cool, but labouring on the ground was hard work. One dash back to the winch with Tony, Trevor and I were in the back of a Rover. Tony floored it, screaming the guts out of the engine; we were bouncing all over the place, and looking forward I saw the needle hit 60mph. We hit a large bump which sent me into the canvas roof, left me on the floor, my glasses askew and my head flat. Trev had also landed on the floor, and we were still bumping about thrashing for a handhold before Tony swung us around to park at the launch point. The brakes squealed as we came to a halt. There was no point in complaining, we always laughed off such incidents. They were funny, but they could also have ended tragically very easily.

*

08.07.79. The next few flights I had were with Scott Wolfson. He was possibly the youngest instructor, certainly the coolest. He wore yellow tinted ski goggles and was around early thirties. As his were my first flights after a break, it always took a couple of flights to reorient yourself before any real learning could begin, such was the haphazard nature of the training schedule. On my first flight, my glasses almost flew away on the launch, so Scott lent me his goggles for the duration. What a nice guy. After that, I bought a pair myself for the remainder of the course. It shows the mind-set of the time as well, that I hadn't realised I could and should have bought some earlier. There is a definite transition in most people when they become self-reliant and make all the decisions relevant to them for themselves, after which, they are ready to assume responsibility for others. I lived with my parents, my mum bought my clothes, and I didn't buy my own food. Institutionalised in education, we don't make our own decisions until suddenly we are thrown into the wider world and have to fend for ourselves. Until it was pointed out there was a need, I hadn't realised there was a need. The transfer to adulthood is recognisable when you can make all your own decisions.

*

15.07.79. This weekend we did some very exciting stuff. That's a polite way of saying I was shitting a brick as it was time to start 'Recovery from unusual attitudes.' It was effectively a misnomer on this course as everyone seemed to have an unusual attitude, let alone recovery from such. What it meant in reality was the instructor would put the glider in impending peril or the precipice facing disaster, and the trainee would have to recover the situation, safely, as per the instructions. Good old Mills was taking me up. He explained on the ground how this would transpire. He would pull the aircraft nose up into a stall, the nose would drop and I would then have to allow the aircraft to gain speed before pulling the nose back up into level flight. As these manoeuvres kill a lot of height, we would need a good high altitude launch to enable time in the air to demonstrate. Mills took us up to around 2,000 feet and as soon as the cable was away, he was barking in my ear behind me.

'Right son, notice as I pull the column back the airspeed is dropping off and the nose is rising...' Certainly it was disconcerting to see the nose go so high in attitude, my view of the field disappeared as per the launch as the glider's nose obscured it. We were pushed back in our seats as the ASI needle dropped to almost zero knots. 'See it takes a little while before we reach about 15 degrees and then we will nose down...' The world appeared to halt and time stood still, for a moment... the wind rush subsided, the nose stopped tilting back, and the control column between my legs cycled around as Mills demonstrated its ineffectiveness without airspeed. My body followed as the nose surged down and forward and within a moment we were vertical facing the fields below. The airspeed picked up in an instant, the ASI needle spun to indicate our acceleration toward the ground.

'And recoverrrrrrrr!' screamed Mills from the rear seat. The column lazily sat to one side so I grabbed it and pulled it back, easing the craft back into level flight and coincidentally pulling G on myself as we defied gravity's intention of obliterating us on the ground. Mills took over again, this time explaining he would add some adverse rudder to initiate a spin. *Please don't*, I thought. This was getting heavy. He pulled us again into a stall, this time the nose went down but we almost went over backwards.

'Recoverrrrrrrrrrrr!' came the cry, a triumphant scream aimed at kick starting my survival instincts as much as an instruction to perform. This time, with the added rudder we were staring at the ground and spinning; slowly at first but we started to spin faster. It was mesmerising, hypnotic; I almost forgot myself. It was if I wanted to hurl myself into the ground so beautiful was the view, the angle, the sound of the air rushing past my ears, but after a second I pulled the column back, again pulling G and slowing to normal speed. Mills said I had not observed the rudder enough to counter it; next time I needed to actually look at the rudder and column positions before applying opposite corrections and before pulling out of the dive. *Blimey, is there time?* I thought. Sure enough, on the next couple of flights, as the scream came from behind to recover, I observed the rudder was pushed left and the column right, or vice versa. I applied opposite rudder, centralised the column and pulled out of the fatal dive. 'Good!' screamed Mills. I was getting it. I was getting it.

That weekend, it was four flights with Mills and that was it. It was half past the summer and I was halfway through the course. I really felt I would run out of time. 24 flights in, it normally took about 40 flights to complete, but with all the interruptions to my training, it took a while to get back in the swing before actually learning new things. Next would be cable break procedure.

*

04.08.79. The day was spent travelling to RAF Leeming in North Yorkshire. Another interminable train ride coupled with some shorter ones at the end. We were given a packed lunch which incorporated some extremely dry Jacob's crackers. When Mark Watson (Wattykins) fell asleep, Cadet May kindly placed some of his cracker in Mark's open gob. Mark awoke after a while, and immediately and unknowingly began chewing the cracker. His face was a picture of discontent when he removed the inedible remains after a few seconds of near ingestion. It was the only excitement within

261 miles of travel. Even Gowland probably let out a little wee, we laughed so much.

Near Northallerton, RAF Leeming was originally a bomber base in the war, home to Stirling, Halifax and Lancaster bombers. Then it became a base for Night Fighters such as the Mosquito and Javelin. Since 1965, it had been home to No.3 Flying Training School and the Northumbrian Universities Air Squadron, which operated Jet Provost trainers. For the next week, it was going to be home to us, too. God help it. We arrived, weary and train sore, to discover we didn't have a billet; we were going to stay under canvas instead.

'Cor, we gonna be staying outside?' asked Cadet Carr.

'It seems so. Coningsby took concentration but this one is in tents.'

Carr looked at me with the dead-eyed look the thick as pig shit tend to. Wordplay wasn't his strong point; nor was thinking.

'So no smoking in these, Carr,' ordered Gowland. Too right. We didn't want a cadet barbecue, well, not of that kind.

I was in charge of our tent. Tent, don't you go anywhere, I order you. I'm the corporal, now. You have to tell these tents, you give 'em enough (guy) rope... The olive green tents were actually quite large, high enough to stand up in, and housed four of us. I was quite shocked to find proper beds inside; I thought we would be in sleeping bags. The beds and wardrobes were placed on wooden duck boards. The guy ropes were a pain, though, we all kept tripping over them. I was to share with Ritchie, Roberts and Watson. *Oh no*, I thought, *I'm going to have to find a cork for Ritchie's arse.* Sharing any contained space was going to be tough.

The only saving grace was that I didn't have to share with Gowland. He was a sergeant now, flying up the ranks. He had his Gliding wings; thankfully his course didn't coincide with mine. I was missing it already, but there would be time to complete it, wouldn't there? The Jet Provosts lay in a line not far from our camp; we could just see the red and white livery of the aircraft over the fence.

Later on, in civvies, we went for a walk around the base. We stopped to pose for pictures under the static Javelin aircraft by one of the buildings. We got a bollocking for that as we were unknowingly next to the officers' mess. It's their mess, let them clean it up. As if we wanted to spy on them stuffing their pate foie gras anyway. We spent most of the evening in the NAAFI, glugging Coke and listening to Meatloaf on the jukebox. 'Bat out of Hell' was played everywhere, it seemed. Ritchie was already a big fan. I was just discovering him. That album was huge, and sold 43 million copies (and counting). It was such an over the top production, you couldn't help but like it.

'Do you like Meatloaf, Carr?' I asked, draining my Coke.

'Only if it's with chips,' he replied. Gastronomy, nor it seems the pop scene, were his strong points.

We settled down for the night in our tents. As was usual, spirits were high. Ritchie was up to his usual antics, which was telling jokes and farting constantly. The smell was awful, the eggy guffs would drift around the tent and overwhelm you. They seemed to be increasing in frequency and potency as the evening wore on.

'Ritchie! Will you stop farting! It's bloody obscene; there must be something very wrong with your guts.'

'They seem well enough to me, to be producing all this gas,' quipped Watson.

'No one asked you, Wattykins,' I said. 'Have any of you read Spike Milligan's war diaries? His mates used to light their farts. We daren't try that with Ritchie, he'd blow up the base.'

'Lighting farts is *easy*,' interjected the pong machine, in-between expulsions.

'Yeah, right.'

'I'll show you,' he said. Right, we gotta see this. We crowded around his bed, torches aimed at his nether regions, holding our noses.

'Go on then.'

'Wait a minute,' he laughed, 'I have to get ready.' He struck a match, and held it to his behind, his legs high in the air. *Poooooof.* His arse gas blew it out, followed by a horrendously awful smell.

'Ritchie! Bloody hell, I'm going to kick you out of this tent in a minute.' We were all laughing so much, combined with the lack of pure oxygen in the tent, I thought we might pass out.

'Hang on, I'll have one more go.' He lit another match, struck the pose with his legs; a long pause. There was a crackling sound.

'Arrgh! I've burnt me pubes!' He grabbed a bottle of lemonade and doused his privates with it.

If there ever was a time I nearly died laughing, that was it.

Eventually, we settled down into our beds, the night cool, and the beds warm. I was nearly asleep, and there was a sharp retort from Ritchie's direction.

'Ritchie,' I drawled wearily, 'I swear I'm going to tie you to that bed and pull the covers over you, you'll suffocate yourself.'

'Sorry,' he lied. 'It was just my nipsy saying Goodnight.'

'Goodnight to it, too. Let that be the end of it, please.'

There was a very long pause. Silence fell on the site. I was again almost asleep.

Paaaaaaaaaaaaaaaaaaaaaaaaaaaaaaaaaaaaaaaaaaarp.

Ritchie's nipsy was obviously snoring.

*

05.08.79. Sunday. I found my way along the duckboards to the toilets. It was freezing and a little misty. Nothing much happens on a Sunday apart from being trooped into church. Oh, and the football matches. As there were ten of us, we took part in five-a-side matches with the other squadrons. For some reason, I was in the team. We played two games against the same squad. They didn't just run rings around us, they ran hexagons and decagons. Chris Tipler looked at me in despair as goal after goal soared past May.

'May! Stand still and they can't get past your bulk!'

'You can talk!' he retorted. 'Get up the field and stick one in!'

Chance would be a fine thing. As soon as we gained possession, a pass or two and we lost it. It was humiliating. Oh well, it wasn't too bad. Only 5-0 and 7-0. I mean, we could have had negative goals. Gowland was horrified at our lack of success. So much so he laughed himself stupid; well, a bit more than normal. Afterwards, we found out they were Wing champions and had the cup to prove it.

'That wasn't fair,' said Dudley. Too right. We would have been ok against a 'normal' team, i.e. one made up of geriatrics and cripples.

*

06.08.79. Something easier today – shooting. Ah, nothing like a nice lay down with a deadly weapon by your side. I fired five rounds with the .22 and 20 rounds with the .303. Afterwards, my shoulder ached like crazy. The smell of cordite was now on my clothes for the rest of the week. I didn't know then it would be the last time firing those weapons, but there would be more to explore later.

We were allowed to visit sections on the base as usual. I chose the Simulator Flight; a couple of others joined me. The Jet Provost simulator had an instrument panel and a control column, but little else. Analogue computers emulated true instrument readouts and traced the virtual aircraft's path on a long piece of paper. It was extremely tricky to maintain the course, height and attitude as set by the instructor, but I battled it for 20 minutes or so and I did very well. My gliding training would have helped. It was great fun but a far cry from modern simulators, even PC-based ones today. It all seems now that 1979 was the transition period between the old electromechanical world and the modern digital one. Even the year 1980 had seemed futuristic, and it was only a few months away.

As is also usual at camp, we had to parade and drill. Carr kept getting things wrong, almost turning the wrong way if it was left or right turn. Come on, Carr, you have a 50% chance of getting it right before you start. We were constantly on at him, and eventually he bit back. It's never fun being perceived as a lummox but in his case it was more than perception. Carr had pale blue eyes and long eyelashes, which he would flutter as smoke emanated from his ever present fag. Unfortunately behind those eyes was a very dim bulb that more often as not was switched off. Therefore, we would be marked down on points because we were harbouring a thick bastard.

*

07.08.79. Another flight in a Chipmunk, this time it was in *WK517*. I felt like an old hand by now, walking like a monkey, parachute hanging off my rear as I clambered into the cockpit. Throughout the 20 minute flight, I took control and noted the differences of response compared to the glider; it was always great fun but again it was over too soon.

*

08.08.79. Wednesday. There's nothing to look forward to quite like an assault course on a midweek morning. We were bussed to Catterick Army base about 11 miles away. Dressed in our denim onesies, we were about to approach all sorts of obstacles and aim not to kill ourselves. This was where they trained the British Infantry and Commandos. Now they had May and Carr. Oh my god.

RAF Leeming Annual Camp August 1979. L-R from rear: Cdt Tipler, Cdt May, Flt Lt Bloxham (VR), Camp Commandant, F/O Wilkie, Mr Keens, Me; Front row, Cdt Dudley, Cdt Ritchie, Cdt Watson, Cdt Carr, Cdt Roberts, Sgt Gowland, Cdt Pomfret. (MOD Photo)

We were shown every obstacle and how to approach it. 'Good morning, Mr set of logs' is the polite way. We looked at the 12 foot wall. We looked at each other. How are we going to get over *that*!

'I wish Mum was here,' stated Roberts.

'Does it scare you?' I asked.

'No, but I'd stand on her head to get over the wall!' Strange chap.

The regulars have the added joy of many pounds of kit and a rifle to hold, we just had to get our sorry asses around it without breaking our necks. After the walk around, we were lined up at the starting point.

'Right, when I blow this whistle, you will have precisely 20 minutes to complete the course I have shown you. Remember, it's racing against the clock!'

'What sort of clock?' I whispered to Pomfret. 'Is it a grandfather clock? We might beat that.'

'It'll be here in a tick,' he said.

Pheeep! We're off. Luckily the ground was quite dry, being August. The six-foot wall was first. Getting over that by yourself was ok. Monkey swinging on the bars was tough. Running on logs was tricky but the worst was the cargo nets. It took all your strength in your arms and shoulders as your feet would be anywhere but beneath you. Up to the top of the net, hold on tight and roll over the top. It was great fun, but extremely knackering. The 12-foot wall was where team play was essential; a leg up to your mate to sit on top, and then he would lend a hand to get others up from a run and jump. It was easier than I thought, except getting May over. After we got around intact, still breathing heavily, they sent us around again. Just for luck, we did it a third time before we broke for lunch.

'Why do they call it an assault course?' asked Carr. 'It should be called an obstacle course.' Wonders will never cease; a logical point from an illogical beast.

'Because if you question the Army they'll assault you,' I said.

Carr looked at me with the dead-eyed look the thick as pig shit tend to. He thought I was serious. He was a lost cause. I was glad I only had three more days of him. He was an ok chap but it became wearing explaining everything three times.

The others were good company. Roberts, diminutive, give him a green hat and he *would* be a pixie; Dudley, equally small, quiet, dependable. Ian Pomfret was Mark Pomfret's little bro, Mark was a contemporary at King's Furlong Junior School. I didn't know then that I would hook up with Ian in a couple of years on a completely different venture.

Watson (Wattykins) was a character. He would often shriek like a girl and gurn the most extreme faces in reaction to conversation. On the official photo he looks like he's sniffing one of Ritchie's. He was very loud and had yet to find the volume control. Chris Tipler had an older brother, Trev, whom I would get to know a bit later on; both good guys. And then there was Gowland. Gowland was Bockhead's number one, and didn't we know it. That leadership distanced him, which I was glad about, but the rivalry we shared that often inspired me to perform better had waned. I didn't need it anymore, and his advance was now out of reach. I had no urge to better him. However, he was on my team, and I didn't want to let him down, either. May and I were corporals, and I took it seriously. When I was in charge of the guys, I wanted for us to do it right, whatever the task.

*

09.08.79. Thursday A free day in York. Not free in that it cost nothing, but we were released from the RAF shackles for a day and allowed to roam the streets of the historic city. Blockhead told us to behave ourselves and he disappeared with Flying Officer Wilkinson and Mr Keens, our civvy instructor. I was keen to see the Minster.

'You're going to *a church*??' mocked Gowland, incredulous that anyone would wish to indulge in some culture. 'I'm off to the pub.'

Well, Tony, you're only 16 for a start; second, you can go to the pub anytime in the future, but you have the opportunity to visit an historic building. Oh, well, who's with me? Dudley, Ritchie, Carr and Watson. Come on, lads.

It was quite a walk across the city to the York Minster

from where we were dropped; but it was worth it. What a building, it was literally jaw dropping, looking up at the nave. There has been a religious site there since 627 AD and the present building took 250 years to build, between 1220 and 1472.

'Lads, we've found something older than Bloxham,' I said. 'But only just.' We wandered around for a while, and then decided we would go to the National Railway Museum. It was less than a mile away and we had time. After wandering around the 20-acre site, viewing all sorts of trains through the ages, I was unsure what was more tiring, the assault course or this.

'I've seen enough steam trains now,' said Ritchie.

'Yeah. I'm chuffed to bits too.'

It's a wonderful museum, Dave Langley heaven, but there was a distinct lack of wings.

We had to save our energies for tomorrow. Orienteering. Yummee.

*

10.08.79. Friday, the last full day at camp; except it wasn't, as we were bussed off with the other squads to yomp across the North York Moors. At least it wasn't raining; in fact, it was the opposite, it had been steaming hot all week. Whereas at Coningsby, it was rain and puddles, now it was flies, shit and more flies. Oh, and mud. Well, most if it was, a lot of it was shit. It became hard to tell. Mile after mile across green fields, yellow fields, brown fields; beside sheep, cows and other things that left a trail of smelly pats across the landscape. It was also extremely hilly, so the heat made it very hard work. We wore our ubiquitous denims, but had them half-mast and tied around the waist. My boots were caked in all things brown, flies forever in my face, but the view was tremendous when you could look upon it. Bulbous white clouds hovered over the hills, and when the sun broke through, shadows chased over the ground in a constantly shifting palette of light and shade. I didn't know where we were heading for, the senior NCOs huddled over the map and we appeared to be walking in a huge circle. After many hours, and late afternoon, we eventually fell off the hillside back to our waiting bus. It fired into life, reverberating noisily whilst we eased off our heavy boots to let our feet breathe.

'Pwoar, put yer boots back on!' ordered Gowland. What's he on about? Any cheese would be outponged by the attached shit, anyway.

We were all absolutely exhausted, but spirits were very high. Someone started a sing song and we all learned the words to 'The Hairs on her Dicky Dido.' I won't elaborate but I added some nice counterpoint and harmonies. We sang all the way home, to the final night in our cosy tents. As I settled down to sleep, the chant from the bus still rang in my ears...

'...One black one, one white one, and one with a bit of shite on, and one with a fairy light on, to show... you... the... way.'

Nice three point harmony at the end.

*

01.09.79. Upavon. The weekend before starting work. I had to complete the gliding or I would run out of time. There was the distinct feel that summer was over; all my mates had completed their courses and I was the only one left from my starting group. The ones who I witnessed going solo, I said goodbye to, others I just never saw again, like Melbourne. It was a real shame. It was a big event when your colleague was about to embark on their first solo flight; the instructor would start tightening the straps in the rear cockpit and add ballast if needed, to emulate the weight of the instructor so the craft would fly in a similar way. This was the sign the cadet was ready. The field would be cleared, as much as possible, for the soloist to enjoy a clear flight without much else in the sky. The instructor would watch, saliva gone, as the young pilot soared into the launch, completed one circuit and came safely into land. I told my instructors how few flights I had during this summer, and they really upped the ante. It also helped there were fewer cadets to take up now. I wondered if this weekend, I might actually solo myself...

'Right,' began Mills. 'We'll have a couple of refresher flights, and then I want to concentrate on cable break procedure. Have you read up on it?'

Read up on it? I practically devoured the gliding notes we were given. I might have got 'D' in geography but I could find RAF Upavon, and knew my notes inside out, back to front and upside down. Just don't test that. Anyway, the basic procedure is below 150 feet, if the cable breaks (or simulated by pulling the cable release knob), stick forward, land straight ahead. Between 150-350 feet, perform an 'S' turn and land into wind, and above 400 feet, complete a shortened circuit. Now I had to learn how to do it properly.

The first couple of flights I had to ease myself back into flying. It had been all of six weeks since I last flew, this time again in *XE800*. Mills was a good teacher; we completed three circuits, and on the fourth flight, he pulled the cable on ascent, without warning; there was a loud bang, and because of the lift on the wings, the aircraft suddenly leapt up by a few feet. It felt like an elephant had landed on my shoulders. I saw the altitude was low, around 150 feet, so as I had just pulled the stick back into the climb, now I instantly pushed it fully forward. The craft still had a lot of momentum from the launch, so it arced over into a nose down dive. As we came over the brow of the arc, the wind hit my face with full force and I could see the whole field below me. It was a wonderful sight, a giant billiard table smoothed out by the height above it, the cable descending beside and under us, toy land rovers driving about in slow motion. I prepared for a landing and steered to the side of the cable path. The ground came up to meet us, grass whizzing past the cockpit before the familiar contact bump of the main wheel.

'Good!' exclaimed Mills. 'I didn't tell you we were going to have a cable break that time. I won't pull it next flight.' Bloody liar. He said that on the subsequent three flights, all to test my reactions. The next one he pulled at 250 feet. Before we took off, I observed the windsock to see the wind was coming from the left, which meant we had to land facing left. As the momentum took us over the arc, the apogee being the highest point, I pushed us into a dive, and then turned to the right, still diving. Straighten up, to the right of the field; at the end of the field, tight turn left at 150 feet to bring us landing to the left, into wind. Turning so low was tremendously exciting; I was really enjoying this part of the course. After seven flights, Mills handed me over to Griffin in *XN238*. There followed three more flights as normal circuits. My goodness, I had covered ten flights in a day; more than I would normally manage in a whole weekend.

That night, as I lay in my bed, I pondered the week ahead. Would there be time to finish my course tomorrow? I didn't think so. The weather looked changeable, and I had to finesse a few things, important stuff, like landing; I still couldn't quite master the act of keeping it in the air for a few seconds more. My thoughts turned to Monday; I would have to start work. As for all of us 16-year-olds, all we had known was school, now our lives were going to change in an enormous way. If I had known what lay ahead, I might have tried to sail the glider across the Channel.

*

02.09.79. Sunday. The weather was definitely looking dodgy; big black clouds interspersed the white, the cloud base pretty low. Still, we were here to get on with it. I had my old mate Scott Wolfson in *WT901*. We had three familiarising circuits, so he could assess my overall flying, and then the fun began. We had five cable break practises in a row; each time, he said the next one wouldn't be. I knew these guys' tricks by now. We had one more normal circuit, and I just had time for one more flight before close of play. Unfortunately, it was with Griffin, in *XN238*.

Griffin had taken Martin to solo, so I think he had an affinity with him. He was the pilot who told him to imagine chopping off the tops of daisies as you skim the grass, aiming to keep the craft flying for the maximum time. For some reason, we didn't get on. I was still very quiet, studious, and mostly unquestioning. Obviously I would ask questions relevant to my understanding of my instructions, or actions, but I would assume that unless told otherwise, I would carry on. My launch on the final flight of the day was a good one; I had bags of height, around 1,300-1,400 feet. I proceeded to exercise some 360 turns at the launch end, to reduce height, but found I still had a lot of height halfway downwind. I allowed the craft to move further out from the field, as I had so much height in store; Griffin said nothing behind me. I brought it back over the perimeter, turned into finals, and brought it into land. After we were safely on the ground, he decided it was time to talk to me.

'Right, to start with, what were you doing taking us right over the road beyond the perimeter fence? You know we don't fly that far out.'

He was calm but was quite supercilious and snotty. Why didn't he say something in the air? The other instructors would. If he was just observing, assessing my suitability toward solo, then I understood his concern, but all he really did was undermine my confidence at this late stage and piss me off completely. He stomped off, and I am happy to say I didn't fly with him again.

I had three more flights, all with pilot Daycombe, still in *XN238*. Daycombe was another old boy, and on the first flight, with the blustery weather and his fairly quiet voice, I couldn't hear a single instruction from the back seat. On the ground, he rigged me up with a headset so he could talk to me through the tube. Nothing fancy like radio. On the second flight, his whisperings were directly in my ear, it was eerie, like he was in my mind. The big downside was, the headset was so bulky I could hardly turn my head. We launched well and settled down into calm forward flight.

'Don't worry about that grey patch ahead, it's only rain,' he murmured. Rain? Only rain? I thought it about it for, oh, a second, and turned to the left crosswind. We couldn't escape it. The rain hit us from the right; the glider became a little toy in God's breath. We also got wet.

'If this weather persists we will have to call it a day,' Daycombe advised as we sheltered under the wing, waiting for the Rover recovery. As it was, we squeezed in one more flight between showers.

I left the airfield that weekend despondent, just wishing it was all over. I had enjoyed my gliding immensely, but now I missed my mates to share my triumphs and disasters. I was doing well, I handled the flying and the cable breaks as I should, but now it was time to sink the pink.

10. We Can Work it Out

03.09.79. The first day of work. As Elvis Costello sang, 'Welcome to the working week.' Well, no thanks. But there was no turning back now; I was to enter the adult world whilst my friends were extending their adolescence at college for the next five years. The week before, Mum had opened the post and called up the stairs as I lay in bed to tell me my 'O' Level results.

'You've done a lot better than you thought you had!' she shouted. She recanted them to me.

English Lit – B. Maths – B. Physics – C. Latin – C. French – C. Art – C. Geography – D. Chemistry – D.

I was pleased with my Bs. Physics should have been a B but it was a tough paper. Yes, they all say that. I scraped Latin, French was about right. Art, C? Everyone's a critic, even the examiner. Cheeky beggar, I spent hours on that. Chemistry? Well, thanks Mr Penman. Somehow, Simon Coates got an A; he taught himself, which was even more impressive. Geography – an unsurprising result, as my Gliding course was in the middle of revision time. I didn't really care, I didn't need it. With these results and my English Language, I had seven good 'O' Levels, which placed me in the top 5% of the national results table. Not bad really. I needed five including English, maths and physics for the apprenticeship, which was starting this very day. Martin had not done as well as he had hoped, and enrolled to retake some of his exams at Queen Mary's, the local sixth form college.

We were to have two weeks' induction at Dan Air

Engineering at Lasham, then six months' basic workshop skills training at BETA. This was Basingstoke Engineering Training Association and was destined to be hell on Earth. Andy Ritchie's dad and brother both worked at Lasham, I was to get to know them all well.

There was a lot of trepidation as I put putted on my moped the eight miles to Lasham. I was yet to meet my fellow apprentices and had no real concept of how things were going to progress. I was to be trained to be an Airframes and Engine Technician, attend college at Farnborough, and it was going to take four years. There was going to be equal amounts of physical work and mental work, learning the craft, the trade, and the academic side of engineering. If I had also known then the amount of homework I would get at college, I might have gone down the A Level route instead. I went to work to escape school!

Arriving at Lasham, I rode up onto the airfield and around the perimeter track. It all seemed very official as I reported to the Security Hut. Vast 727 aircraft sat on the tarmac outside enormous hangars; everything had just gone supersize compared to the RAF fighters and trainers I had been used to up close.

I knew where I was going; to the training hut next to the Dak. The DC3 Dakota was the first aircraft Dan Air acquired, in lieu of a debt, so they started an airline; as you do. This was 1953 and the two original owners were called Davis and Newman (DaN being a bridge of their names). The Dak was painted in the red and white livery of the airline that still adorned the existing, though ageing, fleet of DeHavilland Comet 4 aircraft, the world's first commercial jet airliner.

There were eight apprentices; five 'Heavies' (Airframe/Engine, like me), and three 'Fairies' (Electrics/Instrumentation). It was an interesting split also, as four of us were from the Basingstoke area, three from the Alton area, and one from Fleet.

Loyalties typically fall along geographical or familial lines. Unsurprisingly, two of the Altonians knew each other and so did two of the Basingstoke mob. I was pleased to see my old ATC mate, Ian Ross, who was starting as a Fairy.

'Ian mate! I didn't know you were coming here? What have you done to your arm?' He was sporting a large bandage on his left arm.

'Broke it,' he murmured in his quiet but assured way. 'You know the blue bridge? Someone put a rope swing on a tree up there...'

Ted Snelling was our host and instructor. He was also to become our and certainly my mentor for the next four years. He had a wonderful delivery of words and perfect comic timing. You felt at ease with Ted, but he always imparted the importance and seriousness of what we were going to do: work on aircraft; as dangerous to work on and with, as much as it would be making an error that could lead to a disaster for others, either on the air or on the ground. It was a serious business and no mistake.

We were shown over the vast site, the four main hangars, the sick bay, stores, goods in, goods out, the many production workshops, the director's offices (known as Mahogany Row). We met again the guy in charge of training, Norman Mullen, a former RAF Flight Engineer. He reminded me of Butch from Tom and Jerry. He kind of growled at you. Not that he lived in a kennel. Well, I don't think so.

We were the first year of four sets of apprentices, who were of course all older than us. There were plenty of ex-apprentices also working on the site, and we would get to know everyone in time. The biggest challenge was now we were immersed in a world with people of all ages, backgrounds, and beliefs. We were boys but we wouldn't be for long.

Ted told us we were eight from 200 applicants, i.e. 4% of

us who applied made it. I didn't realise it then, but that was significant. We all were pretty competitive people, although I wasn't yet a confident person. However, that drive and ambition was present, and was the cause of many an upset to come. Let us meet the participants and perpetrators with first impressions.

Jeremy (Jez) Cotterell, from Fleet in Hampshire. Fair hair worn long, crap bumfluffy moustache. Wore a pikey fur-collared check jacket. Rode a Fizzy, an old one to get the horsepower, but it was knackered. His dad worked as head of the Radio Section. Oh, your dad works here, does he? Well, well. Heavy.

Paul Kavanagh, from Four Marks. A little like a young Pete Townshend, an enormous hooter. Seemed alright. His mum worked in the sewing section. Eye, eye? Fairy.

Justin Goatcher, from Alton. Tall, stupid little moustache, obviously loves himself. Curly hair, a big nose, full of mouth, noisy. His dad was Head of Workshop Production Control. Am I missing something here? Rode a Suzuki 50. Heavy.

Chris Bloomfield, from Basingstoke, Hollins Walk no less, close to me in South Ham. Fairly short, slim, cool feathered haircut, little moustache, wore a brown leather jacket. Cool cat. His dad worked as an Electrical Engineer. Now, what is going on? Is this a nepotistic paradise or what? Wouldn't be seen dead wearing a bike helmet, would spoil the hair. Fairy.

Steve Holden, from Alton. Tall, dark unruly hair. Huge nose. Flared nostrils that gave the impression of a Citroen DS. Thickset. His mum worked at the base, also in upholstery. Knew everybody and everything going on, and more that wasn't. Bullshitter. Heavy.

Andy Waller, from Basingstoke, went to Cranbourne School; knew Martin and Colin. Weird, skinny, and ugly with a hooked nose and protruding Adam's apple; longish dark hair, predilection for brown corduroy trousers, clever. No relations on base.

Trevor Heath, from Basingstoke. Spotty, barrel-chested, speccy geek. Won't stop going on about Gliding. Oops that's me. Damn those mirrors. Heavy (well, 10 and a half stone).

Ian Ross, from Basingstoke. Cool, slim dude with glasses. Quiet, measured. Fairy.

We weren't quite the magnificent seven, more the pubescent eight.

It was telling the three more academic lads had no relations on the base. Holden, Goatcher and Cotterell were going to Weybridge College to study as theirs was a craft apprenticeship, and they would attain a City and Guilds qualification. The rest of us were off to Farnborough, for our Technician qualifications. It was such a massive change to our lives; the people we had been surrounded by for the last five years were elsewhere. We had to get to know most of the 600 people on the base, new people at BETA, and the people at College. We would have to start with each other.

Alliances have to start somewhere. Jez and I bonded over our appreciation of Elvis Costello. Jez was affable, garrulous, and keen to be liked. I took an instant dislike to Justin, and I had a certain distrust of Paul and Steve. Justin just came over like the jocks at school; mouthy, confident, and would get aggressive if you disagreed with him. I felt ok with Chris and Andy, and Ian was solid as an old mate. It would be a strange dynamic as time progressed.

We had to enrol at Tech College. Whilst we were there, we had to fill out a questionnaire. One of the questions was: 'What is your ideal profession?' I wrote 'Professional Musician.' Probably an odd answer for an Aircraft Engineering student, but it was the truth. I felt more and more that was what I would aim for. I was still to learn a more suitable instrument.

I had given up the violin now. I had attained Grade V and just stopped. I wanted to play electric guitar. I would pore over the pictures in the Grattans Catalogue of cheap Les Paul copies. It was probably healthier than the underwear section, anyway. When I could afford it, it was gonna happen.

'Sweet 16 ain't that peachy keen...' a short quote from 'I Don't Like Mondays' by The Boomtown Rats. It would be huge on its October release, but I quote it for the term, Sweet 16. Whenever you told anyone your age, they would say, 'Sweet 16, eh?' I'm not sure if they meant I was sweet, or the age. You wonder about some people. It's an invented age, of course; in ages past and other societies, 16 would be considered mature. In our artificially cultured modern world, it was the transition to working life. It used to be 14 for my dad's generation, who would have thought it would extend the other way, to keep more in education as job opportunities reduce?

Lasham had its own volunteer fire crew. They had a few vehicles which attended every Dan Air related take-off and landing at the airfield, and they also closed the perimeter track during these times. The Fire Crew chief gave us a lecture about fire prevention and fire control, and we learnt about the different types and uses of extinguishers. The chief was a disconcerting-looking guy, mid-fifties, bald and quite frankly abominably ugly. He looked like a boiled egg that had been half bashed in. Holden told me he had been in a car crash or something. He certainly looked like one. Bloody nice chap, though. The chief lined up a series of extinguishers, all close to or out of service date that we were to operate to get used to using. He lit a large oil drum, full of oil, outside the fire station that was next to our training room. The flames were huge and the heat was tremendous. We all took our turn to extinguish the flames with different types of extinguisher. It was extremely tricky to get the fire out; the foam extinguisher was the best. We got used to aiming at the base of the fire, not aimlessly at the licking flames. The CO_2 extinguishers were tricky, as they got extremely cold in an instant, and were pretty ineffective against burning oil. It was wonderfully entertaining and enlightening demonstration, and in my first week of work, showed the importance of doing practical things yourself to really take things in. I knew if I would ever have to really fight a fire, I had done it already in practice. Later, when we were at BETA, Holden told me the chief had died of a heart attack soon after this. It was a shame.

During lunchtime, I came across Waller outside with a remote control unit. He was operating a radio controlled plane high above our heads. It was buzzing all over the place. I couldn't see it very well as it was so high, but he seemed to have absolute control. He let me have a go – it was trickier than it looked. The controls were extremely sensitive; you daren't criticise their hairstyles. Martin, Colin and I used to watch older geezers flying their planes and choppers on Basingstoke Common. Back then, radio controlled aircraft were very expensive and invariably petrol powered. It was a proper hobby, not cheap toys from China as they are today. Colin told me Waller was a bit of a geek – he looked odd but was amenable and intelligent. The canteen sold chips; a plateful covered in ketchup was Andy's staple diet.

Earlier in the summer, Martin had bought a line controlled aircraft. It had a small glow plug motor and the elevator was controlled by thin cable attached to a hand grip. It 'flew' around you as you spun in a circle, good fun but characteristically crude compared to radio control. It needed a lot of room so we took it to the Memorial Park to fly. Whilst there, some lad with a terrier took interest. The terrier took interest too; it kept chasing me around the park and leaping up, taking big bites into my buttocks. For some reason, it liked mine better than Martin's. Colin said it looked hilarious, me running in panic whilst this little bastard was flying through the air in direct trajectory with my butt.

Perhaps that's why I never bought a radio controlled plane; it's just another pain in the arse.

I was keen to get back to Upavon and finish my gliding. The other guys were quite impressed about it, except Justin.

He knew it was better than anything he had ever done, so he either said nothing or tried to change the subject back to something he did know about; or thought he knew about. Lasham was home to major international and national gliding championships, and was a constant activity on the other side of the airfield. Unfortunately, it all seemed so prohibitively expensive.

Justin was obsessed with the future transition to a motorbike; which bike would be best, i.e. the fastest. Waller and Holden knew a fair bit about the bike market, as did Jez. I listened and absorbed, and when I had time I popped into the local motorcycle garage, Motts in Basingstoke. A decent 250cc bike cost around £600-700 new. The Honda Twin CB125cc caught my eye so that would become a target to aim for; by the time I was 17, I *would* have one.

*

08.09.79. The first week of work over, albeit induction week, it was back down to Upavon. I really needed to nail this. Interruptions to my training abounded, albeit weather related, camp related, or flying programme related. Mills took charge.

'Right, lad. Let's see if we can sort you out this weekend and get you to solo. Fuckin' ell, you'll be pleased to see the back of this place, won't yer?'

I nodded and grinned; I was keen to get on, but the thought of going solo still terrified me. Mills gave me no time to think. We were strapped in and away; two familiarisation flights, tweaking what I knew, and adding little things I didn't.

'Correct use of spoilers!' he yelled from behind me at 500 feet. 'We use them in five second bursts to lose excess height. Always pull or lower the column in conjunction with spoilers, open the spoilers, pull the nose up slightly, close the spoilers, nose down slightly.' He demonstrated; the spoilers were little flaps that spoiled the airflow over the top of the wings, killing lift; as the lift is two thirds from the top of the wing, opening them drops the aircraft like a brick. Subsequently closing them, the lift returns, hence the need to adjust the nose attitude accordingly.

'Right, turn into the final leg, speed on...' I put the nose down to increase speed before turning into the final leg and then turn in at speed for the final approach. The landings are better but still fast.

We go again; and again. The third launch, he pulls the cable release. I was ready, and pushed the column over to recover from the low height.

'Thought I would catch you out there, but you were ready you bugger,' he smiled when we were on the ground. I certainly was. Every launch, I was primed, pumped up, adrenalin filled. It was an exhausting process, but no time to waste. Two more flights, cable break test. Then another two flights, and break for lunch.

After lunch, full of chips and apprehension, Mills passed me over to Fuller. I guess he needed a second eye on my ability today. I was on a roll, very confident, and felt in control. But was I ready?

Fuller took me up again in *WT901*. The third flight and another cable break test. I reacted well. No hesitation. Complete control. We did another two flights. Waiting for the recovery vehicle, he started to tighten up the straps in the rear seat. I knew what that meant. The growl from the Land Rover increased in volume. It was nearly here. Fuller gently spoke to me.

'Now, Trevor. If you do exactly what you have been doing the past few flights, you should be able to do it yourself this time. Are you ok with that?'

'Yes, sir.' I helped him load the glider onto the trailer. I looked at the wooden structure with a highly critical eye. Now don't let me down now, I'm depending on you, you old wooden crate. Don't become my oversized coffin. We bounced and creaked back to the launch point. Fuller creaked more than the Rover, but I hoped he was right. I should be ready. Bloody hell, most were ready at 40 flights; I had 60. It certainly didn't help having the course spread over 12 weeks.

I sat in the cockpit; the wing was on the ground. The area was cleared for my run. I had been given the ok to proceed. My mouth was dry as I looked at the grass before me, cable running over the field, most of it hidden from view. The control tower was to my left and assorted cadets and instructors awaited my orders.

'Wings level.' The words came out of my mouth but I didn't realise I was saying them. The cadet on the wingtip raised the wings to level. I worked through the checklist, and tested my controls. Satisfied all was correct, I gave the next order.

'Cable on, please.' Some rattling below me and the cable was attached. The cadet slunk away from the bottom of the glider.

'All clear above and behind?' There followed a quick scour of the sky. I was given the all clear.

'Take up slack.' The light beamed and the audible beep filled my senses. There was no other sound, until the cable started to snake and slither through the grass. Suddenly I felt enormous pull and I was going forward. 'All out!' I bellowed, and I raced forward past the tower. I was on my own; completely on my own. With no added weight behind me, I was suddenly shooting up into the sky; 50 knots, 60 knots, far too fast. I stamped on the rudder and pushed it left and right, the signal to the winch to slow down. It did, almost instantly; the sound of the wind reduced to a normal level.

I was tracking upwards, the speed was stable, the craft swayed slowly from side to side. I could feel the tension of the cable beneath me, occasionally groaning, the vibration fed through the cockpit floor and into me. Don't break; just don't bloody break. I was coming to the apex of the climb, and I eased the stick back; I wanted maximum height. Height is good; height is safety. I had so many flights in quick succession that I was on auto pilot; the momentum of it was carrying me. Someone was talking. Who was it? Oh, it's me. I became my own phantom instructor.

'Keep the nose straight, watch that yaw, good... nice and level, over the top of the winch now... nose down, cable release, a couple of Yanks on the handle... cable gone...'

It was a good launch, 1,100 feet. I settled into calm flight and turned left. Stick left with some left rudder, centralise stick. Maintain turn with rudder, to counteract adverse yaw, then right stick, wings level, rudder central, nose down. I had so much height. I realised this view was all mine, and mine alone. The solitude was tremendous. No one in the world could touch me up here. No one could help me either. It was an existentialist moment. I am alive, here, now, master of my own fate. I turned 270 degrees to the right. The winch was in view, to my left. God it looked small. I could see the toy Land Rovers tracking down the field, gliders coming down to land. The alternate circuit operated by the Wyvern club gliders was busy, red K13s filled the sky. It was joyful to fly and have other gliders around you, albeit across the field. I let the craft take me downwind. Before I knew it, I was releasing the spoilers to reduce height, to ensure I wasn't too high at the turn in point. Spoilers open, pull the lever on the left side of the cockpit, pull the stick back to keep the nose up; the rush of air was louder, and I felt the craft dropping out of the sky. The altimeter was reading lower, but not enough. Another five second burst, to lose another 50 feet. That's it, nearly 300 feet. Nose down, increase speed to around 44 knots, turn left for crosswind leg... turn tight left, 200 feet, ready for final approach.

I could almost hear a drum roll, or the dramatic music from 'Thunderbirds' when they have a near disaster. The field was below me, I soared over the launch point. I could hear myself talking me down. Another burst of spoilers. What's this? The Rover is in front of me, bringing cables to the launch point. Why isn't he out of my way? I shook my fist at the cadet driver as I sailed over him. Round out just above the ground, ease stick back – the horizon lowered, I could see only the grass before me now, whizzing past beside me... bang! I hit the ground too fast. I bounced up again; I struggled to keep it straight. Bang! Again. It was a messy landing, but I was down. The craft came to a halt, and the wing fell to the ground. Silence. I had done it. My first solo.

The Rover arrived with Fuller. I leapt out and we put the glider on the trailer.

Fuller was relieved but had a vital piece of advice. 'Next time, Trevor, if you see something in front of you on approach, please make a definite turn away from it before you land, ok?'

'Yes, sir.' I agreed, but I was annoyed. Why had the ginger twat in the Rover chosen that moment to deliver cables? I didn't hit him, anyway, so I didn't really see what any fuss was about. From Fuller's viewpoint, it would have been completely different. All he saw was impending disaster.

The second flight was harder. The first time I was desperate to get it done; now I started to get nervous. That was not good. I performed almost as well for my second flight, but again, the landing was poor. I really needed to improve my landing. I told Fuller it was another heavy landing; I wasn't proud, but I was honest. There was only the final flight to prove myself.

The last flight, I went to pieces. I really didn't want to go again. Instead of increasing in confidence it was the opposite. It wasn't the flying, but the two poor landings. I felt I couldn't do it. Up until then I had landed pretty well, but my confidence shaken, I stopped believing and my performance suffered as a result. The last flight was the worst for launch height and the worst landing of the lot. But hey, I had done it. Fuller and Mills shook my hand and congratulated me.

'Now fuck off,' smiled Mills. Fucking off with pleasure, sir. It was still Saturday, so I said my goodbyes, had my logbook signed, and caught the bus home. Job done. It was the last time I climbed into a glider.

Back home, it was all quite an anti-climax. Mum and Dad were pleased for me, and hopefully proud. Jackie was still at Cambridge, and David was in the Army now. He had been posted to Paderborn in Germany, so it was only really my parents and my sister Alison still around. I took my moped up to see Martin. I had to tell him I had finished my solos. It was only a few weeks after he had finished his, but I always seemed to be behind. At least Colin hadn't done his yet; being born in July, Col had yet to be old enough and find a starting slot. When Colin eventually took his course, it was in the new-fangled powered gliders, the Venture; the poser. That was in RAF Syderstone in Norfolk, and he was only allowed one solo, the swampy cheapskates.

Col had a job at Ambersil with a few other cadets too. It was working on the pressurised can production lines. He and others, bored out of their minds, sabotaged the cans as they passed along the conveyor belt, puncturing them to see the fluid pour out, or aligning them to topple of the end. The supervisor had a word in their ears. That job didn't last long. His first proper job was at RE Cross Engineering. A machine operator cut off his thumb, which scared Colin off engineering completely. He joined the Civil Service at the Commission in Basingstoke.

Through his job, he discovered there as was a 'secret' bunker under the building in case of nuclear attack. We also understood it connected with other key buildings, such as the Police Station. It was supposedly hush hush, but we heard about it at various times. In the noughties, they demolished the building and built a block of private flats and named it Crown Heights. They sold it under the banner of luxury flats, and the bunker was to be converted into a subterranean swimming complex. They built the flats, painted the block an awful yellow colour, but to date, no sign of the pool. It's probably still stocked to the gills with baked beans and toilet paper.

During the seventies, most Brits were sold the most godawful cars by British Leyland. Mum had an Austin Allegro, probably the most inaccurately named car of all time. Allegro translates as 'lively'. To be accurate, it should have been called the 'Sciatto', but the Austin Slovenly might not have sold so well. She hated it. For some reason, they gave it a steering wheel that was square. I suspect the chief tester wrenched off the wheel in a fit of pique and chucked it out of the window. It fell on the ground and dented into a square shape, and the designer refitted it back on the stalk. Then that was the template. Well that's my theory, anyway. To cap it all, Mum's car was chocolate brown. She had, by now, moved onto small Volvos; much better.

I think it had been 1972, when I was nine, but Dad picked me up from school in our new car. It was a metallic green Vauxhall Cresta and it looked amazing, like some American auto. It was huge; it fitted three at a squeeze on the front bench seat and four in the back. It also had 3,300cc of engine, six cylinders producing 140bhp. Top speed was only 100mph or so, but it had bags of torque. Dad was still driving it now, but not for much longer. Being such a large and heavy car, the fuel consumption was high, plus it was getting pretty old. I hoped I would be driving soon enough to be able to take it out at least once.

For now, it was still the moped. I popped into town one evening and after the usual flick through all the latest releases, bought 'Time for Action,' the new 45 from Secret Affair. The Mod revival was in full swing, and The Jam was at the forefront. As I weaved around the old Thorneycroft roundabout, probably the largest diameter one in the town, I heard a loud *twang*; I glanced around, and saw the contents of my bike carrier were empty. I stopped at the side of the road, and in-between traffic, recovered my lunchbox, scarf, bungees and single from the centre of the road. The poorly single was on the tarmac, sans sleeve, and it would have to be the A-side facing down, wouldn't it? I thought it was ruined, but when I played it, the only audible scratches were on the play in groove. Thank goodness. Listening to the track on CD never seems the same without the graunching noises at the start.

There were some fantastic tracks coming through; 'My Sharona' by The Knack, 'Back Of My Hand,' by The Jags. Col and I quite got into Joe Jackson, who sounded a bit like Elvis Costello. The Jags' singer sounded very much like him, but the lyrics were almost incomprehensible at times. They were all blitzed by 'The Eton Rifles'. Blimey, what a record. Weller was having a go at the cadet corps. I didn't take it as an affront as an Air Cadet, because I felt he was attacking the upper classes and the privileged elite. I hope that was the case, Paul. Prime Minister David Cameron later stated it as one of his favourite songs, but as he was an old Etonian, Weller retorted with, 'What part of the song didn't he get?'

At ATC parade, I was proud to show off my new Gliding wings. I would often now take brief lectures, predominantly about the theory of flight, to the younger cadets. One new starter wouldn't stop talking in one of them. After the third time of telling him to be quiet, I wheeled around from the blackboard and flung my piece of chalk at him. It hit him squarely between the eyes.

'Ow!' he retorted as the chalk disintegrated on his forehead.

'What a shot!' observed Roberts.

I pointed to the Marksman badge on my arm.

'Don't mess with me,' I said. I didn't hear another peep.

It seemed violence, or at least the threat of it, was a key part of control. The state maintains order by the threat or use of violence; it appears to be a basic part of the human condition. It isn't restricted to humans either; the animal kingdom is exactly the same. It's a dog eat dog world. The cold war existed because of the mutual threat of annihilation, and the Looney Left wanted to take away our only real defence, our nuclear missile deterrent. Polaris, and later Trident missiles would be the reason why Britain had not succumbed to an Eastern European land force far larger and greater than our own. The debate would last for decades but many CND supporters of the period later publicly admitted they were misguided. Whatever the truth, I hoped I wasn't going to be obliterated in an instant after being blinded by an atomic flash, and the less arms out there on both sides would be a good thing, if you could trust the bally Balalaika players to count fairly.

'Da, Dmitri. Zat vas vun hundred twenty kiloton missiles, or vas it ninety-nine? Who vill miss vun missile? Ho ho ho.'

'Do not vorry, Slobodan. If ve haff vun extra it can be exploded in ze Urals. Ve will not miss a few hundred thousand starving peasants.'

It is difficult to imagine now how imminent an attack seemed in 1979. There were many publications and novels exploring how World War 3 would happen. In one lecture at ATC, the presenter stated the battleground *would* be Germany, as if it were irrefutable fact. I shivered at the prospect and often dreamt of the horror of witnessing an H-bomb. The message was suffused through the media, either deliberately by the government intent on fostering distrust and fear of the East, or by an alarmist conglomerate of journalists, misinformed or genuinely fearful of our future. Spreading fear on a global scale is a constant I have observed as I get older. Today, it is the terrorist threat from unhinged individuals in the Middle East. Although they certainly exist, the climate of fear they openly espouse is amplified beyond reason by the world stage; TV, the internet, radio. Without these modern platforms to stand upon, the fear generated by the hate makers would evaporate, their inhuman acts of violence would remain unseen, and they would exist only as the isolated and sporadic events they often are. As with anything, people imitate what they see. Following the Russian Revolution, western workers became, literally, bolshie (named after the Bolsheviks), and started to cause trouble, which ultimately led to the General Strike in 1926 (I know there were other factors, historians, but this is a book about a Basingstoke geezer, not a Muscovite). Ignorance can be bliss. Such is the modern world.

Anyway, what was the point of all this exposition? Was it to delay starting to talk about BETA? Just like the fact I didn't want to go to BETA? I hated metalwork at school, now I have to go back and do six months of it? Thank God it was only that time; the other inmates would be there for a year.

Basingstoke Engineering Training Association is based in Joule Road, Basingstoke. Housing approximately 70 machines back then, with 80 students, it was the prime training centre for young engineers for miles around. We had to cover the basics of production; milling, turning, welding, forging, bench work, sheet metal working and electrical working. It would effectively be a month on each section. The first thing they gave us was our work wear. It was a horrid green dustcoat, with a horrid green cap and big, black safety specs. Those with long hair had to keep it in a net under the hat. The specs were huge, and had side bars to prevent stray ingress of metal from spinning machines. I had to place them on top of my own specs; great, now I wasn't four eyes anymore, I was six eyes. At least it was a leveller – the rest of them looked like speccy dorks as well.

I was glad to see my old mate, Phil Rolfe there. He was now an apprentice toolmaker for a local firm, SSI Fix Equipment. So Purdey and Gambit were back together again; everybody knew somebody else. There was also Mark Pomfret, Ian's bro, who I knew from King's Furlong, and Peter Deadman, who lived opposite Martin. We had to park our bikes and mopeds in the bike sheds at the back of the building. Greg was a man mountain from Harriet Costello; I knew him only well enough to not engage. One of his weasely mates arrived on his cycle, and Greg just picked him up, still on his bike, and held him over his head. The weasel wobbled and panicked, shrieking like a little girl.

'Greg! Let me down! I'm gonna fall! Woah!'

Greg gently let him down so there was only a slight bounce as the wheels touched. Strong? You wouldn't mess with him.

As well as apprentices, there were the machine operators. These were destined to be the lower skilled underclass, their training a mere fraction of ours. There is always a hierarchy, theirs was a lower of the lowerarchy. Amongst these cerebrum-challenged throng were two girls. It would be fair to say, they weren't; that is, not exactly fair maidens. Oh alright, they were complete dogs, are you happy now? One was quite sweet; with her red lipstick, she reminded me of the glammed up Gremlin in 'Gremlins 2'. Very ironically, someone dubbed her Miss America. That made me laugh.

We were introduced to each section ('Hello, Milling') so we knew what misery would befall us from one month to the next. A huge red button atop a small pillar sat in the centre of the workshop. This, we were told, switched off every machine onsite, as it was the emergency stop. On one side of the large building, were the milling and turning sections, with multiple manual lathes and mills. Behind them, was the sheet metal section. Opposite side of the building was the bench fitting and the welding sections. On the upper floor was the electrical section. There were also classrooms, washrooms and the canteen.

There was a mid-morning tea break. Never have I been so thirsty until I started manual work. Usually the same dark-haired woman with blue eye shadow served tea behind the counter, and you could buy cheese or ham rolls, crisps and biscuits. The menu was unbelievably basic. Anyway, you can't argue with a Wagon Wheel; certainly not with one in your gob. Goatcher was in his element, he had loads more motorbike enthusiasts to talk bollocks with. His favourite word was 'acceleration', except he pronounced it, 'eggceleration'. Both Waller and I noticed it.

'The yoke is on him,' Weller announced. We couldn't believe the crap that came out of these youths' mouths as they stuffed cheese rolls into them.

'Yeah, the eggceleration is amazing on the Yamaha RD250, I've heard they go even quicker if you paint the engine green.'

'Paint the engine green? You're 'aving a laugh, aintcha?'

'No, straight up. I've heard it's a well-known fact that someone told me.'

Waller couldn't take it after a while. 'You're talking absolute bollocks, mate.' Goatcher looked up, affronted, ready with his fists at being sworn at. 'Paint your engine green? It makes absolutely no difference whatsoever what fuckin' colour the engine is.'

Justin couldn't pluck a reasonable argument so he would revert to type, that is, insults.

'And what do you know about it, you spotty cunt?'

'A lot more than you do, it seems.' The tea break bell rang; back to work. That would be Andy Waller all over; he would push a point, regardless of the threat or intimidation. I respected his nerve, especially as he was a skinny Herbert; but I had learnt not to push the nutters of this world. I would let them bullshit away if that pleased them. Unfortunately, it gave Holden the impression I was gullible. I certainly wasn't, but I would rather people think me so then attack their unreasonable rantings and risk a bashing.

The senior instructor was called Mr Pearce. We were all to be known as Mister – Mister Heath, Mister Cotterell. Forever being known as 'boy' or Heath was all to change for the better. We were young adults, earning a (meagre) wage, we commanded the requisite respect. Mr Pearce was very laconic, with a dry sense of humour. He was only a little bloke but he had an unerring edge to him, a steely toughness that remained undefined. It was a mixture of schoolteacher and prison officer – quite apposite for this environment. From the moment I arrived till I went home, I felt sure it was a prison. Sweaty, teenage inmates toiling over hot machinery – to me it was a borstal version of a Gulag. This was the painful bit of the training to get to the final prize, or so I believed. Holden said it would be alright when we got to Lasham, we'd have none of this stuff. Well, apart from the sheet metal. We needed to do that as an Airframe Fitter.

Before we even touched a machine, were given lectures and films concerning health and safety. Keep guards down, make sure chucks are tightened, chuck keys removed, loose clothing tucked away, long hair tucked into nets, be aware of power points, emergency stops; the storage of gas cylinders, the movement of cylinders, how to walk them into place, turn them on, turn them off ('Show 'em Miss America,' said Chris. 'That would turn anybody off.').

We also had a talk about the extra conscientiousness required for the aircraft worker. The lecturer, Mr Burge, used to work on aero engines in the Army Air Corps at Middle Wallop. 'If I dropped my tiny spanner in the engine, necessitating a very expensive strip down, I would have to hold my hand up to say I did it,' he said. 'Better to risk being thrown out of a job than let someone die because I didn't speak up. That's why you all have a special role to perform, always be aware of the dangers of working with aircraft, and the potential consequences.' That message has never left me; I'm sure it has never left the others, either.

We also learnt extremely dry (and very boring) facts about metric and imperial standards, sizes of drills, taps, fasteners, nuts and bolts. It was also extremely important information and we were tested after every stage to make sure we got it.

At lunchtimes, we would walk en masse to the newsagent along the road, just to get out for a bit. Kavanagh and Cotterell started a comedic double act, pretending to be gay. They would hold hands and skip gaily down the road, making the rest of us cringe. They would pretend to kiss, once actually touching lips, which was followed by much disgust and spitting by Jez.

'Kavanagh, you bloody queer,' Jez would laugh.

'I dunno, I actually quite enjoyed it,' said Paul, still in character.

A Honda XL185 trail bike zoomed past. Jez quite fancied the idea of getting one when he could afford it, and leapt up and own enthusiastically on seeing the bike. The rider, nonplussed, turned around and pulled up next to an embarrassed Jez.

'What's your game?' said the young rider, not exactly threateningly, more concerned that Park Prewett had lost a patient.

'Er, the bike, it's great, no offence mate, I just like the bike, like,' Jez mumbled and raised his thumbs aloft. The rider rode off, leaving Jez feeling about an inch tall.

'Well, you certainly didn't lose any self-respect there, Jez, well done,' said Chris.

Life was just a string of embarrassing moments. The awkwardness of the teenage years doesn't last, but it is deeply felt. It was your mates' job to maximise that feeling and make you squirm at every opportunity.

We were beginning to get to know each other. Chris was the cheeky one, and could almost get away with murder due to his infectious grin and one liners. Ian was the quiet one, which I already knew; Jez was the orange juice, a good mixer; Holden was the troublemaker; Kavanagh was odd; Goatcher was the jock and Waller was just Waller. He moved in a slow, strange way sometimes, almost like Jarvis Cocker but with added gurning; he didn't seem to care what he said to anyone, although he was mainly polite.

Taylor was from Stannah Stairlifts, the Andover mob. He was beefy, with a fat head and a stupid little moustache. He looked like a bully and he was. He rode a Honda SS50. He challenged others and me to a race around the roundabout, just along the road. I declined, and told him there's no contest with a PC50. He was crazy. One morning, he turned up for work with not one, but *two* pheasants hanging off his handlebars.

'I hit them on the way to work,' he stated matter-of-factly. Yes, well most normal people don't tie their claws to a moped and ride around, you prick.

We all took turns sweeping the canteen floor. Taylor accosted me one morning because Waller had been cheeky to him.

'Better tell your mate to watch it,' he growled at me.

'Tell him yourself,' I said. I turned my back to him and carried on sweeping. He brought his big, smelly bulk up against me. His face snorted hate.

'No, you tell 'im. Or I'll have both of you.'

'Ok, ok,' I said. It was like being affronted by a bull. I didn't fancy getting the red cape out. I told Waller. 'I'm not scared of him,' he said. 'Let him try. Wankers like him are all mouth.'

Well, he wasn't quite; he was mostly fat and gristle, but hey ho. It all came to a head, but thankfully with someone unconnected with Dans. Taylor picked a fight with someone closer to his own size, Jon Kelly, but he was a good bloke. Taylor broke his nose which left a trail of blood all across the canteen floor. He got removed from BETA after that. I don't know if he lost his job, but he was out of my face, so I was glad.

Our first machine work was on the Milling Section. The instructor was a fat, jolly chap with black curly hair. How nice it must be to love your work, as he so obviously did. I found milling rectangular pieces of metal to various finishes good fun. Quite often, someone would relax and inadvertently sit on the emergency stop button, and with one movement of their butt, effectively kill all the machines on site. The sound of machines running down and the whoops of joy from operators would alert the perpetrator to their crime.

The cooling and lubricating agent was called slurry, a mix of oil and water. It looked just like milk pouring all over the work. Although we used barrier creams, to protect our skin, it didn't agree with me. I began to get warts on my fingers, an affliction I had never suffered from. I was quite horrified by that. Every break time, I washed my hands until they were nearly raw. It didn't matter though, using oils and holding metal all day, my fingerprints became stained with black and my nails would be forever dirty. I cut them as short as possible anyway to try and ameliorate it. A day on the machines and my face would be tight and felt dirty; the hat would make you hot and your hair greasy. I hated it with a vengeance. Let me out of here.

Another storm was rising. The Andover mob was unhappy about losing their psychopathic leader. They blamed us, although the big lunk brought all his issues onto himself. They wanted a fight; it was going to be outside, straight after work. I couldn't believe I was hearing this. Malicious intent spread faster than wildfire; threats were made. Kavanagh picked up a long piece of iron and hid it under his dustcoat. 'You're not serious about using that, are you?' I was incredulous. Goatcher and Holden were making battle plans and who to attack first. Everyone wanted to avoid Greg. I saw other lads hiding weapons. I couldn't stand it. Why should I get my head kicked in for nothing? They were all a bunch of pathetic nutters who didn't seem to realise this wasn't the school playground anymore. I went to see Pearce. I told him straight, there was going to be a fight and it wouldn't happen if he came outside to the bike shed just before we all left. He could sense my panic. I only had a PC50, I'd have no chance of escape otherwise.

Someone must have seen me talk to Pearce, or even hear. Within minutes, I saw the same head cases removing the same weapons and hiding them in their lockers. 'It's off!' one hissed to another.

'What do you mean, it's off?' the other snaked back, upset his violent evening was ruined.

Sure enough, Pearce was standing there as we all duly collected our vehicles and left. I never told the others I was the sneak. Who cares? I survived because I'm not bloody stupid.

*

We received our first pay packets. They were delivered in small manila envelopes and we collected them from the office. Chris was shocked and horrified by the measly amount.

'Twenty-nine fifty? *Twenty-nine fifty?*' He said it slowly to emphasise his disappointment. 'I thought we might get more than that! Twenty-nine bloody fifty!?'

It was my first ever pay, more than I had ever received before, so I was happy. It was the start toward my new motorbike, although I was quite miffed that Mum demanded housekeeping money now I was earning. A fiver it is, Mum.

It was only the first week it was so low; it went up to £33 or £34.50 after that, probably a tax issue or start date thing. It certainly wasn't a fortune, but I was determined to afford that Honda by next March.

I could also afford records. I bought my favourite album of all time, 'Setting Sons', by The Jam in October. Weller was so insightful, it was if he peered directly into our lives and reported on it. 'Saturday's Kids' was the ultimate depiction of teenage life in suburbia in three minutes flat. I also bought 'The Raven' by The Stranglers. I took the display sleeve up to the assistant in WH Smith, and she pulled out a sleeve with a beautiful colour lenticular image on the cover. I thought that one might cost more but it was a limited edition of 25,000 as a promo. It became my favourite record sleeve. I reluctantly sold all my vinyl later down the line, but I bought that one again and framed it. Classic.

We had another group of people to get to know at Tech College. Wednesday was college day. I caught the train from Basingstoke which collected the city gents from Fleet and beyond. It was 'Smithers-Jones' from 'Setting Sons' come alive.

'Here I go again, it's Monday at last, sitting on the Waterloo line...' starts the song. It continues to tell the tale of an overworked commuter who gets made redundant, and the only one smiling is 'the sun tanned boss.' It would become the soundtrack to my own experience more than once.

'Farnborough, this is Farnborough...' The recorded voice echoed from the station speakers. It was a 20-minute walk from the station to Farnborough College, past the Tumble Down Dick pub, across the car park, and into the old grounds. The building used to be a convent, it was full of Gothic arches and red brick Victorian design. The newer building was on the other side of the main road. At least we could mix with the totty here, not like at BETA.

The class at College was a rum mix of Dan Air, Rae Farnborough, Asian students and oddballs. RAE (Royal Aircraft Establishment) Farnborough was literally along the road. Every day at College, fighter jets screamed low overhead, and being an Aerospace Engineering course, we would legitimately watch them and discuss the aircraft with certain teachers. Amongst those from RAE there was Ben Bonnick, Steve Page, a guy called Sharples (who we called Ena, naturally), and a biker mate of Ben's; from Dan Air there was me, Waller, Stan Higginbotham, Martin Smith and Mark Etherington, all third year apprentices. They had already taken City & Guilds and were being pushed forward for a higher qualification, TEC (Technician version of ONC). There was also a *really* old guy who must have been at least 35...

The third years were all nice guys. Stan was a humorous chap with glasses and straggly hair, who looked like a manic Graeme Garden from The Goodies. He rode a Triumph 650 Tiger, twin cylinder thing that made an absolute racket. The bass note of the firing cycle was so low it would put modern sound systems to shame. It could be heard for miles away before he eventually arrived. Similarly, Martin rode a Triumph Bonneville. What was it with these old British bikes?

'They've got character,' Stan would say. 'Not like the modern, plastic Jap crap!'

Well, if you define character as noisy, leaking oil and would hardly ever start, then yes, they had character. They also had arcane controls, sited at weird places compared to modern bikes.

Martin was a slim, long-haired cool dude. His dad was Ron Smith, one of the Dan Air directors, eventually, if not then, MD. I would get to know Ron, for my sins. Thankfully, Martin was nothing like him. He reminded me of Scott Gorham from Thin Lizzy, another band I loved. He played guitar in bands, so I was keen to soak up knowledge from Martin. Etherington was quiet, although friendly. He always seemed to sit in Stan's shadow, I suppose he had the personality of two men away; Stan was loud, a little mad sometimes, but God, he made me laugh. He started posing on his Tiger in the car park, revving up and pulling away and tipped himself off it. A forward roll later, he was sheepish but fine. He wore a mid-brown leather jacket with long tassels; a little bit Easy Rider mixed with Monty Python.

There were quite a number of Iranian students at the college. This was around the time western relations with Iran began to get fraught, following Ayatollah Khomeini's reinstatement and the coup against the Shah; US diplomats were seized in the Iranian embassy and held for 444 days. We viewed the Iranians with suspicion for a while but these guys were just students, really nice guys. They just looked uncool with their revolutionists' moustaches. Mr Nagresheth was quite matey, so was his fat friend whose name escapes me. Mark Lennards was an RAF technician on our course; one evening, he had a disagreement with the fat guy over some obscure issue and had a minor tussle with him. The fat one was inexplicably on the floor and Lennards was kicking him; I heard, 'Stay down there, you cunt!' from the back of the class, all seemingly oblivious to the teacher.

The classes were very interesting; Mechanical Science, with Mr Martin, Aeronautics with Mr Oldham, Mathematics and Electrics, and Propulsion with Mr Peter Pock. Mr Martin was very straight laced which opened him up for instant ridicule. He got teased at times but he knew his subject. We had many practical experiments including stretching and testing small test pieces in various machines. On site, there were also a couple of small wind tunnels for aerodynamics testing.

The Maths and Electrics teacher's name escapes me, but he took us for the evening classes. By that time, 6-9 pm, we were pretty tired and not really ready to embrace new concepts. What better time, then, to teach us advanced calculus! We had to learn and use Trig identities until the cows came home. Unfortunately, the cows couldn't do it, either. They just sat there munching grass and asked if it was raining yet.

'My brain juice is bubbling,' said a confused and weary Stan. 'I need a beer!'

We rarely did go for beer, though. After College, it was the walk to the station and train home.

We hardly saw the Fairies; they were on a different course.

Lunchtimes, we would walk into Queensmead Shopping Centre, before it was majorly revamped. I would buy cheap books or records in some of the little shops. On return to class one afternoon, possibly with Steve Page, Waller was behind us. An attractive student walked past us, and Waller shouted, 'Eh eh, sexy!' and immediately ducked behind a car. The girl turned and saw us, smiled and walked on. Waller emerged, grinning from ear to ear as if his face had been slashed in two.

'Waller, you bastard,' I said. 'Good one.'

Waller and I chatted to another guy in our class who had a big bike. Turned out he was 19. That seemed so old as to be possibly nearly pushing up daisies. We were so young; we thought 40 years old meant you were completely past it.

Peter Pock was a former BA engineer, and knew just about everything you could regarding aero engines. He would drone on and on about the HP cock being open and the LP cock being closed, the left legs connected to the thigh bone, or some such nonsense, and straight after lunch too. I would be drowsy after our excursion to town and back, and would lose concentration. He shouted at me once, in his whiny voice, to 'Wake up Mr Heath!' it was so loud and such a shock, it was quite upsetting. Suddenly, I was back in Latin class with Miss Bagley, telling me to stop looking outside and at the Latin. Yes, Teach... zzzzzzzzzzz. Pock had a real thing for young mothers, which he would sometimes reference in a light hearted moment. We didn't know what his attraction was, he seemed a right old perv. I know now, with the benefit of experience, what he was going on about. Dirty old sod.

Between last afternoon lesson and the evening, we had an hour to get tea. That was the only time we used the canteen. I never felt like I was a proper student, as we were part time. The girls seemed to eye us with suspicion, as if we were invaders. Maybe I was just self-conscious and paranoid. I would often have cheese on toast with chips, because I liked it. Waller would have chips, ketchup and more chips.

I would do well at College.

11. Hip to be Square

Jez's Fizzy was a wreck. The stand was broken, so he would lay it against a fence. The starter was dodgy, so to get it going he would bump start it. It didn't matter though, it got him around, and coming from Fleet every day, a distance of 15 miles or so it was quite invaluable. Home time at BETA was dominated by the blue smoke haze of fifty mopeds, mostly Fizzies, and the wasp-in-a-can rasp of the tinny engines. My little Honda may have looked uncool, but it was relatively quiet, 4-stroke and didn't produce pollution emulating a Commando raid on a stronghold.

Although most of us want to fit in, I was always happy to be an individual. I'll go my own way, thanks, has always been my attitude if I disagreed with the common herd. It was less arrogance, more a distrust of the judgement by those I saw as lesser qualified or intelligent. The only other person who matched my academic standard was Rossi; but my practical skills were definitely lacking. Therefore, away from the classroom, the others would find their mark and pummel it relentlessly.

Mr Hickmott took Bench Fitting. He was a tall, middle-aged Scot with half-moon glasses. Bench fitting consisted mainly of filing blocks so that they were square. It took hours and hours. Using Verniers and micrometers, we filed and filed until the material was the requisite thousands of an inch within tolerance. Being little gobshites, we would often stop filing to continue our conversations. Burge would appear from nowhere, peer down on us under his glasses, and boom, 'File, Laddie!' He seemed to pop up from anywhere. He would be out of sight, but as soon as the file stopped moving, there he was, to repeat his familiar two word catchphrase.

The files would clog constantly, especially with aluminium. It would be file, file, file, file, declog, file, file, file, file, declog. You had to use a wire brush to remove the bits of metal from the file's teeth; a bit like flossing but with super strength floss. I had spent a very long time on a pair of blocks, and when I returned from a trip to the stores, sitting in my vice were imposters. I know they were, because they weren't square.

'Right, which one of you sods has switched my blocks? I know it was one of you, so stop mucking about.'

'Wot you on about, Heafy?' said Holden. 'You 'aving a funny turn? No one's touched your blocks. So get filing.'

I wouldn't have it. They were definitely switched. I remonstrated with Holden. He kept turning on me loudly, making out I was a fool in front of the others. I couldn't prove it, but these were not mine; they were terribly concave and beyond rescue, as to get them square would push them out of tolerance. I had no choice but to do my best and present them for marking. I told Hickmott they had been switched. Holden again took the piss. I suspected he had done it, so vigorously did he deny it. I hated him for that. I was marked down on those test pieces, and I needed all the points I could get. I didn't need sabotage; I had already done that to my wellbeing by going into Engineering.

Steve Holden and I would become better mates, but I never trusted him after that. He had lost his dad fairly young, so I forgave him for his constant bullshitting. I guess the anger of the bereavement kept surfacing in attacks on others too. Or maybe he was just mean. I made excuses for his behaviour, but it didn't mean I accepted it.

*

Turning, as in the use of lathes, was also good fun. With our milled and turned sections, we made tools for our future use at Lasham, such as riveting blocks and deburring tools.

We made them well, as they are still in my toolbox today. As I stood behind my lathe, one of the dipshit operators in front of me started his; unfortunately, the chuck key was still in it. The machine was turning at full speed within a second, and the key rattled loudly until the rotation threw it at high speed past my left ear. I handed it back to the dipshit, who had ducked and hid during the brief rattling instead of hitting the off button.

I didn't like being near the operators; they were dangerous, like lit fireworks. The same dipshit was in the forging area, supposedly to hammer hot pieces on the anvil. His first strike, the large hammer rebounded off the anvil and he hit himself on the head, knocking himself out.

Mr Gurd took us for Sheet Metal. He had a West Country burr and was a balding ginger with a beard. He called me 'Misturr Reath' and was quite talkative outside of work time. Jez and I were chatting to him and Jez asked his age. Foolishly, Gurd told us to guess. '40?' I said.

'How dare you?' he said, looking hurt. 'I am 30.' Well, Hurdy-Gurdy, you look older. Get rid of the beard and apply the hair to your thinning thatch, old son.

One of the test pieces I made for Gurd didn't look all that, but every time I measured it, it was completely within tolerance. Jez annoyed me, because as Gurd measured it, he was decrying its lack of visual appeal.

'That looks like a dog's dinner, Heath. There's no way you're getting full marks for that.'

Gurd looked at him. 'The vurrniur does not loy, Mr Cotter-ill,' he said. 'Full marks. 10 out of 10.'

'What? I don't believe it!' Jez grabbed the vernier and started checking my piece. 'Look at that! You can see that isn't square! It's got a hump in it!'

'You'll get a hump in yoor face from Mr Reath in a minute if you don't poipe deown,' said Gurd. 'As I said, the vurrniur duzzen't loy.'

Yeah, shut up Jez. Are you my mate or not?

There were times when laddish enthusiasm obscured any sense of professionalism. This was one of them. Transport the scene five years, and it would be totally unacceptable and likely to end in fisticuffs or legal action. This wasn't a game, or a friendly making things competition. Thankfully, it wasn't for production either.

Waller was good at using his hands. Give him a hammer and he would bash the fuck out of anything. It's possible he had a mild version of Tourette's – he would, jokingly, tell most people to fuck off. It got him into trouble; sometimes he would be forced to apologise to the instructors. He was actually pretty intelligent and well spoken, but the demons would take over, and he would lose himself in silliness. I kind of liked him and was embarrassed by him at the same time.

I started to see Jez socially. We would go to each other's homes, hang out, and play music. He had a mate called Sean who was also in the ATC, so we all got on well. There was a great music shop in Fleet that Jez turned me on to, Kingfisher Music, and I would go in and salivate over the Rickenbacker guitars. They didn't appreciate dribble on the lacquer so they kicked me out.

We were still having cinema duty nights at ATC. I got to see Monty Python's 'Life of Brian' twice for free. It was brilliant, one of the funniest films ever. It was banned from certain towns due to the outcry from Christians, saying it was mocking Christ. It wasn't, but it was having a go at organised religion and blind faith. 'He's not the messiah, he's a very naughty boy.' Quite.

I also went with Colin and his mum to see 'Alien'. That was an X-rated film, i.e. 18s and over, but we got in ok. The queue snaked around the block as you had to queue outside in those days; it also rained. That film seemed terrifying, I suppose because we had never seen anything like it.

In December, Martin and I took ourselves to see 'Apocalypse Now' at the Mercury Hotel cinema. It was a tiny place, but had plush seating and was a comfortable way to view a film. It completely blew me away, and changed my whole perspective on lots of issues; totalitarianism, the obscenity of war, the journey into darkness and madness, it covered many major themes; the basic premise of the boat trip to hell, and the fact that 'you never know what's around the next bend.' It was a statement describing life itself. Martin and I discussed it passionately all the way home.

The NME had some good articles around that time. One was all about state power and totalitarianism, the inevitable rise of increasing police control and CCTV. It happened. So much so we tend to forget today that we are constantly on camera. It's insidious and unsettling, irrespective of any intention to commit a crime.

On 06.11.79, I was awarded my leading cadet badge. The only way up now was to become a staff cadet, which I had no plans to achieve. Martin was promoted to Sergeant. All I had plans for now was to go to Germany camp next year; after that, I thought I might leave.

Some days at BETA were so cripplingly awful, I cried off with a migraine headache. Although I still had migraines from time to time, it was a good, unprovable excuse not to go to work. It was only a couple of times; the others were literally making me sick. The ribbing from Holden and Kavanagh, and the nastiness spat from Goatcher often combined that I wouldn't take it anymore. It didn't matter what subject it was, they would deem me inferior; I dressed 'like a turd', I didn't have/couldn't get a girlfriend, I rode a slow moped, I was 'gullible', I was spotty, I was skinny – hang on, I was what?

A few months after leaving school, and all my residual weight fell off me. I went from 10 ½ stone to just over 9. I didn't really notice it but it was quite a dramatic change. I just knew I was ravenous more often. I don't know exactly what caused it, but I suspect it was through stress; the change in lifestyle from school to work, being amongst a highly critical peer group, and physical work. I had said hello to an old schoolmate in the cinema – he didn't recognise me. It had only been six months.

'Have you been ill?' he asked. No, I haven't been ill. What are you talking about? Jez advised me on new clothes, and I bought some skinny jeans. My legs looked like two pieces of string coated in denim. At least they looked better than the flares I had been used to. It was time I bought my own clothes, anyway.

For all the others' bravado, we were all, without exception, virgins. There was a hilarious exchange at lunchtime between Paul and Justin, describing the nether regions of certain young ladies they had intimate encounters with, but not, the whole hog, so to speak. Supposedly trying to impress with each other's gynaecological knowledge, in the same vein as the Monty Python Yorkshire men, Justin exclaimed, 'Yeah, but women pee out of their bums, don't they?'

Holden and Paul looked at each other, quite alarmed.

'Women don't pee out of their bums, you idiot,' laughed Kavanagh. 'What are you thinking? Next you'll be saying they crap out of their armpits or something!'

Justin looked confused. He may have fiddled with the intricate switchgear nestled within a temptress's labia, but he lacked basic sexual knowledge the average 11-year-old learnt in junior school. He went bright red and refused to discuss it further. Brilliant. We'd wheel that one out whenever we could, the twat. Waller would, especially.

The Welding section: In my opinion, the most dangerous and horrible part of the BETA course training. Pearce gave us a good health and safety going over before we started using welding equipment. We would learn arc welding and gas welding. Arc welding involves passing an electric current through the welding rod that ignites an 'arc'; the material in the welding rod melts and fuses with the material on the bench. The major issue with it is that you can't see what you're welding until you 'strike' the arc, similar to striking a match, and viewing it through a visor, as the light is too bright. Through the dark glass of the visor, you can determine the small area of flux that is being welded; too far away, and it won't fuse, too close, and the rod can fuse to the work, and get stuck. It's all quite unnerving. Pearce warned us of arc eye – a painful condition caused by exposure to welding glare without the use of goggles or a visor. The worst part was the fumes. One hour of welding and the lining of your nose was black. It was foul; all the pollution breathed in was like a day in London reduced to minutes. Of course, being warned about arc eye was an incitement for abuse; separated in welding cells, you would ask your mate to assist, then strike an arc, blinding your would-be assistant. Kavanagh was very keen on this one.

Gas welding was a different story, though. No less dangerous; we were dealing with oxygen and acetylene under pressure, and lit, the temperature of a fully flamed welding torch is around 3,500 degrees C. That is effing hot. For some reason, they gave the bloody things to operators, who thought it funny to lick each other's arse with the flames, sometimes setting their overalls alight. If you brought the flame too close to the work, it would blow up in a big bang, showering sparks and material everywhere. It made you jump a mile. It seemed a lot more controllable though, not least that you could start the flame and aim it before putting the goggles down. I was determinedly better at gas welding. I don't think I was ever truly successful with the arc; holding my breath didn't help.

Oxy-acetylene cutting was the worst of all. Pearce explained that if the gas ignited back down the hoses, i.e. a blowback, the cylinders could effectively explode, blowing us all into kingdom come. The cutter was sited near the back door to the building, and if it started making noises consistent with a potential blowback, we should turn off the taps and the cylinders themselves. Jez and I were operating the cutter when it suddenly started making loud whooshing and popping noises above its normal sound. With one leap, approx. three yards, I exceeded my own standing long jump record and disappeared out of the door. Pearce came over and calmly helped Jez turn it off.

'Mr Cotterell,' Pearce said drily, 'please turn off the taps at the cylinder end. And while you're there, please fetch Mr Heath a clean pair of underpants, would you?'

Classic. He delivered the line with a wonderful comic timing. Even I was impressed, despite my embarrassment.

The Madness single 'Baggy Trousers' was a big hit with me and Chris. The follow up, 'Embarrassment' pretty much became our teenage catchphrase. As I worked at BETA, I would be constantly singing, more often than not, lines from 'Setting Sons'. One of the songs has the line, 'Think of Emma, wonder what she's doing.' Jez was going out with an Emma. He liked the idea of the song from my singing of it. When he eventually heard the track, he was disappointed; so was I when I met Emma. Jez was to have a lot of teenage angst issues with Emma; break ups and getting back together again.

Someone was to be picked from each time to be Safety Officer. The rotten buggers voted for me. It meant a brief meeting each month to raise any concerns. I moaned about the fumes from the arc welding, and Pearce insisted the extractors did their job. My lungs said otherwise. Nothing changed. Anyway, once I had finished in that section, why would I worry? It was actually worse on the Electrical section. We had to solder joints together, and the solder fumes really made my breathing hurt; I don't know the exact constituents of the solder that did it, but it certainly wasn't healthy.

Mr Payne was the Electrical instructor. This was a reasonably clean environment for a change, on the upper floor and away from the oil and the yobs. Of course, there was still the danger element of potential electrocution to look forward to. We had to rig together simple circuits and test them. Ian spent ages on one and switched on the power. There was a loud bang and a flash, as bits of Mr Ross's circuit rained down on the rest of us. That gave him quite a fright; it was also bloody hilarious.

'Get it right, Ian. You're supposed to be a bloody electrician!' pseudo-mocked Kavanagh.

It was also up there that Jez and I were discussing music with Gerard Law, from Snamprogetti Limited. Law and Tim Corso became good mates while we were there. We were espousing our love for the 'Bat out of Hell' album so I sang the whole title track, dramatically, the others joining in. When I got to the line, 'just like ringing a bell', I rang one of our circuit testing bells, which at the time, was pretty funny. I doubt anyone else in earshot appreciated the impromptu performance, but we had a whale of a time.

Interspersed with the practical workshops were the theory tests. I always did well in those. It was an opportunistic two fingers to Justin because my lead in that area was unassailable. Everyone got through BETA though, failure was not an option. We learned skills for life, not just for Christmas.

1980. We were finally at the future, immersed in it. There was still no moon base, except for The Police, who were 'Walking on the Moon'. As slight compensation, I had a flight in a Chipmunk from Hamble on 12.01.80, It was in *WK630* for 21 minutes, and it was my final ever Chipmunk trip. I would have liked to have obtained a Flying Scholarship, but had I no idea how to; I don't recall anyone at 443 Squadron receiving one. Little Dudley became a Corporal and then a Sergeant; I was obviously becoming more and more disenfranchised by being ordered about because I wasn't being promoted. I was a working boy now, and making time for parades was getting hard. Rolfe and Ross left and some of the other elder boys, and it wasn't the same anymore. I was determined to hold out for Germany camp as a swansong.

Around February time, we were all invited to a party in Alton; I can't remember whose 17th birthday it was, but we all piled up to a respectable house on a housing estate on our mopeds. It was a Saturday evening, still light, so the neighbours must have had a panic at the sight of all these noisy yobs arriving. I hadn't really drunk much before then, and certainly didn't go in pubs until I was 17. Holden and Goatcher were our Alton guides, and we decided to visit the Off Licences to buy beer. About 20 of us set off to the High Street. The word was out there were some lads 'wanting a fight.' We start chasing them. The word goes up, 'They have knives!' We run away again. Such is the folly of youth. Back at the house, the music started, teenagers got pissed, the music got louder; at one point, we were all hushed up as the phone rang. The resident answered it; it was the parents, away for the evening. 'Yes, Mum, all quiet here.' *Tring.* Loud yells erupt, music back on, partay!

The house resembled closely the 'Quadrophenia' party scenes; dark rooms, boys and girls dancing in various ways and at varying levels of intoxication. No one took drugs; it was booze all the way. Jez and Sean were doing the hip swaying dance to 'Down Down' by Status Quo. It involved standing opposite each other, spinning hips then ducking to your partner's left and right alternately. They got the rhythm out of sync and smashed faces. Jez held his nose; he had broken the bridge of it. It was crooked for years. As we got progressively pissed, 'Hersham Boys' arrived on the stereo. We all started pogoing en masse, and changed the words to 'Beta boys.' It felt great, altogether, having fun, drunk as skunks.

There were train wrecks. I went into the loo and found Mr Saines, an Eaton apprentice, sitting on it, scratching his wrist with the sharp part of a pin badge. He was scraping lines in his arm. I left him to it. Later, I heard he was seen holding his dick, exclaiming, 'This isn't any bloody good to anyone!' I dubbed him Insaines after that.

Most of us had to crash overnight. Bedrooms were the privilege of the coupled, so it was grab some space time. Ian Ross and I were to grab a settee. The settee said, 'Let go.' It was a very cold, uncomfortable night, especially as we were both sitting upright. In the morning, I found someone had left their toe in my mouth; at least, that's what it tasted like. It was absolutely freezing. As the house slowly came to life, I scavenged for tea and toast. Everyone was worse for wear. What a great night!

Holden and I inspected our mopeds in the harsh February light. The sun was bright but weak; the ground was frozen and there had been a sharp frost. Beside the mopeds, which were on a steep drive, was a frozen trail of vomit, multi-coloured, disgusting. We boiled a kettle and used it to help defrost our bikes. It also released the sick, which trailed further down the drive on a sea of kettle water. Party goers emerged at regular intervals, and upon witnessing the mobile spew, retreated back inside. Eventually, we all went home, leaving the internal detritus to be cleaned away prior to the return of the owners. I don't know what they did about the sick.

It was soon to be March; my seventeenth birthday was coming up fast. That meant only one thing; I was soon to be old enough to ride a proper motorbike. I had saved the money, and Mum and Dad took me to a good bike shop in Southampton. I found a beautiful black Honda CB 125 T2, with a red and orange design on the tank that was definitely for me. I paid the deposit. I had already applied for the provisional licence. The day I rode the bike away, I was the happiest I had been in my life. Not only was it the bike I wanted, but I had bought it with my own money, brand new, in cash. I had a hand me down racing bike from David, a hand me down moped from David, this one was *mine*. Mind you, David had put money into a savings account for me when he started in the Army, so he definitely had helped me toward it. I'll always be grateful for that.

The new bike was wonderful because I could suddenly go faster than 30mph. Being another 4-stroke, it wasn't a speed merchant machine but it did have a top speed of 80mph; fast enough. It was the envy of all my mates. Now I could ride to college on it instead of using the train. Before all of that though, I enrolled on the Silver Star Rider course. This was a locally run training course, the next stage up from the Bronze that I had taken the previous year. It was supposedly above and beyond test standard, so after completing it, the driving test should be a breeze. It was helmed by a local policeman, who was the brother of the Beta Training Centre manager. I bought a white Bell helmet from Motorcycle Village in Farnborough. Stan had taken me there on the back of his Tiger. The vibration on that thing was phenomenal. Common themes bring people together; we were a close community because we all rode motorbikes.

Other third year apprentices were also heavily into music. Eugene Dabrowski (Huey) lived on South Ham, and he played bass and guitar. His parents were Polish; there weren't many living locally back then. Woody (Simon Wood) was a Fairy into sound design and recording; he would become very useful later on. Mitch Mansi was another third year but I never really engaged with him. He was wearing what I thought was a cross around his neck, and he turned on me vehemently. 'That's an *ankh*, you *cunt!*' I decided not to speak to him after that; pretty much ever. He was a crazy rider; he tipped himself off at high speed racing around the peri-track at Lasham. He was lucky he survived it; mind you, the track is bordered by open field, ploughed and seeded by a local farmer, so there was nothing to actually hit. Mark Gregory was another Fairy, we always got on well. The Fairies in the third year were great blokes and became my best mates at Lasham. The Heavies were not so friendly. Richard Carter was Pete Carter's son, one of the directors. Pete was alright, his son was a right bastard. Richard Carter had an excoriating tone to his voice, sarcastic and nasty; he would emphasise his cutting words by glaring his big eyes at you. He was also out of his head on drugs half the time so that probably explained it. The other was Keith. His dad worked in the Design office. I went to find Jez once and he was talking to Keith; he glanced at me, dismissively, and turned back to Jez. 'Who's Joe 90?' he asked, as if I wasn't there. There are all sorts of bullying, but this was pretty low, displaying his arrogance and perceived superiority. I never spoke to him on a personal basis, ever; first impressions last. Keith didn't end well.

*

Nan Heath was now 83 years old. She was finally going into wardened accommodation, in Love Lane, Mitcham. 18 Milton Road was sold, and the proceeds were divided amongst the family. Dad and his sisters received a few thousand each, and all the grandchildren £100. Fantastic, I now had the money for an electric guitar! I wasted no time in getting Mum to order a Gibson copy Hondo Les Paul in gloss black, small amp and fuzzbox. Oh, and don't forget the curly leads. When it arrived, I bought a 'teach yourself guitar' book from one of the town music shops, and attempted to put my fingers on an 'A' chord. *Bluk* went the strings. I don't think it's meant to sound like that. I tried again. *Bluuuk*. I'll work on that. And work I did, for an hour a night, every night. The fuzzbox was great, when I tired of struggling to pick the notes cleanly, I switched on the fuzz and let the sound descend into demented mush; instant heavy metal. Perseverance though, pays off. Within a few months I was getting quite good. Having played a stringed instrument for years, it definitely helped; the finger picking style Jackie taught me years before on acoustic, I still remembered how to do. I listened intently to records, and tried to emulate on my guitar what I thought I heard. It's a classic way to learn. Martin and the other playing apprentices showed me things, drew me chord diagrams; and when bands played on TV, I watched intently what they did with their hands.

It wasn't long before I outgrew my amp. A local music

shop by the bus station sold Vox amps. I bought what I believed was an AC30 'just like The Jam play through,' except it wasn't. It was a cheap transistor version, not a pucker valve amp. It was loud but a mere sonic shadow of the real thing. Apparently, Status Quo and Queen used the solid state versions in the seventies, but God knows why; the valve version, overdriven and wound up, was sonic heaven. This thing was bland and artificial, like aural nylon. Jazz players like transistor amps because they produce more clean tones. Rock players choose valves because that *is* the sound of rock. Ironically, if I had held onto it, it would have been worth using today as an occasional alternative, and a bit rare. At the time, I was peeved and desired to move on up to the real McCoy. It was still unbelievably heavy though; it would give you a hernia if you weren't careful. AC30s house two 12" speakers in a wooden cabinet. The green Celestion speakers (Greenbacks) are good, which these were, but it's the blue speakers that are the business.

March 1980. We finished at BETA. Hoorah! It's over! It really was like being released from prison after a dark, dreary winter. Everyone else at BETA had another six months to do – unlucky for them. We were to start properly at our big, green airfield. Holden suggested we go out for a ride on our bikes now that we were all riding better machines. I met him at The Avenue, the road that encircles the airfield. We rode into Alton, picking riders up along the way. A lot of them rode 250cc bikes, as that was the largest capacity you could have with a provisional licence. Against them, my poor little 125 struggled to keep up; plus, it was dark, and I had no idea where we were going. Every stage of the way, I was left behind. I ultimately decided it was a rubbish evening and thought better of going for an aimless ride again. It was certainly a freedom to ride to college on my motorbike, although the quickest route would be on the M3 motorway; as I had not yet passed my test that was not an option. On long rides it would get very cold; my hands would freeze although I had silk inner liners and thick gauntlets. It was a good job the weather would now get warmer. The most bizarre experience I had was riding in freezing fog; I could see virtually nothing around me, it was all whiteout and the visor kept covering with ice. It was very scary and slippery under the wheels to boot. On a bike, you can never be unaware of the road conditions; you feel it through the machine instantly.

Mum and Dad bought a little shed and gave it to me to house my motorbike. Every week, I washed it down and polished it so it was forever gleaming. Chris used to joke about the cleanliness of it, asking if he could brush his teeth in front of the exhaust pipe. He wasn't knocking the effort, though. Chris's dad drove him to work so he did not feel the need for transport of his own. It was also the time Sony launched the Walkman. I used to wear mine and listened to cassette copies of my records as I cleaned my bike.

The warts on my hands were horrible; the only way to truly get rid of them is to freeze them off with CO_2. The nurse at the local surgery, Brambly's Grange, tried at first with orange-coloured drops but ultimately resorted to the dry ice treatment. It was pretty painful having the super cold material applied to my fingers. Bound up with dressings, I could barely put my gloves on, let alone ride home. Thrashing my guitar one night, I realised the bridge area was covered in blood; I had sliced off a wart with the strings, unaware due to my immersion in concentration. It was a good solution but it stung like a bastard afterwards.

We started at Dan Air properly, straight into the classroom. Over the next couple of years, Ted would teach us about all the separate areas of an aircraft in specific subjects; airframe, engines, pressurisation, hydraulics, electrics, oil systems, fuel systems, pneumatic systems, wheels, tyres and brakes; there was a huge amount to learn. We would also spend a month at a time in a workshop, office or hangar. With over 600 people on site, it was a big place to get to know. Our first classroom sessions focussed on aircraft construction, learning about the earliest fabric covered aircraft to the modern aluminium and carbon fibre structures. We all thought it a bit anachronistic to learn how to apply dope to a biplane's wing, but that was what we had to learn; the method, the temperature, everything.

Pretty much every day, Holden, Kavanagh and Goatcher attempted, and mostly succeeded in winding me up. They would hide my notes during breaks, and I would struggle to find them before Ted started his lessons. Once or twice, they hid them in the room's loft; Ted was bemused to see me stand on desks and retrieve my work, but he knew what the buggers had been up to. He had a false upper plate, and after asking one of us to describe something he had taught earlier, he would slowly push the plate with his tongue, so his teeth would slowly advance through his upper lip. It always had us in stitches. Being constantly picked on by the Altonians though wasn't fun. It was akin to water torture, drip, drip, drip; after a while, those drips become as heavy as an ocean.

Ted was a natural orator. He told us that we were 75 more times more likely to be injured on a motorbike than in a car. 'And you know what the average age of a killed motorcyclist is? Twenty-nine. Twenty-nine years old!' He looked at us around the room. 'So when you're twenty-eight... (comedy pause)... you only have a year to go!'

My first assignment was in the stores. There was one central stores area, with hatches that opened into the corridor between Bay 1 and 2, and also in Bay 1 and 2. These Bays were the largest hangars, Bay 3 being ok for a 737 sized aircraft. Bay 4 was the newest hangar, and could just fit in a Boeing 707. Bay 1 would take the VC10, albeit with the tail in separate docks outside. We serviced and maintained Dan Air's fleet of Comets, B727s, B737-100 and –200, Bac 111 and various third party aircraft. The VC10 was the Sultan of Oman's private plane, complete with gold fittings. There were some very expensive sets of kit on that base. Tony was the storeman I had to work with. He issued out various tools and fittings to the hangar staff, cleaning agents and chemicals. Dan Air was absolutely choc a block with characters, and they all stuck their heads through those hatches.

'Tone, mornin' mate. Stick a glug of MEK in there, would ya? I also need some 15mm screws inch long and a cardboard box if you've got one mate, please.' It was Sean Walsh, an absolute livewire, ex-apprentice and future adversary. He was smoking a fag, illicitly, in the stores area and where inflammable chemicals were prevalent.

'Yes, I've got a box here with your initials on it Sean, look, C-U-N-T.' He pointed to imaginary writing on the cardboard.

'Ha bloody ha,' said Sean, sucking on his fag; he noticed a couple of the Asian fitters behind him were laughing. 'You can stop laughin' an' all, you bastards. All you do is come over 'ere, take our bleedin' jobs and shag all our wimmin.'

Walsh's jibes aside, it was a very cosmopolitan microcosmic society, elitist in many ways, but race and colour were irrelevant here. I had never seen such a diverse group, let alone meet them. We had Sikhs, Muslims, Christians and sinners all working together. Lead Technician (red collar) Kapur, 'Kappy' was a great bloke, he pretty much ran Bay 1; Sammy Sampson was a black Leading Mech (yellow collar) who ran around supporting everyone else.

I always got on well with the Asians. They kept themselves to themselves and took the ribbings well. Little Ollie was about five foot tall and had a nervous twitch. The more they took the piss out of him, the worse the twitch. He had been a Mahout in India, and sent money home every month to his wife still living there. Fred Sarkar was a middle-aged guy with black hair. Apparently he had been blown up in a terrorist incident in Nigeria and had a metal plate in his head. I don't think anyone was 'normal' at Lasham, and that included myself.

There were specific crews that worked out of particular bays. Sean was undoubtedly Bay 1, the busiest hangar and home to the more extreme chancers I had ever met. Drew had a dry sense of humour and was in charge of a pretty extensive porn selling and sharing operation. The video generation was good to him, he must have made a fortune renting dodgy European hardcore. Steve Emerson was pretty posh and was a stand out in this place; he went to a good school and was mercilessly mocked for his accent. He was very laid back and he became a very good mate. Everyone had additional skills they utilised whenever they could for an extra buck. Steve was a good photographer and took all the Dan Air photos on site.

After a while doling out various pieces of kit, including the largest spanner in the world named 'King Dick' (embossed on the side no less), I spent some time at Goods In/Goods Out. We had to learn the paperwork process of receiving and despatching goods, and it was pretty basic prior to the full introduction of computers. One of the store men tried to send me back to the main store for 'a tin of stripy paint.' I sussed it immediately and turned on my heels. They all tried to catch us out with tricks; the favourites they would send us for would be a left handed screwdriver, a long stand, bubble for a spirit level, tartan paint, a tin of elbow grease, skyhooks; I never fell for it. Jock was another store man. His real name was Davy but Jock sufficed. 'Alright, mite?' he used to say in his strangulated Scottish/Cockney hybrid. He would often disappear with his cart, dispensing rotables, i.e. repaired components that had been returned from repair. Many of the aircraft components were serviced on site, and we would become adept at servicing them.

Ernie Vorstat was a jolly fellow. He had a German accent and walked slowly around the site. He was a portly old boy, very friendly and genial. It turned out he was an ex-POW and decided to stay in England, because 'I like it here.' The whole world seemed to converge at Dan Air. Locked in our parochial schools for over a decade, we were suddenly exposed to real life. All my friends at sixth form, surrounded by their contemporaries, would take years to catch up with the life experience.

I was walking around the back of the workshops when I bumped into Holden. 'You heard the news? We've lost a 727 in Tenerife. No one can believe it.' It was April 25th. DA Flight 1008 had indeed crashed into the mountains in Tenerife, killing 146 people, at that time, the worst ever air disaster for a British-registered aircraft. The base was stunned, in shock. Everyone tried to carry on as normal but everyone's thoughts eventually turned to themselves; is my job safe? Why did it crash? Was it anything I did, or didn't do? That 727, G-BDAN, had flown from Manchester.

As apprentices, we hadn't even touched an airplane yet so we knew it was all outside of our experience. Nestled in the centre of the workshops was a small little area where they looked after the FDRs, or Flight Data Recorders, aka the 'black box'. I don't know why they called them that as they were anything but black; usually yellow or other bright colour to be easily found in aircraft wreckage. I don't recall the exact last words on the recorder but it was something like 'Shit.'

It took a long time, as it always does, to get to the bottom of the crash causes. There is never one thing that causes a crash, it is a series of little incidents that taken together, add up to a major disaster. In this case, the aircrew were instructed to fly into an approach pattern that was different to what they were used to, and for what they no procedure for; also, the Spanish air traffic control kept talking in Spanish instead of the official English they were supposed to. This confused the crew, who were tasked with descending into cloud very close to a large mountain. They effectively were in the wrong position, and when the GPWS (Ground Proximity Warning System) whooped at them to pull up, they had no chance to overcome the situation; a tight ascending right turn with power full on was not enough to clear the mountain and they crashed right into it. The inquiry determined the pattern set and heights were actually incompatible with the aircraft's performance envelope; it was effectively unflyable.

As horrific any air crash is, and the subsequent loss of life, many at Lasham would have breathed sighs of relief; at least it wasn't mechanical or servicing failure. I was to witness plenty of that in future.

In the classroom with Ted, we would learn about the bureaucracy of the aviation business, Air Navigation Orders, the Civil Aviation Authority, the Federal Aviation Administration, Airworthiness Directives, the Maintenance Manual, Repair Manual, Overhaul Manual. It seemed never ending. We learned the ATA 100 chapters by rote – pneumatics was chapter 36, power plant 71 etc. It was technical shorthand adopted by the Air Transport Association in 1956 and became a standard used in all commercial aviation.

We all had to spend time in the Technical Records department. It was like walking into a morgue. The man in charge, John Mac, short for McLaughlin, was a tall, bespectacled misanthrope with the air of a dead librarian. He spoke quietly but authoritatively. He was in charge but he didn't possess any spark whatsoever. The room was full of filing cabinets and semi-filed personnel. It was a young team, seemingly struck dumb by the orders of the boss to maintain the decorum of a church. The only sounds were coming from the teleprinter that occasionally displayed internationally transmitted telexes and aviation gobbledegook. We had basic VDUs around the base, but there were no personal computers back then. The VDUs had a green display and the processing power of a fridge.

Malcolm Vincent was second in command. Malcolm had two other brothers working on site; Brother Alan also worked in the offices. Malcolm was wispy haired, nearly bald, fat with ever depleting teeth. A mate later dubbed him 'Central Eating' because he had a gap right in the middle of his plates. I liked Malcolm though, at least he was breathing. The other resident of note was Dawn. She was gorgeous, about a year older than us. She sat there, lovely, whilst each successive apprentice lusted after her. She was bloody moody though. Good job it was only the one month in residence. Mac tested me on my ATA100 knowledge; I knew it inside out, that impressed him. I learnt what I needed to in that department, but I came out metaphorically covered in dust.

Our final year would focus on power plant, the first three on airframes. Therefore, we wouldn't spend too much time yet on engines. Ted briefed us on what to do when we went into the Wheel Bay.

'When you go in there, and inflate aircraft tyres, you WILL use the cage. The safety cage is there to protect you if a tyre overinflates. The guys in there don't use it; YOU will.'

That's great, Ted. But as soon as you entered a workshop, local rules apply.

Paul was the head guy in the Wheel Bay. There were only two of them. Paul was a cool bloke who rode a large Honda but also drove a Mini. He had thinning black hair and sideburns, and was quite powerfully built. His sidekick was wiry but apparently quite strong; you had to be, to manipulate the huge aircraft wheels.

'We don't use the safety cage,' started Paul. 'It just gets in the way. We've never had a problem, anyway.' We've never had a problem anyway; it's like saying, I haven't died yet, why worry?

Nose wheels and main wheels from all the aircraft would come into the bay. 727 main wheels were the largest – they came up to the top of my chest. The tyre, wheel core and brake pack were extremely heavy, and the normal way to transport them around site was by rolling them. Between hangars were ramps that made controlling errant wheels very tricky; quite a few times, I lost a 727 main wheel only for it to crash into a wall or door. Thankfully I never injured anyone, except myself; if they toppled, it took two people to lift it.

Once inside the relative safety of the bay, the first task was to let the air out of the tyres, then to 'crack the bead'. We did this with a pneumatic press. The alloy core was cleaned and degreased in a detergent bath, scrubbed by hand; the tyres would be inspected for damage. The brake pack, which consisted of the hydraulic anti-lock brake mechanism on a mount plate, was sent to the Brake Bay for separate servicing.

We lifted the wheels with a block and tackle, and would check for leaks by lowering them into a huge tank of water. I could see why using the cage was cumbersome but it wasn't that time consuming; the idea was you inflated the tyre in the cage to avoid damage from an exploding wheel. I later got to know a colleague who was badly injured in that very scenario.

The hardest job was to tighten the wheel nuts to the correct torque. Even with a metre long torque wrench and hanging off it with my whole bodyweight, I couldn't torque a 727 main. The other guys thought it hilarious, and said I looked like a monkey swinging on the wrench. It was embarrassing; I wasn't a very heavy 'heavy'. It was a small site; the other lads took the Mickey when they learnt of my difficulties. It seemed everything we did was reported back to each other through the medium of the gossip internet. Who needed Facebook?

Jez told me that Weybridge College was unbelievably lax. The guys seemed to spend most sessions in the pub. We worked hard at Farnborough. It just confirmed what I felt about Justin and Steve, not clever enough to follow our college course but with mouths bigger than their brains, and the ability to criticise everyone else.

Scrubbing aircraft wheels whilst inhaling the sharp smell of detergent gave me the distinct feeling that I was definitely in the wrong job. I thought that working with aircraft would somehow be, well, *cleaner*; they never seemed to give the impression they got so dirty. I enjoyed acquiring the technical knowledge, but the practical, I hated. Thankfully, I was given a temporary reprieve.

Mark Gregory was working on a project with one of the technical staff. Geoff, the Tech Director, had to reverse engineer a series of modifications and employed a few apprentices to draw up the technical specs. I was brought in to help. I spent a few months drawing sub-standard drawings, basically as I was instructed, for the whole exercise to be scrapped. It put me in the frame with the senior staff though, which had been a good thing. Plus, it was clean in the drawing office. I never was much cop at Technical Drawing, although I liked it. It was a pleasant, although fruitless, diversion.

Waller had bought himself a silver RD250, a Yamaha 2-stroke that was became almost ubiquitous as the Fizzy; it was popular with speed freaks and had the requisite 'eggceleration' Justin craved; however it was tinny and noisy, and pumped out reams of blue smoke. Justin bought a Suzuki GT250, Ian went very boutique and obtained a Harley-Davidson Cagiva 185. It was an easy rider style bike with a lazy, laid back riding position. He loved it. It didn't last too long. Still with a cripplingly long HP schedule in front of him, he collided with a young cyclist who jumped off the pavement into his path, and virtually wrote off the bike. He assured me it was completely the lad's fault, who wasn't hurt, but now Rossi had no bike and a huge debt to boot. It took a long time for him to recover from that one.

Holden bought himself a trail style bike. Jez liked trail bikes but eventually he outdid us all. He bought a Honda Superdream CB 250 in blue; the bike I had set my heart on next. The bigger the bike, the more the insurance turned out to be. It worked out approximately a pound per cc back then, i.e. I paid around £120 and therefore Jez had to find double that. It was a lovely bike, though. The more we mixed with other bikers, the more incidents you heard about. One of Jez's mates, whom I had met at a party, left another evening do and crashed straight into the back of an unlit skip. He was out of action for a little while with that one.

Jez was so up and down with Emma. He came into work with a bandaged hand. He went to a party where he had an argument with her, and ended up punching a tree, breaking a bone.

'That was pretty bloody stupid, Mr Cotterell,' I told him. 'Now you can't even pleasure yourself if you do break up.' Jez let out a wry grin; he didn't want to face the inevitable. It all seemed such a pointless charade; he kissed her, she kissed him, he fancies her, she storms off. Teenage love? Bah.

Justin thought himself the Valentino of the indentured. Oh how could any girl resist; surely not the fatuous dialogue, the bulbous lips, or the tickly little bat under his nose? The only thing he had over me was around two inches in height. I stood up to him once against his aggressive attitude and he squared up to me. 'I'll 'ave you, yer cunt.' It didn't command respect, only pity. He was a sad individual, cowering under the cloak of intimidating stock phrases and repellent dialogue. How I despised him. I was getting to the point when I would crack. I didn't know how much more of the constant wearing down I could take.

Anyway, I met all the others' girlfriends. Only at Crufts could you assemble a better set of dogs.

The music of 1980 was proving to be as great as the previous year. Spandau Ballet broke through and introduced New Romanticism into the charts. I loved Gary Numan's solo work such as 'Cars', The Vapors' 'Turning Japanese' and The Specials' 'Too Much Too Young'. My old favourites, Elvis Costello and The Jam were still riding high. Mum and I visited Jackie at Cambridge the weekend when 'Going Underground' by The Jam was released. It was an unbelievably prescient track; during our time there, there was an anti-nuclear rally and CND march, and Weller had just released a song about going underground to escape politicians, rockets and bombs. I saw the video on a telly in a shop window but I was still yet to hear the music. I bought the single in Cambridge and was dying to play it. Finally, in the car on the way home, I heard it played on Radio 1. I was enraptured. The best three minute pop single ever made, never surpassed, and never will be; especially as it was only two minutes 50.

12. Bombs Away

RAF Laarbruch, Germany Annual Camp 1980. I'm sixth from the left at the rear. P/O Ratcliffe is at the RH end. (MOD Photo)

I had been chosen to attend RAF Germany camp. I was over the moon. I could also pay for the trip myself. It was to be at RAF Laarbruch, close to the Dutch border. It was a fully operational fighter base on the front line; exciting. The downside was, I was the only one from 443 Squadron to go, as there were limited places.

The only time I had travelled abroad before that was a day trip to Calais with the family. We had two holidays on Guernsey but they didn't count. The Calais trip was on the SRN4 hovercraft from Ramsgate in 1977. We had a lovely time in the market town of Calais, stuffing lots of wonderful French cheese and baguette. Unfortunately the crossing on the channel on the way back was 'moderate to rough', according to the captain. I found it very rough; I managed to review my lunch about four times in the brief 40-minute return journey, as did many others.

The Germany trip left from Luton airport, late August 1980. I was in the queue to board the Britannia 737 when a cadet behind me said, 'Oy, mate.' I turned to see him open what appeared to be a flick knife. I jumped a foot till I realised it was a flick comb. He laughed, as did his mate. Yeah mate, very funny. Fuck off.

It was only a brief flight, less than 90 minutes, until we touched down at RAF Wildenrath, or 'Wilders'. There were a few airfields close to another, the other main one apart from Laarbruch was Bruggen. I caught sight of the HAS, or Hardened Aircraft Shelters that housed the Harriers, Jaguars or Phantoms on the front line. We were definitely not in Kansas anymore, Toto.

We were bussed to RAF Laarbruch, on the western tip of Germany. There seemed to be a lot of forests; the Germans are big on trees. The station motto was: 'Ein feste burg', which meant a mighty fortress. The first thing I saw was the bank, the word 'Sparkasse' detailed across the building. I had never studied German and it seemed a funny word. It was greener than a UK base; the trees were taller, denser and lined all the roads. We were emptied into a long barrack block with uniform square windows. It was a working military base, everything was perfunctory; nothing was pretty.

In our billet, we had a decent enough Flight Sergeant in charge of us. Most of the lads were aged 17 or 18, the oldest in our billet was 19. They were a good bunch, and although there was to be competition with the other billets, we all mixed pretty well. The first thing we all noticed was the tone. The regulars were very serious, almost embittered; it was a tense, terse atmosphere, a front line station. If Russia kicks off, it kicks off here. There would be many opportunities for the camp personnel to express their frustrations.

I became friendly with two guys, Ollie and Daryl. Ollie was from Fordingbridge, in south west Hampshire. He was a sandy-haired little guy, quite cheeky but amenable. Daryl was darker, with a Hampshire accent; both were a bit younger than me. I tended to avoid the jocks, because they were always wankers. We had a couple in the room but there was no major animosity. One guy from Oxford was very well spoken and was in the middle of his Flying Scholarship – the Holy Grail. I surmised he was public school and somehow wangled it through the right connections. The black guy thought he was the dog's bollocks, and his attitude reminded me of Justin. Avoid. To a point, I could be someone else here; no one knew me, we were all blank pages to one another. I had learnt to keep my personal cards to my chest; the Dan Air apprentices knew each other inside out and abused that knowledge to mock mercilessly.

A junior RAF officer was to look after all us during our week's stay. Pilot Officer Ratcliffe was a fresh-faced young thing straight out of Officer School. He was a very pleasant chap and had a keen sense of humour. We were given the dos and don'ts whilst on the camp, and it was a lot more stringent on the already apparent security of a UK base, as would be expected.

Our building was on the edge of the woods. We were told not to go wandering too far at night, lest we walk too close to the radar and ended up sterile. Good warning. Also, the RAF regiment, who protected the regulars, carried out regular patrols with dogs, normally German shepherds. As the dogs didn't speak English, it would be best not to engage with them either. No one warned us about the other assorted nut jobs but we would come across them in our own time.

It was warm; very warm. The cicadas would chirp into the night, and the air felt, well, foreign. The humidity was a lot higher than at home. The first and every morning, we woke up to find half of us savaged by mosquito bites. The black guy suffered the worst; they seemed to love his skin. His face was covered in lumps and bumps all week. It was a good wake up, so every night I wore my long-sleeved rugby top; I was hardly bitten.

I had been writing a diary assiduously for a few years. Each evening, I would jot down my thoughts and feelings of the day, and I stored my diary in my locker. I didn't bring much else from home, except my trusty Agfa camera. This was effectively the apotheosis of summer camps, both in my abilities and the location itself. I had learnt to fly, to command weapons, to navigate, to present myself smartly, even to iron a bloody shirt (although I swiftly lost that skill). It all fostered discipline, temperance, equanimity and a steely attitude. I was on my own here, although amongst equals, and I wasn't letting anyone in too close.

We were given a basic agenda for the week. There was a billet presentation competition, so the standard routine; cleaning, mopping floors, bed packs, smart drill, etc. We would be training with SLRs, the 7.62 Self Loading Rifle; we would have a night exercise with the RAF Regiment, oh goody, we were all looking forward to that one... We would also explore the environs of the base, have some demos from the demolition squad, and some visits to Holland war cemeteries. It was quite a mixed bag, but it would keep us busy.

We lined up for the standard photo, all of us in front of a Hawker Hunter. I wrote all the names on the back but after 34 years and being stuck down in an album, I tore it trying to peel it off. All the names are there but inaccessible. Damn.

We were all keen to fire the SLR. It had been used by the RAF for some time but up until now we only had access to the ageing Lee Enfield. We had to learn to strip it completely and reassemble it before we were allowed anywhere near the range. Some of us were also blindfolded and told to assemble the weapon. That took a bit longer. We eventually lined up on the outdoor range to fire a dozen rounds or so.

As we lay on the grassy bank, going through final rehearsals with empty weapons, a black RAF sergeant dressed in camouflage gear drilled us one by one. As I waited for my turn, I felt something nip me. Ouch. There it was again; and again. I looked down to see I was lying on an ants nest. These weren't the average British ant; these were Teutonic monsters, bred on euro rations and nuclear mutation. They were huge with red thoraxes and a really bad attitude. I started, or tried, to brush them off. No sooner had I removed 10 I gained 20. In the end, I stood up, raised my hand to the Sergeant that I required assistance, and wriggled and writhed to remove myself from my denim overall. The Sergeant came over and was quite amused; he helped me brush the little critters off. That certainly amused the other lads, at least I was a talking point for something I couldn't foresee or control.

On the range itself, I found the SLR a surprisingly difficult weapon to use. The recoil was pretty low, much less than the .303, but having the ability to fire without reloading caused me to fire off too quickly, so my aim suffered. Plus, I forgot the number of rounds I had fired. I certainly wouldn't achieve the marksmanship badge again based on this performance, but it was the first time. I had also been bitten to buggery, the little bastards.

In the evening, we were allowed off base and sauntered down to the local town. There was a wide cycle track next to the pavement and the locals seemed to actively encourage riding bikes. It was quite disturbing to see young lads without helmets riding mopeds, which they could do at 15. It all seemed a lot more laid back compared to the UK. One of the lads bought some chips and shared that you had to order 'frites'. I joked that if we ordered Fritz then his wife might get jealous.

Early in the week, we were taken aboard the bus to the town of Nijmegen, in Holland, and to the Philips museum in Eindhoven. We passed over the bridges at Arnhem. We also visited the Overloon war museum and cemetery. It was a lot of travelling, but there was a lot to see. In Eindhoven, the Philips museum was a real place of wonder. It resembled a huge saucer-shaped spaceship. Inside, there were prototype mock ups of the new digital medium, compact disc. This would be the future, they said – they were right, it was. We were let loose for a couple of hours on the streets of Nijmegen. Ollie, Daryl and I looked in a few shops, and resisted the urge to buy clogs. One wag did, the same guy who bought the 'frites'. He was a bit like Neil from 'The Inbetweeners', but with a no. 1 haircut.

Crossing the Arnhem suspension bridge was quite an evocative moment. I had seen the Attenborough film 'A Bridge Too Far' many times, and knew the story of Operation Market Garden. This was the allied assault on Hitler's troops on the Rhine, prefaced with a large paratrooper and glider assault that ended in failure. It was strange standing on one of the very bridges, the scene of those battles. Overloon museum brought the same feelings, as we sat on tanks from the period and read all the history. There was a lot of information and photos of the death camps, which was very upsetting. The worst of all, we walked along the lines and lines of graves in the war cemetery. Row after row of gravestones, many of which had no names, only 'a soldier killed in the conflict, known unto God.' There were so many of them. All of them died so we could live in freedom. I felt I owed them all. They would have been young men, some not much older than me. All of us were sobered by that visit; the bus was noticeably quieter on the way back to camp.

There were great facilities on site at Laarbruch, a really good NAAFI, a bowling alley and a cinema. One night we watched Blake Edwards' '10' with Dudley Moore and Bo Derek. They had popped by for a coffee and decided to watch the film with us. Afterwards, we were ordered to stand, the Union flag appeared on screen, and the National Anthem played. Good old, jolly old England. Rather, what what. Except, we weren't in England, we were in Germany. It all felt a little surreal.

We were expected to walk to the destinations we were

assigned to in a smart, dignified manner. One of the lads couldn't find his beret. Oh, dear. We only progressed 100 yards or so and there was a yell from above.

'Oi! You! Yes, you? Where is your beret?'

Someone indeterminate was shouting from the top window of a barrack block. The hatless one offered a weak, 'I don't know.' The shouting thing continued for some time, asked the lad's name, squadron and the name of his NCO. Then he went. We walked on. That was a bit harsh and unnecessary, I thought. It seems the tension on this base was so high the residents needed to find an excuse to let off steam.

We visited the Harrier and Jaguar squadrons and got up close and personal with these high-tech fighters. One of the most interesting areas was the Bloodhound missile section. At a separate location on the edge of the base, approx. 40 or so of these pointy wonders stood, sentinel, all pointing east. Nearly 28 feet long, these Surface to Air Missiles (SAM) were one of our main defence systems during the Cold War. Supposedly the top speed was Mach 2.7. The following is according to the internet: "By the time the missile has just cleared the launcher it is doing 400mph. By the time the missile is 25 feet from the launcher it has reached the speed of sound (around 720mph). Three seconds after launch, as the four boost rockets fall away, it has reached Mach 2.5 which is roughly 1,800mph."

I asked the guy showing us the missiles what explosive was used. He was dismissive.

'I think they stuff these things with nuts and bolts,' he said. 'If it hits you at the speed it does, you're done for anyway.'

I felt I was a Russian target just standing there. It was all a bit unnerving.

That evening, I went for a shower with the others at the end of the corridor. As I walked back, alone, someone shouted at the top of their voice, 'Freeze, you bastard!'

I looked right toward the source of the sound. It was coming from a man in a room off the corridor, who was pointing his Colt service weapon right at my head. I looked into his squinting eyes. Go on mate; shoot. Go on, shoot. I *dare* you. You fuck. After an eternity, probably five seconds, he raised the muzzle toward the ceiling and started laughing hysterically. I continued at the same pace the final few yards to our billet.

Heads were peering around the billet door, alerted by the commotion.

'What was that, Heathy? What's going on?'

I told the lads who were all intent on knowing what was going down. I told them what had happened, that I had calmly stared down what I believe to have been a loaded weapon. Then I started to shake, involuntarily.

The Flight Sergeant was helpful. 'He's Regiment. They are the guys with the weapons, and they keep them loaded at all times.'

Great, and we were going on exercise with these madmen?

Tonight though, was an exercise of a different kind. We went across the base in the 4-tonner, all piled in the back. It bumped and jostled for ages until we were well into the woods. An explosives team were to give us a demonstration of how to blow shit up. Great, as long as it wasn't us. It was all outside, on a tarmac area, blown up cars and bits were all around. To begin with, the lead guy showed us thunderflashes. He explained we would see a lot of these this week. We exchanged knowing glances. Then he lit a few, to demonstrate how loud they were.

'If you see one near you, or coming towards you, go in the opposite direction. Under no circumstances, pick one up when lit! It will blow your hand off.'

No shit, Sherlock. He set a few off. Bloody hell, they were

bright and loud, just as states on the tin. It was indeed a 'thunderflash'.

Next, he showed us a handful of what appeared to be plasticine.

'This is plastic explosive, about half a pound. This small amount will happily punch a hole in a vehicle or building. If I explode it in my hand, it will damage me, but if I contain it, with my fist, it will take half my arm off. It needs to be packed against something to be effective.'

An explosive demonstration, RAF Laarbruch 1980.
(Trevor Heath Archive)

To demonstrate, they set it up under a heavy ammo box. We were retired about 70 yards away. PO Ratcliffe ensured we were well back.

We put our fingers in our ears, not knowing quite what to expect. There was a long delay, and suddenly there was a huge flash, followed by an almighty bang. Smoke billowed everywhere. The box had disappeared. It was a good few seconds before large chunks of it rained down from the heavens.

'Jesus! That was only half a pound?'

They told us they were setting up a bigger bomb, to blow up the already blown up carcass of a car in a walled area across the way. They tried, we stood way, way back, but they failed. For some reason, it didn't go off. Oh well, never return to a lit firework.

It had been a very interesting evening. We were taken back to the NAAFI for a late supper. We were always hungry.

As usual, just before bed, I wrote down my thoughts for the day in my diary. Someone was obviously keen to know what I was writing.

With all the trips in the bus, the evening activities and the evening cleaning, we were getting worn out. I slept absolutely soundly all night. We would start the week ebullient and raring to go, by midweek we were all flagging and falling asleep on the bus.

During this night, I was woken by an aggressive, drunken voice. It was a cook, who had found his way to the Flight Sergeant's bunk just down from mine. He was shining a torch in the poor lad's face, ranting in a Scottish accent. Cooks in the RAF were *always* Scottish.

'We're goin' to get you, you bastards. You wait for the night o' the exercise, we're goin' to do you all good and proper!'

We all acted immediately. By acting immediately, I mean we all lay there, immobile, terrified to move. It was still an action, just without movement. Eventually, the less than jocular jock sloped away, and we all let out an audible sigh of relief.

'Anyone wishing to leave the base form an orderly queue,' joked the Flight Sergeant.

It was mind games, but we couldn't be sure. It was meant to rattle us, and it certainly did.

One of the lads, called James, had bought a flick knife in the Dutch shops. James had gained something of a reputation all week as a bit of a prat. We were warned the purchase of such knives was not allowed, nor would it be acceptable through customs. On the bus returning from a shopping trip, the public schoolboy let rip with a loud diatribe, berating his stupidity. It was quite funny and the rhythm of his delivery predestined his predictable future as an after dinner speaker.

'Hey lads, we all went shopping today. Most of us bought biscuits for Mummy and Daddy because we're good little cadets, but not James; no, he bought a HUGE fucking knife, cos he's REALLY ROCK, and he has to show the world that he's tougher than everybody else. And James got to play with some big rifles this week, not a puny .22 like he's been used to, but an SLR, which James thought was REALLY ROCK,' etc., etc.

I suspect James had used the phrase 'Really Rock' and this was his reward. Poor sod.

I rang home a couple of times. It was pretty expensive; the payphone gobbled all my change like it hadn't eaten for a week. It was good to hear their voices, though. I was alright, I was enjoying it immensely. The sense of trepidation was building though, due to the impending evening with the Regiment guys, the 'Rock Apes.'

I returned to the billet, and went for a shower. When I returned, I noticed something was not quite right in my locker; my diary was missing. I was instantly incensed; how dare anyone, especially anyone in this room, think it acceptable to rifle through my things, let alone take my diary? It was full of intimate thoughts and observations, and more pertinently, slagged off a number of cadets within the immediate vicinity.

'Right, you lot, who has taken my diary? No fucking about, I want it back NOW, no messing about! If it doesn't come back RIGHT NOW you'll be in deepest shit!'

I used my most shouty voice possible; until now, I had been amiable, reasonable, without authority. I felt it appropriate to unleash my dark side to get results.

At first, everyone feigned ignorance. I stamped my feet louder until there was movement; the black guy retrieved it from his locker and handed it back.

'You know you should really watch that temper of yours,' he said, with less threat implied than surprise at my reaction. That was the point; I went from cold granite to volcano in less than a second; the way psychos do. It was an act but it got results.

It was a good job no one had a chance to read it; I was more scathing about the black guy than any of them. His kleptomania proved my point; he wasn't to be trusted. But then, now I couldn't trust anybody. I didn't know this bunch; we weren't from the same squadrons. We were all getting on ok and then he had to spoil it. Years later I saw the film, 'Biloxi Blues'. There was a scene very close to my experience when the main character, played by Matthew Broderick, has his diary stolen and read out aloud to his billet buddies; they are sceptical until they realise he has appraised them in his writing. I might have got beaten up.

The week was coming to an end; the Thursday evening was to be the exercise with the Rock Apes.

After dinner, on a warm, sunny evening, we were all loaded into the back of the 4-tonner. As the vehicle bounced and jostled around the tracks into the woods, we held on tight to the sides of the tarp. We were all feeling a large sense of trepidation, but we were vocal, noisy, in good spirits. Suddenly, we were all thrown forward on top of one another as the truck screeched to a halt. Outside all hell was breaking loose; machine gun fire opened up all around us and we all instinctively hit the deck. Explosions were going off and the side of the truck was being hit loudly, amid lots of shouting and general ruckus. He was very noisy, was General Ruckus. When Dad was in Palestine, he said when he had to duck for cover on hearing gunfire, that his arse was going 'half a crown/sixpence.' I finally knew what he meant.

We lay on the floor of the truck, looking at each other, wild-eyed, desperate to work out what the hell was going on; no one spoke.

'Come on out you fucking bastards!' screamed a voice outside. The sides of the truck were being hit again; it was a 360 degree aural assault. No one moved a muscle.

'Right, if you won't come out, we'll fucking smoke you out!'

I could see figures moving about through the back of the truck, but I couldn't see much; there was smoke everywhere and explosions going off at intervals.

Insidiously, red and orange smoke rose through the floor. Within seconds, it filled the cabin, and we all moved to the tailgate and jumped out into the daylight. I tripped over the tailgate and effectively fell onto the tarmac a few feet below. Blinking into the light, able to breathe again, I could now see what was causing all the noise. Twenty or so camouflaged rock apes with blackened faces surrounded the truck, aiming weapons at us that had yellow muzzles. Some were lying on the ground, others were standing; thunderflashes were the cause of the explosions. Yellow and orange smoke drifted around the truck and dissipated through the woods.

The voice ordered us to the ground; we didn't argue. Eventually, he spoke again.

'Right, first lesson: Why didn't any of you try to get away?'

It was almost a comical line. Try to get away? How? We

were in the back of a closed truck without any firearms and they have machine guns! At least, it seemed like a friendly voice set in the heart of a snarling lion.

We were allowed to get up, weapons were lowered. Ratcliffe appeared – ah, this is the exercise and not the breakout of World War Three. We had absolutely no idea what was happening, although we knew that we had an evening with the regiment. It was the element of surprise, an ambush. Our hearts could now beat a little slower; for a little while.

We moved on to another area, well away from the main buildings of the base. The guys showed us the weapons they were using. They had BFAs on, the yellow muzzle attachments. These were Blank Firing Adaptors, which capture the debris produced from the blank round, otherwise they can cause injury. We were told that blank ammunition would be used throughout the evening, but not to deliberately get too close to the muzzles as they could still be dangerous, and the warning about running away from thunderflashes was reiterated.

Ollie asked one guy about his sten gun. He wanted to know what it sounded like and felt like to fire. The ape aimed it in the air and let off half a dozen rounds. The sharp crack of each round being released echoed around the woods; unfortunately for Daryl, the expelled shell casings poured out in a line from the weapon and straight down the neck of his open shirt. He started dancing a jig as he struggled to retrieve the boiling hot metal from against his skin. It was hilarious and scary at the same time. The night was an open book and we had just started the chapter.

We were lined up to listen to the Chief Rock ape. He told us that we were to imagine we are on a guard post and an individual was trying to get past. He handed an SLR loaded with blanks to the first cadet.

'You are not authorised to shoot unless you believe your life or the lives of others are in danger. Now, defend your position.'

A heavy, thuggish-looking Rock Ape, the 'intruder', tried to saunter past the cadet.

'Halt!' the cadet ordered, his weapon aimed at the thug. 'Who are you and where are you going?'

The thug employed various tactics; silence, bullshit, any old story.

Chief broke the play acting scenario with punch in information.

'Well, what do you do? How so you prove who he is?'

The cadet rang an imaginary telephone to an imaginary assistant.

'The phone's cut off. Isn't it best to ask for some identification?

The cadet tried that next, still aiming the weapon at the thug, who stood there with his hands up.

'Do you have ID?'

Thug reached in his top pocket, and threw down what looked like an identity card. It plopped to the feet of the cadet. As soon as he lowered his gaze, the thug took his opportunity; he grabbed the muzzle of the weapon, and pushed hard, jabbing his accuser in the ribcage. As the cadet buckled in pain, and the rest of us stood shocked at the viciousness of the assault in which was supposed to be role play, the thug took the weapon, aimed at the cadet and 'shot' him.

The echo from the shot attenuated.

'Second lesson; do not lose possession of your weapon! You are now dead and cannot defend your position!' He had a very droll sense of humour. Maybe the cook was right; they were out to get us.

Ratcliffe helped the cadet get up, still nursing his ribs. *That's not happening to me*, I thought. The next guy obviously thought the same. He didn't let the thug get too close, but was unsure what to do when he started walking away. The cadet moved the selector switch from 'Safe' to 'Repetition'. Ratcliffe put his fingers in his ears. He wouldn't, would he? Bang! He certainly would; he 'shot' the intruder in the back. He got an earful for that.

'We don't shoot people in the back,' said Chief, retrieving the weapon from the hapless murderer. 'We will work down the line until you get it right.'

It was my turn. Oh Jesus. I didn't want to make a fool of myself and be made an example of. I took my position. Thug came a walkin'. I raised the weapon, and ordered him to identify himself. As before, he threw down a plastic card. I ordered him back, well back... and I picked up the card. It was a joke ID, stating 'Member of Playboy Bunny club'.

'This isn't valid identification,' I barked. 'Do you have valid identification?' I kept the weapon raised. Thug started toward me, pretending he had, but was trying to get closer.

'Stop right there!' I shouted. It was an impossible situation to control with blanks, as it wasn't real. I had no means to communicate with others who should be around to assist; it could only end in stalemate. Thug performed the same tactic and walked away. I saw Ratcliffe put his fingers in his ears; my finger was on the trigger but I knew I wasn't going to fire. The thug walked away and I lowered the weapon. I was intact, no injury to me, but I didn't get an ID and thug boy was on the loose.

'Ok', said Chief. 'He didn't illegally shoot the intruder but he was shouting at him so much he was starting to enjoy it.' Was I? Not so sure about that, Chief. More like I didn't fancy a butt in the ribcage. The first cadet was rubbing his chest all evening.

'Make sure you ask for valid identification. If they can't produce valid ID then they are not getting past you. If they try to go where they are not allowed, then you can place them under arrest. Only as a last resort, if your life is in danger, are you permitted to shoot. We do NOT shoot people in the back just because they walk away!'

Lesson over; it was beginning to get dark. The Apes showed us their image intensifiers; they could see in the dark with infrared technology. Look through the viewfinder and everything is green, but figures stand out a mile. The final part of the exercise was to protect our VIP; in this case, the Flight Sergeant. It was a highly weighted game of hide and seek. We would have 10 minutes to hide and they would come and find us, one by one. If they captured the Flight Sergeant, it was game over.

Right, we're supposed to hide and they have night vision? It was a bit of a joke. I secreted myself in a small bushy area under a tree; as it was dark, I couldn't see well enough to securely secrete myself in the foliage. I was found in minutes. Blanks were going off everywhere; muzzle flashes lit the scene at various times. A fizz, a whoosh... thunderflash! Make sure you're nowhere near it. It was half an hour of sonic mayhem in the dark. I had no idea what was going on. A call went up; they had caught the Flight Sergeant. Game over.

It was pretty late now; probably all of 9:30 pm. It seemed like a very long but enjoyable few hours of terror. Before we retired, the Apes let us fire the weapons in the dark; a machine gun sat on its support legs, and I was able to fire off some rounds into the darkness. Shell casings zinged everywhere onto the tarmac, all types of weapons were being let off in a cacophonous orgy. It was time to go. We loaded onto the 4-tonner and were dropped off at the mess for a late supper of fish and chips. Wonderful. We had survived.

0500 hours. We had to get up and start cleaning the mess for final inspection. Yawning, I helped move beds, sweep floors, dust and clean. An hour later, we went back to bed for another hour or so. Then it was up again, make bed packs, and prepare for the verdict. We had done it; we had achieved the most points and had won the best kept billet award. Our prize was a copy of the RAF magazine each. I was pretty pleased with that, and our efforts. We pulled together well as a team, although at the start of the week, nobody knew anybody else. We had travelled for miles around Holland and had been given an insight into the workings and mind-set of personnel on a front line operational base. I had met many taciturn and serious individuals on my time in the ATC, but never so many aggressive and uncompromising individuals as I had in the past week. It changed me. I had stared down the barrel of a gun, and aimed one at someone else. I had been terrorised but wasn't reduced to a tearful wreck; on the contrary, I had taken it all in my stride, as did everyone else. I felt independent and sturdy; I felt as if I was no longer a boy, although not quite a man. I was now able to stand on my own two feet and didn't need to rely on anyone else. It was nice to be picked up by Mum and Dad at Luton airport, though.

Being back home was very strange. It was another period of transition. I knew I was going to leave the ATC now, as they had nothing left to offer me. I had taken all I needed from the organisation and it was time to move on. Gowland left just before me. I sat and chatted with him in the car park about our shared experiences. He was no longer a rival but a contemporary, about to start his career. He had been accepted for Pilot training in the RAF. As we talked, he suddenly looked troubled.

'Did I hit you once?' he asked.

'Yes,' I said. I reminded him of the circumstances.

'I'm very sorry about that,' he said. He seemed genuine. We shook hands and wished each other good luck. I meant it. I never saw again him after that.

I returned my uniform and said goodbye to the cadets who were around that evening. Bloxham was supposed to sign my logbook but he wasn't around either. It was a damp squib, no fanfare, no parade. I just slipped away and rode my motorbike home.

It was an end of an era for me. My whole life had been consumed by the cadet force and the pursuit of a career in the RAF. That had all dissipated. It was no longer my path. I couldn't face someone ordering me about anymore. The experiences had instilled a deep sense of discipline but I had started to resent authority, certainly authority poorly exercised. I had kept my repressed anger from my persecutors; the other apprentices were now the bullies in my life and I would have to deal with them. I wasn't their stooge; I wasn't going to take their shit for much longer, although Goatcher and Holden especially would keep doling it out. It was all building to a breaking point; but this worm would turn. This worm had grown teeth. They had better watch out.

I would have to progress through the different workshops and get to know all the various characters; to hold my own with the baying mob of Bay 1 and attempt to dispel the malicious disinformation that Goatcher had fomented in the minds of Lasham folk who would judge me on his hearsay before I had even met them.

I continued playing guitar as if my life depended on it. I would get good enough and start a band, I thought; anything to escape the awful day to day grime of working in Engineering. I enjoyed playing for its own sake, but it became an instrument and symbol of escape, if only from reality for a little while. My English teacher had advised I take a career as a writer, or at least as a serious hobby. Pah, what did she know? Maybe it would be song writing – I could feel the overwhelming desire to express myself to the world. Express what though, frustration? The urgency of punk and new wave music enthralled me and I wanted to join the party. I didn't have answers, only questions. I was young, and I had no idea where everything was heading. It was familiar marker points in time, exams at college, different years of apprenticeship, I just had to put my head down and get through it. To quote Weller in 'When You're Young,' I was 'just waiting for the right time.' I didn't know for what exactly; but I would probably recognise it when I got there. It would take another four years.

Reunion July 2015. Martin, Trevor and Colin first time together after 33 years (Trevor Heath Archive)

CPSIA information can be obtained at www.ICGtesting.com
Printed in the USA
LVOW10s1611041015

456850LV00025B/561/P